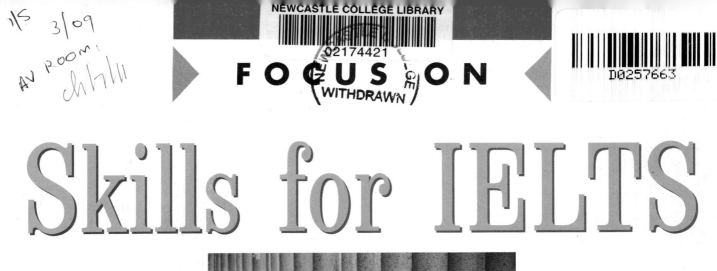

FOCUS ON

Skills for IELTS

Foundation

PEARSON
Longman

MARGARET MATTHEWS
KATY SALISBURY

Map of the book

▶ Introduction

What is *Focus on Skills for IELTS Foundation?*

Focus on Skills for IELTS Foundation offers systematic preparation for students wishing to take the IELTS exam. It provides training for students taking the Listening, Speaking, Writing and Reading modules. The level is suitable for mid- or lower intermediate students who would like to take the IELTS exam but who may need some extra support with grammar, vocabulary or skills.

Focus on Skills for IELTS Foundation offers:

- detailed **information** about the four modules of the exam, including all task types
- **guided practice** for all four skills
- **language input** for the different parts of the Speaking and Writing modules
- **hints and tips** to help with special areas of difficulty
- intensive work on **academic English**, including collocations and useful phrases as well as key language for specific academic topics
- **four Progress Checks** which recycle key language and skills in new contexts
- **Examples of answers to Speaking and Writing tests** with detailed assessments by an examiner
- **recordings for comprehensive Listening practice**, with a range of accents, including British, US and Australian English, that may be used in the exam

How can *Focus on Skills for IELTS Foundation* be used?

- **To accompany the coursebook *Focus on IELTS Foundation***
  Focus on Skills for IELTS Foundation reflects the structure and organisation of *Focus on IELTS Foundation,* and can be used to accompany the coursebook either in class or for homework activities. Each of the units 1–12 in *Focus on Skills for IELTS Foundation* relates to the same unit in *Focus on IELTS Foundation,* covering the same general topic area and reinforcing and extending the skills and language work and the examination training provided there. Cross references are supplied for key activities and language points to help teachers and students use the two books together.

- **As a short intensive course to help students to prepare for the exam**
  Focus on Skills for IELTS Foundation can also be used on its own as a short intensive course for students who only have a limited amount of time to prepare for the exam. It may also be used by students who have already used *Focus on IELTS Foundation* but who wish to do more preparation for the exam. The book offers a full introduction to all the tasks the students will meet in the IELTS exam, together with the key language and skills needed. Used in this way, the book could be completed in about 30–40 hours.

- **For students to use to prepare for the exam on their own**
  Students can use *Focus on Skills for IELTS Foundation* on their own at home or in a self-access centre. The book provides clear guidance and useful tips on all tasks, and full answer keys and audio scripts are provided. Training is given on self-assessment of writing and speaking, and students are encouraged to record themselves for speaking activities wherever possible.

Recommended procedure

- Work through the units in the order they are in the book. Although all the tasks are of exam level, the book is graded, with more support being provided at the beginning.
- Work through the different sections of each module in order. Earlier sections will provide language and ideas for the later parts of the module.
- Don't use a dictionary while doing reading tasks. However, once a task has been completed, go back over the text to highlight and record useful phrases – including new collocations of words that are already known. (The same procedure should be followed with Listening. After the task has been completed, listen again – with or without the audio script – and note useful words and phrases.)
- Students should evaluate their own work critically and use the answer keys appropriately.

The IELTS exam

What is IELTS and where can I take it?

IELTS stands for International English Language Testing System. The IELTS examination is taken by students who want to live, study or work in an English-speaking country, and especially by those who are going to follow academic courses at a university or similar institution, or more general training courses. It can be taken at Test Centres world-wide on fixed days throughout the year.

Exam overview

The examination tests all four language skills: Listening, Reading, Writing and Speaking. There are separate Reading and Writing Modules for those requiring qualifications in academic skills or more general skills. This book focuses on Academic Reading and Academic Writing skills.

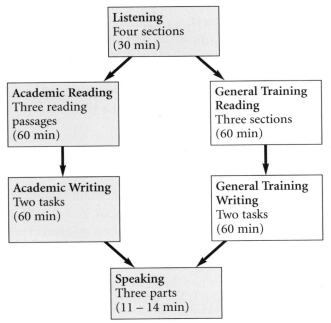

Results

You will get your IELTS results within two weeks of taking the exam. You will not be given a pass or a fail grade, but instead you will receive a Test Report Form giving you a band score for each of the four skills, and a final overall band which is an average of these. These band scores are expressed on a range of 0 to 9 and cover the whole range of language ability.

For more information, look on the IELTS website www.ielts.org.

THE IELTS NINE-BAND SCALE

Band 9 – Expert User

Understands and uses the language extremely well: produces appropriate, fluent language with no mistakes; understands everything.

Band 8 – Very Good User

Understands and uses the language very well: only occasionally makes mistakes; may misunderstand some language in unfamiliar situations; is able to give complicated explanations clearly.

Band 7 – Good User

Understands and uses the language well: occasionally makes mistakes, and uses inappropriate language in some situations; generally uses complex language well, and understands complicated explanations.

Band 6 – Competent User

Generally understands and uses the language well: may make some mistakes or misunderstand things, but can use and understand fairly complex language in familiar situations.

Band 5 – Modest User

Uses the language fairly well in several situations: generally understands things in most situations, though is likely to make a lot of mistakes when speaking or writing; can usually manage quite well when dealing with familiar topics.

Band 4 – Limited User

Is only able to use basic language in familiar situations: makes a lot of mistakes, or uses language inappropriately; is not able to use complex language; often has problems understanding things.

Band 3 – Extremely Limited User

Is only able to produce and understand general meaning in very familiar situations: communication often breaks down completely.

Band 2 – Intermittent User

Can only talk/write about very basic information on familiar topics, using single words or short phrases: has great difficulty understanding.

Band 1 – Non User

Has no ability to use the language except a few words.

Band 0 – Did not attempt the test

No language is provided which can be assessed.

Listening

Time and organisation

The Listening Module has four sections of increasing difficulty, with a total of 40 questions, and takes about 30 minutes. Each section has 10 questions and is heard **once only**. You have time to look through the questions before you listen, and also time to check your answers after each section. You write your answers on the question paper as you listen, and you then have ten minutes at the end to transfer your answers to a separate answer sheet.

Content and task types

Sections 1 and 2 develop the listening skills needed for survival in an English-speaking country, in situations such as shopping, accommodation, etc. Sections 3 and 4 have a more academic context – for example, they may be a recording of part of a tutorial, seminar or lecture. You will hear a variety of accents including British, North American and Australian English. The following task types may be included:

- multiple choice
- matching
- classification
- short-answer questions and lists
- note/table/flow chart completion
- sentence or summary completion
- labelling a diagram, map or plan

Marking and assessment

All the answers have one mark. Any answer which is above the word limit specified for that task will not receive a mark, so it is important to read the instructions carefully. Spelling and grammar must be correct. The final score is converted to a whole or half band on the IELTS band scale.

Academic Reading

Time and organisation

The Academic Reading Module has three reading passages, and a total of 40 questions to be answered in one hour. The first two reading passages have 13 questions each, and the last one has 14 questions. The total length of the three passages is between 2,000 and 2,750 words. All your answers must be written on a separate Answer Sheet **during the exam**. No extra time is allowed for this at the end of the exam.

Content and task types

The reading passages will be on academic topics of general interest. You don't need to have specialised knowledge of the topic, as any specialised vocabulary needed for the task will be explained in the text or in a glossary. However, you need to have a good understanding of more general academic terms in order to cope with the tasks successfully in the time given, and it will help you if you have some awareness of the types of general issues covered in this book.

The following task types may be included:

- multiple choice
- matching lists or phrases
- matching headings to sections/paragraphs
- classification
- identification of information – True/False/Not Given
- identification of writer's views – Yes/No/Not Given
- locating information in sections/paragraphs
- short-answer questions and lists
- note/table/flow chart completion
- sentence or summary completion
- labelling a diagram, map or plan

Marking and assessment

All the answers have one mark. Any answer which is above the word limit specified for that task will not receive a mark, so it is important to read the instructions carefully. Spelling and grammar must be correct. The final score is converted to a whole or half band on the IELTS band scale.

Academic Writing

Time and organisation

The Writing Module consists of two different writing tasks and the whole paper takes one hour. You do not have any choice of tasks. Task 1 must be a minimum of 150 words and it is recommended that you spend no longer than 20 minutes on this. Task 2 must be at least 250 words and carries two thirds of the marks, so it is recommended that you spend 40 minutes on this. Underlength answers lose marks.

Content and task types

The Task 1 prompt is always a type of diagram. You have to write about the information shown, describing the main features, trends or differences. You have to refer closely to the diagram and, where relevant, illustrate your main points with figures. You are **not** required to give any explanation for the data, but have to describe only the information given in the task.

Task types may involve describing information from:

- a graph, chart or table
- a flow chart or process diagram
- a plan or map
- a diagram showing how something works
- a diagram showing or comparing objects
- a set of small diagrams

In Task 2 you are required to discuss an issue, question or opinion of general interest, and to give your own point of view. The topics do not require you to have specialist knowledge, but you have to be able to present ideas on general issues. The prompt is usually a background statement introducing the topic, followed by an instruction to the candidate. This instruction tells you how you should approach the topic and it is very important that you spend time analysing exactly what you are expected to write about.

Instruction types include:

- giving and justifying opinions
- comparing opposing opinions
- evaluating advantages and disadvantages
- comparing arguments for and against
- analysing problems and suggesting solutions
- answering direct questions on an issue

For Task 2 you are expected to write in a formal style, appropriate for an academic exam.

Marking and assessment

Task 2 carries more marks than Task 1, so you should take care to spend a full 40 minutes on Task 2.

Task 1 is assessed in terms of:
Task fulfilment: how well you have reported and illustrated the main points of the information.
Coherence and cohesion: how well you have organised the information across your answer and how you have linked the ideas within and between sentences.
Vocabulary and sentence structure: how appropriately and accurately you have used a range of language.

Task 2 is assessed in terms of:
Arguments, ideas and evidence: how well you have been able to present relevant ideas and opinions and develop these into a well-supported argument/opinion.
Communicative quality: how well you have organised and linked your points and ideas.
Vocabulary and sentence structure: how appropriately and accurately you have used a range of language.

Your scores on these criteria are combined to give you a Task Band for each task. These are then combined to give you a Final Band for Writing.

Speaking

Time and organisation

In the Speaking Module, each candidate has a face-to-face interview with an examiner. The interview consists of three parts and takes between 11 and 14 minutes. The examiner records the interview.

Content and task type

Part 1 lasts for 4 to 5 minutes and begins with introductions. The examiner then asks you a series of questions on two or three different topics connected to your life, your interests or what you do.

Part 2 lasts 3 to 4 minutes and is based on the candidate giving a short talk. You are given a card with a familiar topic and several prompts. You then have one minute to make notes on what you want to say before speaking for two minutes on the topic given. You do not have a choice of topic but the topics are based on your own experience, such as a person or place you know, or an event or activity you have experienced.

The examiner may ask you a brief question at the end.

Part 3 lasts for 4 to 5 minutes. Here the examiner asks you more abstract questions related to your topic and develops a more general discussion.

Marking and assessment

Candidates are assessed on all parts of the interview. Remember that if you give very short answers, the examiner has very little language to assess.

The criteria are:

Fluency and coherence: how well you are able to maintain the flow of conversation, and how clearly you can express and link ideas.
Lexical resource: how appropriately and accurately you use a range of vocabulary.
Grammatical range and accuracy: how appropriately and accurately you use a range of structures.
Pronunciation: how clearly you speak and how well you use the different features of English pronunciation.

The scores on these criteria are combined to give the Final Band for Speaking.

1 ▶ Read all about it!

Focus on reading 1 *About the Reading module; reading strategies*

▶ About the Reading module

1 **Read the following information and then answer the questions below.**

The IELTS Reading module has three sections and lasts one hour. Each section contains a reading text of 750–950 words and has two or three different tasks. There are 40 questions in total.

The first reading text is the easiest and the third is the most difficult. The texts can come from newspapers, magazines, books and journals and cover a range of subjects, e.g. physics, biology, architecture and history, but you don't have to be an expert to understand them. The tasks are intended to test understanding of English, not subject knowledge.

1 How long does the IELTS Reading module last?
2 How many reading texts does it contain?
3 What is the maximum length of each text?
4 Which text is the easiest?
5 What do tasks in the Reading module test?

SKILLS PRACTICE
▶ Reading strategies

▶ Skimming
Focus on IELTS Foundation, p.8

You will use a variety of reading strategies when you do IELTS Reading tasks.

Sometimes you may want to look quickly through a text to get a general idea of what it is about. This is called **skimming**. One approach to skimming is to read the first sentence of each paragraph. This is usually the topic sentence, which introduces the main idea of each paragraph.

2 a) Skim read Texts 1–5 opposite. They are all about the same thing. **What are they all about?**

b) Look at exercise 4 on p.9.
Which of the following do you have to do for each text?

A Answer a question
B Tick a box
C Match two numbers
D Complete a sentence

▶ Scanning
Focus on IELTS Foundation, p.8

At other times you may want to search a text for a specific word, number or phrase. This is called **scanning**. In the IELTS reading module you will save valuable time if you can locate the information to answer a question quickly, without re-reading the whole text.

TIP You should look for the same word(s), and also others that mean the same thing.

3 a) **Find a reference to computers in Texts 1–5. Which text is it in?**

b) **Scan Texts 1–5 for references to the USA. How many are there?**

Text 1

The earliest libraries that we know about were different from present-day libraries, as their contents were mainly government records. Archaeological findings from ancient cities of Sumer revealed temple rooms full of records of commercial transactions, or inventories. Things were much the same in the government records of Ancient Egypt. The earliest private or personal libraries containing both non-fiction and fiction books appeared in classical Greece.

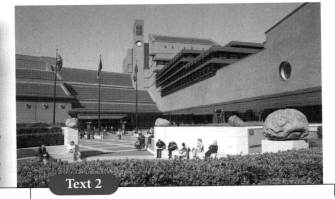

Text 2

Library materials such as books, articles and CDs are usually arranged in a certain order, according to a library classification system, so that you can find particular items quickly. In addition to public areas, some libraries have additional rooms where reference materials are stored. Often a professional librarian works from a reference desk or other central location, to help users find what they are looking for.

Text 3

Many visitors to a library do not know how to use the library effectively. This can be because they are shy and embarrassed to ask questions, or because they are not used to libraries. These problems were behind the library instruction movement in the U.S., which encourages library-user education. In fact, library instruction has been practised in the U.S. since the 19th century.

Text 4

Managing a library involves tasks such as planning what new books to buy, designing classification and borrowing systems, preserving materials (especially rare and fragile manuscripts) and developing library computer systems. Long-term tasks include planning library extensions and developing community services such as adult literacy programs.

Text 5

In North America, among other countries, libraries in poor communities are relatively expensive to run, but arguably less important to the community than essential services, such as police, firefighters, schools, and health care. At any rate, many communities are beginning to feel they have no option but to close down, or reduce their library services to balance their budgets.

4

Look at this list of topics.

i   Library management
ii The history of libraries
iii Library-user training
iv Financial problems for libraries
v   The organisation of libraries

Which text (1–5) deals with which topic? Write the number of the text next to each topic. The first one has been done for you.

	Text	**Topic**
Example	1	*ii*
	2	
	3	
	4	
	5	

Focus on grammar *Present simple*

Focus on IELTS Foundation, p.7, KLB p.153

1   **Answer the questions below.**

1   How many verbs are there in the present simple in Text 1?

2   How many verbs are there in the present simple in Text 4?

2   **Circle the correct letter.**
The verbs in Text 4 are in the present simple because the text is about:

A   regular actions
B   general facts
C   mental processes

3   a)   **Why do we use the present simple in the sentences below? Look again at the options above and write A, B or C in the spaces provided.**

1   The university library **opens** at 8 o'clock on weekdays.   ......

2   The Dutch Royal Library **contains** almost the entire literature of the Netherlands, from medieval times to the present day.   ......

3   Research **shows** that girls are generally better at reading than boys.   ......

4   My daughter's teacher **thinks** she might be dyslexic.   ......

5   The publishers **produce** their sales list every January.   ......

6   Memory probably **plays** an important role in reading ability.   ......

b)   **Underline the verb in the exercise above which is in the plural form.**

4   a)   **The verbs are missing in the sentences below. Which of the missing verbs are singular and which are plural in form? Write S (for singular) and P (for plural) in each case.**

1   Many students .... to read Internet articles rather than books.

2   Ultra-violet light and humidity .... printed material.

3   One leading educationalist .... that current methods of teaching reading should be reviewed.

4   Librarians usually .... special gloves to handle old manuscripts.

5   In a few countries, a single publisher .... books to all schools.

6   Poor reading ability .... children's performance across all school subjects.

b)   **Complete the sentences using the verbs from the box below. Remember to change the verb to the correct form.**

| *supply* | *believe* | *damage* | *affect* | *prefer* | *wear* |

Focus on vocabulary 1 *Dictionary skills*

TIP Whatever your own special subject is, you should try to learn these frequently-occurring words.

A good English–English dictionary is a very important tool for the learner. In addition to giving word meanings and examples, a good English–English dictionary will give you information about pronunciation and grammar. To get the most from your dictionary, you need to understand the abbreviations and symbols which are used, so make a point of studying the pronunciation table and the other keys, which are usually at the beginning.

1 a) **Underline these words in Text 2 and look at how they are used.**

classification   reference

> **Text 2**
>
> Library materials such as books, articles and CDs are usually arranged in a certain order, according to a library classification system, so that you can find particular items quickly. In addition to public areas, some libraries have additional rooms where reference materials are stored. Often a professional librarian works from a reference desk or other central location, to help users find what they are looking for.

b) **Read these extracts from** *Longman Exams Dictionary***.**

> **clas·si·fi·ca·tion** /ˌklæsəfəˈkeɪʃən/ *n* [C,U] a process in which you put something into the group or class it belongs to, or the group it belongs to ➡ **CLASSIFY:** *the classification of wines according to quality* | *There are five job classifications.*

> **ref·er·ence** S3 W1 /ˈrefərəns/ *n*
>
> **reference book** *n* [C] a book such as a dictionary or ENCYCLOPEDIA that you look at to find information

c) **Using the information from the dictionary, choose the best word to complete these sentences.**

1 The most general classification of library books is based on .... (size/colour/subject).

2 The main stress falls on the .... (first/ fourth) syllable of classification.

3 An example of a reference book is a .... (novel/ dictionary/ biography).

4 The main stress in reference falls on the .... (first/ second) syllable.

d) **Write the verbs which relate to the nouns** *classification* **and** *reference***. Use your dictionary if necessary.**

classification   ....

reference   ....

▶ Classification systems

> **TIP** Diagrams or 'mindplans' like this can be a useful way of recording information about vocabulary. For an example, see *Focus on IELTS Foundation,* p.29.

2 a) **Complete the mindplans below.**

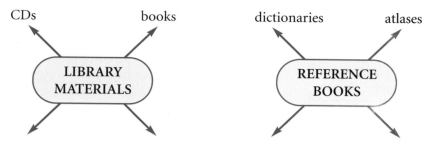

b) **Choose one of the topics below and produce your own mindplan like the ones above.**

- climate
- schools
- animals

3 a) *involve*   *include*

The two words are close in meaning, but not exactly the same. Look again at how they are used in Text 4, p.9.

b) **Study these extracts from** *Longman Exams Dictionary.*

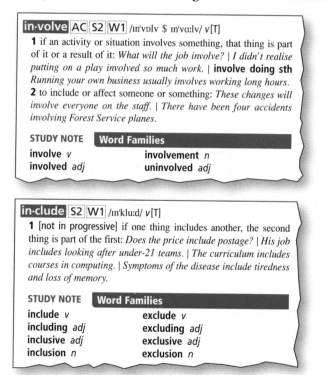

in·volve AC S2 W1 /ɪnˈvɒlv $ ɪnˈvɑːlv/ *v* [T]
1 if an activity or situation involves something, that thing is part of it or a result of it: *What will the job involve?* | *I didn't realise putting on a play involved so much work.* | **involve doing sth** *Running your own business usually involves working long hours.*
2 to include or affect someone or something: *These changes will involve everyone on the staff.* | *There have been four accidents involving Forest Service planes.*

STUDY NOTE   Word Families
involve *v*   involvement *n*
involved *adj*   uninvolved *adj*

in·clude S2 W1 /ɪnˈkluːd/ *v* [T]
1 [not in progressive] if one thing includes another, the second thing is part of the first: *Does the price include postage?* | *His job includes looking after under-21 teams.* | *The curriculum includes courses in computing.* | *Symptoms of the disease include tiredness and loss of memory.*

STUDY NOTE   Word Families
include *v*   exclude *v*
including *adj*   excluding *adj*
inclusive *adj*   exclusive *adj*
inclusion *n*   exclusion *n*

The abbreviation *v[T]* after each word means that they are transitive verbs. In other words, they are followed by a noun (e.g. *involving Forest Service planes; includes courses*), or a noun phrase (e.g. *involves working long hours; includes looking after under-21 teams*).

c) Complete these sentences using involve(s) or include(s).

1　Being a successful student .... studying hard.

2　Countries which import rice .... the USA and Canada.

3　Learning a musical instrument .... practising every day.

4　Winners of the Nobel Prize for Literature .... Naguib Mahfouz and Elfriede Jelinek.

5　New ideas to improve road safety .... special training for lorry drivers.

6　Accurate weather forecasting .... the use of electronic equipment.

Focus on speaking *About the Speaking module; communication strategies; understanding questions*

▶ About the Speaking module

1　Read the following information and answer the questions below.

The Speaking module consists of three parts. In the first part the examiner asks questions about you, your opinions, your likes and dislikes. In the second part you talk for up to two minutes about a topic chosen by the examiner. In the third part the examiner asks extended, general questions connected with the same topic.

1　In which part(s) of the Speaking module do you have to answer questions?
2　Which parts of the Speaking module are connected with each other?

SKILLS PRACTICE
▶ Communication strategies

When you are talking to someone in English there will be occasions when you don't understand. Get into the habit of asking for help.

If you didn't hear properly, you can say:

Sorry? I didn't catch that.
Could you repeat the question, please?

If there's a word that you don't understand, you can say:

Could you repeat X, please?
What does X mean?

▶ Understanding short questions

Short questions can be difficult to understand. If you don't understand them quite quickly, you will not be able to give a suitable, prompt answer. You will need practice in listening to short questions and responding quickly.

2　a) ∩ Listen to these questions about reading and fill in the gaps.

1　Do you .... ?

2　What kind of things do you .... ?

3　Is reading a .... in your country?

4　How often do you .... ?

5　..................... read to you when you were young?

b) Which of the five questions above could be answered with *Yes* or *No*?

3 a) 🎧 Below are some short answers to typical Part 1 questions about reading. Listen to the six questions and match them to the appropriate answer. Write an answer a)–f) in the spaces provided below.

Questions	Answers
1	a) About three times a week.
2	b) My favourite books are history books.
3	c) No, not really.
4	d) In my bedroom.
5	e) I always get them from a library.
6	f) When I was about five years old.

b) 🎧 Listen again and make notes on how you would answer the questions.

▶ Prediction

4 a) Look at some possible answers to the question, 'Do you enjoy reading?' Notice how each person gives some details, to make the answer more interesting. Before you listen, try to guess the answers.

Do you enjoy reading?

1 Yes, I do, but I don't get .... these days.

2 Not really. I prefer ....

3 Oh yes. I've always loved reading, ever since ....

4 Yes. It's my .... !

5 No. I only read when I have to. I . ...

> **TIP** If you don't understand a question, make sure you ask the examiner to repeat or explain! You will lose marks if you say nothing but you won't if you ask for help, so practise replying to short questions quickly.

b) 🎧 Listen and see if your answers were correct.

EXAM PRACTICE
Part 1

5 🎧 Listen again to all the questions in exercise 2. This time, practise answering. Try to answer quite quickly. If possible, record yourself and then listen to what you have said.

> **TIP** If the examiner asks you a question about you or your life which doesn't really seem relevant, use your imagination to answer! Remember that you are marked on how you answer, not on your opinions or ideas, so it doesn't matter whether your reply is strictly true or not.

Focus on reading 2 *Skimming; choosing paragraph headings; guessing unknown vocabulary*

SKILLS PRACTICE

▶ Identifying topic

Focus on IELTS Foundation, p.12

1 You're going to read about people who can't read and write. Thinking about the topic of a reading exercise may help you to predict some of the ideas and vocabulary that will be in the text. Think about the topic of reading and writing using the questions below.

1 In your country, are there many adults who can't read and write?
2 What are the reasons why some adults can't read and write?
3 What problems do adults have when they can't read or write?
4 How can adults get help with reading and writing?

EXAM PRACTICE

▶ Matching

> **HELP**
>
> To make the task easier, there are only six titles for six paragraphs. In the IELTS test there are extra titles.

2 The text on Literacy on p.16 has six paragraphs, labelled A–F. Read the text and answer the questions below.

Questions 1–6
Choose the correct heading for each paragraph from the list of headings below.

List of Headings

i   Early mention of the problems

ii   The link between adult and child literacy

iii A new attempt to improve literacy

iv   The great variety of reading material

v   Present levels of adult illiteracy

vi   Lack of progress

Write the correct number i–vi for each paragraph.

Paragraph	Heading
A	....
B	....
C	....
D	....
E	....
F	....

LITERACY

A We live in an age when we are surrounded by information. Apart from information in notices, books and newspapers, we receive information in our email, from the Internet, and from text messages on our mobile phones. So
5 it is ironic that with so much information available to us, more people than ever before are unable to access it because they are not able to read and write.

B Adult literacy is a very important, but often overlooked part of any basic education programme. Most programmes
10 focus on children, but research and experience show that if children come from homes in which the adults have low literacy skills, those children will have a very high chance of becoming low-literate adults themselves.

C The number of illiterate adults in the world is now over
15 900 million, nearly equivalent to the population of India. Two out of every three of those adults are women. That shocking figure gets worse if you include individuals who are not completely literate, so they lack the level of skill required to be successful in the family, at work, and in the community.

20 **D** The international community has been calling attention to the problem of illiteracy for a long time. As early as 1948,
education was among the basic human rights included in the United Nations Universal Declaration of Human Rights. More recently, at a meeting of the World Conference on
25 Education in 1990, it was stated that 'illiteracy is a significant problem in all countries, industrialised and developing'. Delegates to the meeting agreed to try and reduce the adult illiteracy rate to one-half of its 1990 level by the year 2000, and to reduce the difference between male and
30 female illiteracy rates. The goal was repeated at various conferences throughout that decade.

E However, by the end of the century statistical evidence showed that efforts to improve literacy were still failing. Although some progress had been made, 113 million
35 children still remained out of school and although the overall numbers of literate adults had risen, many remained illiterate.

F At the beginning of the new millennium, an organisation called the World Education Forum published six education
40 aims. These range from providing care and education in early childhood, to improving the quality of all aspects of education. One of its goals was a 50 per cent improvement in levels of adult literacy by 2015, especially for women. In addition, in 2001 every member of the United Nations
45 General Assembly voted to call the years 2003 to 2012 'the Literacy Decade'.

▶ **Guessing unknown vocabulary**
Focus on IELTS Foundation, p.10

If you try to understand every single word in a text, you will slow your reading down and reduce your understanding of the whole text. It is often better to guess words/phrases which you don't know and continue reading. Your guesses will often be right, because there are usually plenty of clues to their meaning. For example, words in one sentence may be explained in the sentences that follow.

3 When you first looked at the text, you may not have been familiar with the word *literacy* in the title. However, at the end of paragraph A there is a phrase which has a similar meaning. What is the phrase?

Sometimes you can use your knowledge of grammar or vocabulary, or your knowledge about a topic, to guess unknown words.

4 Look at the word *overlooked* in paragraph B and answer these questions.

1 What kind of word is it (noun, adjective, verb, etc.)?
2 Does it have a similar meaning to *important* (in the same sentence), or a different meaning? How do you know?
3 Which of the following is it likely to mean?
      main   missed out
   Why?

Sometimes you don't understand the exact meaning of a word or phrase, but you can be satisfied with having a rough, general understanding.

5   Look at the word *delegates* in paragraph D.

1   What kind of word is it (noun, verb, etc.)?
2   From the rest of the sentence, can you guess the approximate meaning?

Sometimes you can't guess what a word or phrase means. In this case, ignore it and move on quickly.

6   **Complete the summary using the most appropriate verb from the box below. Remember to change the verb to the correct form.**

Although there **1** .... a lot of written information around us, large numbers of people **2** .... still unable to read and write. There are more illiterate females than illiterate males and children whose parents are illiterate often **3** .... illiterate adults themselves. Although governments generally **4** .... the problem and frequently **5** .... new measures to deal with it, little has changed over more than fifty years. Universal literacy will not happen overnight, but it is a process which **6** .... serious commitment.

be (x2)   agree   recognise   involve   become

Focus on vocabulary 2 *Academic vocabulary*

1   The following words from the Academic Word List (see *Focus on IELTS Foundation*, p.138) appear in the text on *Literacy* (p.16). Study the way they are used in the paragraphs shown and then say whether each one is a noun (N), verb (V) or adjective (A).

1   *access* (paragraph A) ......
2   *focus on* (paragraph B) ......
3   *equivalent to* (paragraph C) ......
4   *lack* (paragraph C) ......
5   *significant* (paragraph D) ......
6   *range from … to …* (paragraph F) ......

2   Look at these less formal words. Match them to the academic words in exercise 1 as these are used in the text on *Literacy*.

a) *get*
b) *concentrate on*
c) *large*
d) *go between … and …*
e) *don't have*
f) *same as*

3   Choose a word or phrase from the list in exercise 1 to complete these sentences.

1   In some rural primary schools the ages of children in one class .... five .... ten.
2   There will be no .... improvement in health care unless investment in training increases.
3   Government efforts will .... the needs of the elderly.
4   The spread of disease is faster in villages which .... clean drinking water.
5   Rainfall during the storm was .... the average rainfall for one month.

2 ▶ Take note

Focus on listening 1 *About the Listening module; listening for gist; prediction; recognising spoken numbers and letters*

▶ About the Listening module

1   Read the following information and answer the question below.

The IELTS Listening test has four sections and lasts about 30 minutes. There are 40 questions in total. Sections 1 and 3 are based on a conversation between two (or sometimes three) main speakers. Sections 2 and 4 are based on a presentation given by just one main speaker.

In terms of topic, Sections 1 and 2 are similar, because topics are based on common situations from everyday life, such as shopping or finding a job. Sections 3 and 4, on the other hand, are based on topics connected with training or study.

Tick any of the following characteristics which relate to the first section of the IELTS Listening module:

A   there is one main speaker
B   there are usually two main speakers
C   the topic is connected with study or training
D   the topic is usually a social one

SKILLS PRACTICE
▶ Listening for gist
Focus on IELTS Foundation, p.18

The general sense of what speakers are saying is called 'gist'. In real life, we can get the gist of things we hear more easily if we are familiar with the situation. If we understand the gist of conversations, we can understand the details more easily.

Section 1 deals with common, social situations.

2   🎧 Listen to five short conversations and decide what the context of each one is. Circle a letter A–C for each conversation.

1   A   booking a hotel
    B   discussing hobbies with a friend
    C   joining a sports club

2   A   taking part in a market survey
    B   buying clothes
    C   registering for a course

3   A   seeing a doctor
    B   buying new shoes
    C   explaining absence from work

4   A   booking a cycling holiday
    B   enquiring about a second-hand bicycle
    C   admiring a friend's new bicycle

5   A   buying a new car
    B   reporting an accident to the police
    C   asking a car repair company for help

► Prediction

Make sure that you listen very carefully to the introduction so you know **who** is talking, **what** the topic is and **where** they are.

When you recognise the general situation, you can usually understand the details of a conversation more easily too. In fact, in common situations you can sometimes predict what people might say.

3 Look at the three advertisements, A, B and C, below. What questions might a telephone caller ask? Match questions 1–10 with the adverts.

A
For Sale
3-drawer desk, good condition, £35.
Tel: 662918

B
On tour now at the Pavillion Theatre
Joe Cole and his Crazy Band
For ticket information, call: Tel: 499449

C
WANTED
Part time waiters and waitresses. No previous experience necessary.
To apply call 792004

1 Do you take phone bookings? ......
2 How big is it? ......
3 How soon can I start? ......
4 Where is the restaurant? ......
5 How much are the tickets? ......
6 What should I wear? ......
7 Where do you live? ......
8 What time does it start? ......
9 What's it made of? ......
10 What are the hours of work? ......

► Recognising letters and numbers
Focus on IELTS Foundation, p.17

In the first part of the IELTS Listening module you hear people providing simple, factual information. Sometimes this information involves names which are spelt out, letter by letter.

The names of some English letters sound very similar – for example M and N, B and P, D and T, or J and G. The only way you can improve your ability to recognise the letters is by practising.

TIP Get to know which letter sound(s) you have a problem with and practise these.

4 a) ∩ Listen and tick the letter that you hear from each pair.

1 C; S   2 J; G   3 L; N   4 Q; K   5 M; N   6 O; U   7 T; D
8 I; Y   9 B; P   10 A; E

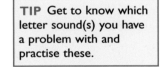

b) ∩ How old do you think the men in the pictures are? Listen to some information about them and match each description to a picture.

Description 1 = Man ......
Description 2 = Man ......
Description 3 = Man ......

c) ∩ Listen again to the same descriptions. Write the three men's names and the dates they were born in the table below.

Man	Name	Date of birth
A		
B		
C		

Focus on grammar 1 *Quantity*

Focus on IELTS Foundation,
KLB p.144

SKILLS PRACTICE
► Describing data

In Writing Task 1 you sometimes have to summarise information presented in figures, e.g. from a graph, chart or table.

We often use these words when we want to summarise a set of figures:

+ ←————————————————————→ −
       all   most   many   few   no

All and *no* describe 100% and 0%. The other words under the line describe quantities in an approximate way.

1 **Choose one of the words above to complete these sentences. (Check the facts in a reference book if necessary.)**

1 .... penguins live in the southern hemisphere.
2 .... types of bird are able to fly.
3 .... tigers are found in Africa.
4 .... writers of fiction become world-famous.
5 .... employers now offer their workers shares in the company.
6 .... children begin to walk at around twelve months.
7 .... human societies have a spoken language.
8 .... types of plant can survive in desert.
9 .... desert animals are active at night.
10 .... form of life has been found on Mars.

► *Few* or *A few*
Focus on IELTS Foundation,
KLB p.144

These share the same meaning, but *a few* is a more positive expression, while *few* emphasises how small a quantity is in a more negative way.

2 **Choose *few* or *a few* to complete these sentences.**

1 Although some regions of the world have many natural resources, ... countries have everything they need.
2 Exposing ancient cave paintings to light damages them but .... remain open so people can see them.
3 At one site, archaeologists found .... skeletons and some pottery.
4 The pilot managed to land the plane safely and .... passengers were hurt.

► How many? (Using figures)

When we use figures, we often use one of these words/phrases to show how accurate they are.

> *just under   almost   exactly   around   just over   approximately*

3 **a) Answer these questions.**

1 Which one is the 'odd-man-out'?
2 Which pair(s) have the same meaning?
3 Which pair(s) are opposite in meaning?

b) Use the information in the table to complete the summary.

Expenditure on public health in 2001 varied considerably. While the **1** .... spent almost $5,000 per person, **2** .... spent just over half that amount. Both **3** .... and **4** .... spent around $2,900, and **5** .... just over $3,300.

Expenditure on public health in 2001 (per person)

Country	$US
USA	4,887
Switzerland	3,322
Norway	2,920
Luxembourg	2,905
Germany	2,820
Australia	2,532

c) Draw lines to match the figures below to one of the phrases.

76%	Exactly a half
29%	Around five hundred
50%	Nearly ten thousand
9,998	Just under a third
497–503	Just over three quarters

Focus on vocabulary *Media*

1 Read the list of words in the box. Put them into the correct column of the table. Some words may go in more than one column. Use a dictionary if necessary.

> broadcast   turn off   circulation   channel   column   print
> station   watch   read   advertisement   journalist   publish
> tabloid   broadsheet   weather forecast   headline   editor   listen

Television	Radio	Newspaper

2 The underlined words in the sentences below are incorrect. Replace them with a word from the table above.

1 An <u>editor</u> writes stories for a newspaper.
2 I often listen to the <u>headlines</u> on the radio to find out whether it will be hot or cold tomorrow.
3 A <u>tabloid</u> newspaper is full of serious, important news but a <u>broadsheet</u> newspaper is shorter and has lots of gossip about celebrities.
4 If a newspaper has a large <u>broadcast</u>, it sells a lot of copies.
5 This is my favourite radio <u>channel</u>.
6 The television <u>publishes</u> a lot of different kinds of programmes.

21

Focus on writing 1 *Task 1: Skills*

Focus on IELTS Foundation, p.21, KLB p.142

In the IELTS Writing module, Task 1 you may have to compare and contrast figures in different ways, e.g.

less … than   fewer … than   more … than

1 a) **Study the statements below and say whether they are true (T) or false (F).**

1 There are fewer snakes in Scandinavia than in Australia. ......
2 Light colours reflect less light than dark ones. ......
3 There are more people in China than in India. ......
4 There are now fewer craftsmen and craftswomen than in the past. ......
5 Bicycles are less harmful than cars to the environment. ......
6 There are more Chinese speakers than English speakers in the world. ......

b) **Write similar statements, using the words given here.**

0 people – Egypt – Jordan – more
There are more people in Egypt than in Jordan.

1 sleep – adults – babies – need – less
2 German speakers – Spanish speakers – fewer
3 science – women – men – study – fewer
4 electrical goods – Thailand – Germany – export – more
5 environmental damage – nuclear power – fossil fuels – cause – less

▶ **How much more or less?**

When we compare two quantities without figures we can use *slightly, considerably, much* or *far* with the comparison, to be more exact.

slightly	more …
considerably	less …
much/far	fewer …
	bigger …
	smaller …

NB *Much* cannot be used with *fewer*. Instead we say *far fewer*.

2 a) **Which two words from the right-hand column above can be used with words like oil and gas? Which of them can't be used with words like these? Why not?**

b) **Study the information in the table and use the prompts below to write sentences comparing types of energy. One example has been done for you.**

World energy use 2004	
Type of energy	**Percentage of total energy used**
Oil	37.3
Coal	26.5
Gas	23.9
Nuclear	6.2
Hydro	6.1

0 gas/coal
In 2004 we used slightly less gas than coal.

1 oil/coal ....
2 oil/hydro ....
3 hydro/nuclear ....
4 coal/gas ....
5 oil/nuclear ....
6 gas/oil ....

Focus on grammar 2 *Expressing frequency*

Focus on IELTS Foundation, p.19,
KLB p.140

1 **Study the adverbs of time and frequency and answer the questions below.**

> *always   often   never   occasionally*
> *rarely   seldom   sometimes   usually*

1 Which pair(s) of words are similar in meaning?
2 Which pair(s) of words are opposite in meaning?
3 Put all the words onto the scale below.

How often?

+ most often   least often −

←   →

....

Expressions of frequency appear in different positions in a sentence. Some can only appear in one particular place, but others can appear in more than one place.

2 **Below are some of the findings from a survey about the media. Choose the correct expression in brackets to complete the sentences below.**

1 Most older people listen to the radio .... (in the mornings/usually)

2 People under 20 .... listen to the radio. (about once a week/seldom)

3 .... teenagers play computer games in their bedroom. (generally/always)

4 Forty-two per cent of retired people read a newspaper .... (hardly ever/every day)

5 Fewer than five per cent of people .... watch television. (never/only once a week)

6 More women than men listen to the radio .... (always/frequently)

Focus on writing 2 *Task 1: Interpreting visual data*

In Task 1 of the IELTS Academic Writing module you have to describe the data presented in tables, graphs, pictures or diagrams. You have to write up to 150 words for this.

SKILLS PRACTICE

▶ **Reading the data**

Focus on IELTS Foundation, p.20

In order to be able to describe the data in Task 1 accurately, you have to understand visuals such as A, B and C below.

1 **Look at the diagrams A, B and C below and answer the questions.**

1 What are visuals like these called?
- pie charts
- line graphs
- bar charts
2 Which one(s) compare(s) two different areas?
3 Which one(s) compare(s) two types of phone?
4 Which one(s) give(s) information about numbers of people?
5 Which one(s) give(s) information about amounts of money?

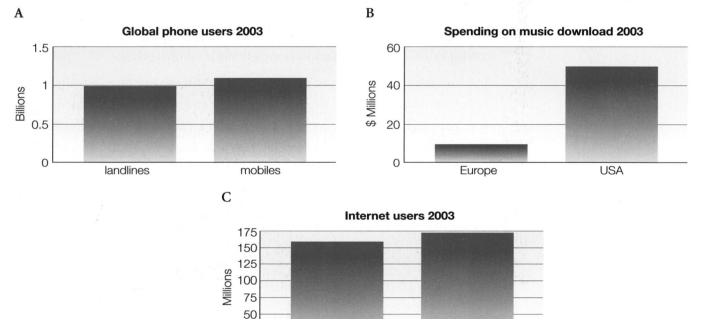

A

Global phone users 2003

B

Spending on music download 2003

C

Internet users 2003

2 **Complete the following statements by choosing the correct option.**

Chart A

1 There were approximately 0.5/1 billion/1.5 billion landlines worldwide in 2003.
2 In 2003 there were just over/just under/exactly 1 billion mobiles worldwide.
3 In 2003 there were slightly more/slightly fewer/considerably more landlines than mobiles worldwide.

Chart B

1   In 2003, Americans spent approximately
    £40,000,000/£50,000,000/£60,000,000 on downloading music.

2   In 2003, approximately/far less than/much more than £50,000,000 was spent
    in Europe on downloading music.

3   In 2003, considerably more/slightly less/considerably less money was spent
    on downloading music in Europe than in the USA.

Chart C

Decide whether the following statements are true (T) or false (F). Correct the
false one(s).

1   In 2003 there were more than 175 million Internet users in Europe.

2   There were approximately 175 million Internet users in North America in
    2003.

3   There were slightly more Internet users in North America than in Europe in
    2003.

▶ Describing the data
*Focus on IELTS Foundation,
Essential Language* p.21

3   **Look at the bar chart below. Choose a suitable expression from the box to
complete the sentences below.**

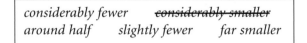

considerably fewer	*~~considerably smaller~~*	
around half	*slightly fewer*	*far smaller*

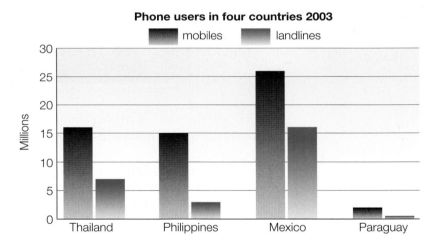

Phone users in four countries 2003

0   The number of mobile phone users in Paraguay is *considerably smaller* than
    the number of mobile phone users in Mexico.

1   There are .... mobile users in the Philippines than in
    Thailand.

2   The Philippines has .... landlines than Thailand.

3   Thailand has .... the number of landlines that Mexico has.

4   Paraguay has a .... number of mobiles and landline users
    than all other countries shown here.

Focus on listening 2 *Getting ready to listen; Completing a form*

▶ Preparation

In the first section of the IELTS Listening module you hear an everyday conversation between two people. Before the conversation starts, you hear an introductory sentence describing the general situation. You also have a few minutes to read the first few questions. Remember to read them carefully and try to predict the answers.

EXAM PRACTICE
▶ Section I

1 🎧 **Listen to the introduction to a conversation.**

1 What will the topic of conversation be?
2 How many questions should you look at before you listen?

2 🎧 **Look at the form below. Listen again to the introduction, the instructions and the first part of the conversation. Answer the questions below.**

1 How many speakers are there?
2 Are the speakers talking face-to-face, or are they on the phone?
3 Where is the woman?
4 What does the man want to do?
5 Which speaker has a form to fill in?

In the first section of the IELTS test you hear the beginning of the conversation twice. This is the only part of the test where this happens. It helps you by giving you the opportunity to get used to the voices.

3 🎧 **Listen to the first part of the conversation and complete questions 1–5 on the form opposite.**

4   a) Look at questions 6–10 and think about the type of word/number you
       might need to write.

    b) 🎧 Listen to the second part of the conversation and complete the form.

Questions 1–10
Complete the form below.
*Write **NO MORE THAN THREE WORDS AND/OR A NUMBER** for*
each answer.

KINGSBURY
Adult Education College

Student Enrolment Form

Example	*Answer*
Enquiry about:	*an evening course*

PERSONAL DETAILS

Name: *Peter* **1** ....

Age: **2** ...... *years*

Occupation: **3** ....

Address: **4** ....
                   Kingsbury

Phone number: **5** ....

COURSE DETAILS

Title: **6** ....

Start date: **7** ....

Method of payment: **8** ....

Reference: **9** ....

SPECIAL REQUIREMENTS (if any)

        Needs access for a **10** ....

3 ▶ It goes with the job

Focus on grammar *Past simple*

▶ Describing past situations
and events
Focus on IELTS Foundation,
p.32, KLB p.150

1 a) You are going to read a short passage about the career of **Richard Branson. Do you know anything about him already, e.g. nationality, company, interests, etc.?**

b) Read the text quickly and answer the questions opposite.

Richard Branson

▶ *The entrepreneur and adventurer's story so far.*

Richard Branson began to publish Student Magazine with the help of friends, before he left school at the age of sixteen. The following
5 year, aged seventeen, he set up a Student Advisory Centre, a charity to help young people.
10 In 1970 he founded his first commercial company called Virgin, to sell music records by mail order. Not long after that, he opened a record shop in London and a recording studio in Oxford. The company then continued to
15 expand into other areas.

In 1984 Branson established Virgin Atlantic airways. This company is now the second largest long-distance international airline in Britain. In 1997 Branson took over two of Britain's
20 rail companies and immediately began to modernise them. He also established a music store chain, Internet and mobile phone companies and hotels. The Virgin company now has over 200 businesses altogether, in more than
25 30 countries.

Besides being a businessman, Richard Branson is also an adventurer. In 1986, for example, his boat crossed the Atlantic Ocean in the fastest recorded time ever. A year later, he crossed the
30 Atlantic in a hot air balloon. This was not only the first hot air balloon to do this, but it was the largest ever flown, and it reached speeds of over 209 kilometres per hour. Between 1995 and 1998 Branson tried several times to fly around
35 the world in a hot air balloon, but he was unsuccessful. A Swiss team achieved that record first, in early 1999.

1 When did Richard Branson first run a business for money?

   A when he was at school
   B when he was 17
   C in 1970 ✓

2 What kind of business did Richard Branson run during the 1970s?

   A magazines
   B music ✓
   C travel

3 Which company did Richard Branson buy and develop in the 1980s?

   A a train company
   B a phone company
   C an airline ✓

4 How did Richard Branson cross the Atlantic faster than anyone else?

   A in a balloon ✓
   B in a boat ✓
   C in a plane

▶ **Uses of the past simple**

We use the past simple for completed actions (e.g. *he founded his first commercial company*). The past simple form of verbs consists of one word.

Regular verbs form the past simple with *–d* (if the word ends with an *e*), *–ed* (if the word ends with a consonant), and *–ied* (if the word ends with a *y*). Sometimes *–t* can be used as well as *–ed* (e.g. The past simple of *learn* can be *learned* or *learnt*). These are the main rules.

Your dictionary will tell you whether a verb is regular or irregular. Some of the most common English words are irregular, like *be* (past simple *was/were*), *have* (past simple *had*), or *say* (past simple *said*).

For information on how to form the past simple, including questions and negatives, spelling tips and time expressions, see *Focus on IELTS Foundation*, p.150.

TIP There are no rules for forming the past simple of irregular verbs, but your dictionary will tell you what the forms are.

2 Look again at the first two paragraphs of the text on p.28. Underline all the past simple verbs.

3 Complete this summary by putting the verbs in brackets into the correct form.

Richard Branson is an entrepreneur. He **1** .... (publish) a magazine while he **2** .... (be) still at school and when he **3** .... (leave) school, he **4** .... (open) a music business. He called his company Virgin. During the 1980s and 1990s Branson **5** .... (set up) businesses in areas such as transport, telecommunications and tourism.

As well as being a businessman, Branson is also an adventurer. In the 1980s and 1990s he **6** .... (break) several world records, especially with his hot air balloon. However, he **7** .... (do) not succeed in flying around the world in it.

Focus on reading *Identifying topic; short-answer questions*

One of the task types which you might meet in the IELTS Reading module asks you to identify the main topic, the main idea, or the best title for a reading text. You have to choose the phrase or sentence which summarises the text best. There are four options.

1 a) If you look quickly at paragraph 1 of the text below, you will see that it is about coral reefs. Think for a minute about coral reefs (there is a picture to help you) and anything you already know about them. Note down a few words/phrases that come to mind.

b) Read the text quickly to get a general understanding of it. Remember, <u>do not</u> try to understand every word as you read.

Coral reefs are found in tropical seas throughout the world and provide shelter for hundreds of different plants and animals. They look like flat beds of rock, but in fact they are formed from the skeletons of tiny
5 sea creatures. Almost one half of the world's coral reefs occur in shallow seas, near to the coastline of over one hundred countries.

Millions of people depend on these coral reefs for their livelihoods. The majority of
10 natural products which come from coral reefs, such as fish, shells and seaweed, can be sold, either locally or in export markets. Not only does the person who collects the products earn money, but also those people
15 who prepare, market or sell them. In some countries, coral reefs are the main natural resource. In the Maldives, for example, 25% of the workforce is employed in fishing. In addition, 56% of the national economy
20 comes from reef-based tourism. This means that a substantial number of people are employed in tourism-related jobs.

Fishing is normally an occupation for adult males, particularly where it involves the
25 use of boats, and other people are often excluded from it. Coral reef fisheries, on the other hand, are usually accessible on foot, so work is not restricted to men. In fact, collecting fish and other products from the
30 reefs is generally the job of women, children and even the elderly.

Women's occupations are not limited to reef fishing. In India and the South Pacific, for example, women help to make and mend
35 the fishing equipment. Fish processing is often done by women too. Such employment brings both direct and indirect advantages. For example, on Ulithi Atoll in Papua New Guinea, women can obtain mahogany wood
40 for fishing boats in exchange for cloth they make and so gain more control over the household income. They can also apply for loans or credit. This gives them more independence and status, both in the family
45 and in the community.

EXAM PRACTICE
▶ Reading for overall meaning

TIP In the exam, the same type of task might ask you to choose the best title, or the writer's purpose, or any other *general aspect* of the reading text.

2 Decide which answer A–D best expresses the main idea of the text.

A The structure and location of coral reefs.
B Fish exports from Papua New Guinea.
C The economic importance of coral reefs.
D Female unemployment in coastal villages.

3 Three of the phrases or sentences suggested above are incorrect. Below are the main reasons why a phrase or sentence might not correctly summarise the overall meaning of a text. Match each incorrect answer to a reason.

Reasons
A The phrase/sentence describes a detail, rather than the main topic of the reading text.
B The phrase/sentence contains information which is not mentioned in the reading text.
C The phrase/sentence contains a statement which is the opposite of the information in the reading text.

▶ Short-answer questions
Focus on IELTS Foundation, p.35

Another task type in the IELTS Reading paper is short-answer questions, where you answer using a few words from the reading text. When you answer these questions you should pay careful attention to the **words/phrases** which introduce them. These tell you what **kind of answer** you are probably looking for, e.g. if the question begins with the word *Who*, the answer will be a person or people (usually their name(s)), but sometimes a characteristic such as their job or their age).

4 Look at the two lists below. Match the question words/phrases on the left to the type(s) of answer they might require.

NB There may be more than one type of answer for some question words/phrases.

Question word/phrase	Type of answer
1 Who …	number/amount
2 How many …	object
3 In which parts of the world …	reason
4 For what purpose …	activity
5 How much …	place
6 How often …	person/people
7 What …	method (way of doing something)
8 Why …	
9 How …	
10 What proportion …	

The maximum number of words you can write is specified and might be one, two or three. **If you write more than the maximum number you will not get a mark**, so you need to choose your words carefully. Make sure you choose the most important ones. Articles such as *the, a, an,* etc. are not included in the three words.

5 a) **Look at the first paragraph of the text and question 1 below. Which answer below would be correct for question 1 and why?**

A flat beds
B flat beds of rock
C beds of rock

The answer is *C – beds of rock*. This is because answer A does not contain the most important noun, *rock*, while answer B has four words and so it is too long.

b) **Do the exam task below.**

EXAM PRACTICE

> **TIP** The questions are always in the same order as information in the text

Answer the questions below.
Choose NO MORE THAN THREE WORDS AND/OR A NUMBER *from the passage for each answer.*

1 According to the writer, what do coral reefs look like?

2 How many countries have a coral reef close to their coastline?

3 What proportion of workers in the Maldives fish for a living?

4 Which activity is more than half of the Maldives' economy based on?

5 How can people usually get to reef fisheries?

6 What do Indian women often help to make?

7 What is usually exchanged for wood by women on Ulithi Atoll?

▶ Linking expressions

In the text, there are many examples of words and phrases which connect ideas between different sentences or paragraphs. These are sometimes called linking expressions. Different linking expressions for different types of connection help you to understand texts more easily.

6 a) **Look at the way these linking expressions were used in the text on p.30.**
 - for example (line 17)
 - In addition (line 18)
 - on the other hand (line 26)
 - In fact (line 28)

Note that linking expressions most often appear at the beginning of sentences and are followed by a comma. Where they occur later in a sentence, they normally have commas before and after.

b) **Answer these questions and use your dictionary if necessary.**

1 Which of these linking expressions means the same as *but*?
2 Which one means the same as *also*?
3 Which one is used to signal that the writer is going to emphasise something?
4 Which one means the same as *e.g.*?

c) **Complete the summary by choosing the correct linking expressions.**

Coral reefs are often situated near to the coast and they provide a useful source of income for local people. 1 *For example/On the other hand*, fish, shells and seaweed from reefs can be sold. 2 *In fact /In addition*, tourists often come to explore the reefs and the tourist industry provides jobs.

Fishing in the open sea is normally an occupation for men because it is a dangerous occupation. 3 *For example/On the other hand*, fishing on coral reefs is safe. 4 *In fact/On the other hand*, the work is usually done by women and even the elderly are able to join in.

In conclusion, coral reefs provide both economic and social benefits to communities living near them.

d) **Read the sentences below and decide whether they are true (T) or false (F).**

1 The majority of coral reefs are in shallow waters. ......
2 Many people make a living from coral reefs. ......
3 The only way to make money from coral reefs is to sell the products. ......
4 Women do not normally go fishing on boats. ......
5 In India, women often help to wash and prepare fish before it is sold. ......
6 Women cannot borrow money in Papua New Guinea. ......

Focus on vocabulary *Work; generalisations*

1 a) Scan the text on p.30 for the words and phrases connected with work in the left-hand column below and underline them. Match the words in the left-hand column as they are used in the text with the meanings in the right-hand column.

1 occupation(s)   a) money earned from working

2 livelihoods   b) job(s)

3 income   c) a way of earning money to live

4 workforce   d) gain money by working

5 earn   e) a group of workers

b) Complete the mindplan below, using information from the text.

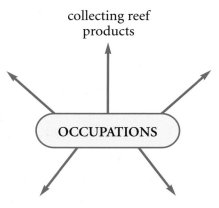

collecting reef
products

OCCUPATIONS

▶ Generalisations

In academic texts we often describe facts which are generally, but not always, true. In English there are several ways of making sure information is presented accurately. One of these is the use of certain adverbs.

Here is an example from Text 2:

- *Fishing is <u>normally</u> an occupation for adult males, particularly where it involves the use of boats…*

2 Scan the text and find three other adverbs with a similar function.

▶ Work

3 Complete the sentences below with a form of the word given in brackets. Use your dictionary if necessary.

0 I'm studying chemistry at university because I want to be a ..*scientist*.. (science).

1 You have to write lots of job .... (apply) when you're looking for work.

2 I like my job but my .... (manage) isn't very nice.

3 It's a small company with only twelve .... (employ).

4 She has a very good .... (qualify) from university.

5 There are fifty .... (work) in this factory.

6 If you are good at your job, maybe you will get a .... (promote).

7 I am in .... (retire) because I feel too old to work anymore!

8 I would like to be a .... (write) because I love books.

4 Answer these questions. Use your dictionary if necessary.

1 What is the difference between *an employee* and *an employer*?
2 If I don't like my job, do I *resign* or *retire*?
3 I am good at my job but my company doesn't have enough money to pay me. Will my manager *give me the sack* or *make me redundant*?
4 I receive my pension every week. Am I *too sick* or *too old* to work?
5 If you apply for a new job, will you have *an interview* or *a conversation* with the manager of the company?

5 Match the sentences in column A with the best response in column B.

A	B
1 I had an interview yesterday.	a) Congratulations!
2 I got a promotion today!	b) Are you going to accept it?
3 I've been offered my old manager's position.	c) Why?
4 I'm thinking of leaving my company.	d) Are you looking forward to it?
5 My boss is sending me on a training course.	e) How did it go?

Focus on speaking *Part 1 Answering personal questions*

In the first part of the IELTS Speaking test you have to answer short questions about yourself, your family and friends, or your opinions.

SKILLS PRACTICE
Focus on IELTS Foundation, p 29

1 🎧 **Listen to these questions about housework and answer each one as quickly as possible. Don't worry about the length of your answer at the moment.**

> **Housework**
> *How often do you do housework?*
> *Which job do you least enjoy doing in the house?*
> *Which job do you most enjoy doing in the house?*
> *How much time do you spend doing housework?*
> *Did you help with the housework when you were a child?*

2 🎧 **Listen to the same questions and the answers given by a man.**

The man gives a short answer to each question, followed by extra information. In the IELTS test you will get better marks if you extend your own answers to give extra information.

3 **Look at what the man says in answer to one of the questions.**

Q *How often do you do housework?*

A *I do a little bit every day, like washing dishes or making beds, but I do most jobs at the weekend.*

He gives *examples* of things he does every day. Giving examples is one way of extending your answers.

TIP If necessary, you can invent answers. For example, if you don't know the English word for a particular household job, just use another that you do know.

4 a) Look at what the man says in answer to another of the questions.

    Q *Did you help with the housework when you were a child?*

    A *No, never! My mother thought that housework was for girls, so I wasn't expected to do any.*

    b) How does the man extend his answer to this question?

5 🎧 Listen to and answer the same questions again. You can use the same answers as before, but this time add one more sentence to give extra information.

6 Look at the pictures below and answer the following questions.

    1 Where do the people in the pictures work?
    2 Have you ever worked in places like these? If not, would you like to?
    3 What other jobs can you name (e.g. police officer, teacher, etc.)?

7 a) 🎧 Listen to these questions about work and complete the gaps.

    1 Do .... job?
    2 Is your .... ?
    3 Do you .... in your work?
    4 .... your work?
    5 .... have you done this job for?

EXAM PRACTICE
▶ Part I

    b) 🎧 Listen again and practise answering. If you don't have a job, imagine that you have one and make answers up.

PRESENT SIMPLE

1 Use the correct form of the words in brackets to complete the text.

Using a Thesaurus.

A thesaurus is a bit like a dictionary, but it **1** .... (group) words with similar meanings together. Sometimes you can't find exactly the right word for what you trying to say. At other times the right word **2** .... (be) on the tip of your tongue, but you just **3** .... (not remember) it. You can use a thesaurus to find a word with the exact meaning that you want to express.

The thesaurus is divided into two sections: an index section and a reference section. Start with the index and **4** .... (look up) the word which is closest in meaning to the one you are looking for. Underneath the word you will see one or more alternative meanings. When you find the one you **5** .... (want), look for it in the reference section and you will find a list of words to choose from.

PAST SIMPLE

2 Use the correct form of the words in brackets to complete the text.

Printing

Before the 1400s people usually **1** .... (produce) and **2** .... (copy) books by hand. This **3** .... (take) a long time, so they were rare and expensive. However, in about 1450 Johannes Gutenberg **4** .... (invent) a printing press. This **5** .... (allow) a lot of books to be produced in a short time, so it was a very important development.

Gutenberg **6** .... (build) up words from separate pieces of type. He then **7** .... (put) ink on the words and **8** .... (press) paper against them. Printing by this method was widely used for newspapers, books and magazines up to the end of the twentieth century.

LINKING EXPRESSIONS

3 Choose a word/phrase from the box to complete the paragraph below.
NB There is one extra word/phrase.

> *In addition* *Therefore* *For example*
> *In fact* *However*

Farming

Nowadays, machines play an essential part in producing enough food for the world's needs. Machines can perform most of the jobs previously done by men or animals quickly and efficiently. **1** .... , machines can be used to milk cows. The milk can then be weighed, cooled and placed in containers in a series of automatic operations. This saves time and money. **2** .... , it reduces the risk of getting germs in the milk through handling.

3 .... , the farmer's skill is still very valuable. **4** .... , the best results in farming can only be obtained when the farmer's knowledge and experience is combined with the speed of his machines.

THE HIGHEST/LOWEST; MORE/FEWER…THAN

4 Complete the sentences, using information from the bar chart.

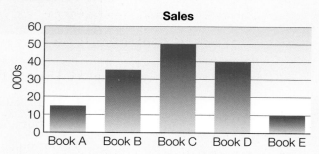

0   Book C had *the highest* sales.

1   Book E had .... sales than Book A.

2   There were .... sales of Book B than Book D.

3   There were .... sales of Book B than Book A.

4   Book E had .... sales.

5   Book A had .... Book D.

HEADINGS TASK

5 **Choose the best heading for this text. Circle the correct letter, A, B or C.**

A Joining a library
B Useful websites
C Electronic books

Academic libraries are increasingly using their budgets to buy online materials rather than physical books. There is also increasing take-up of online materials by public libraries, particularly of dictionaries and other reference material.

Agents known as *electronic aggregators* specialise in supplying these e-books. The agents first make a deal with the publishers (and through them the writers) for material. They then use a suitable format to produce the files, which they market and sell.

SHORT ANSWERS TASK

6 **Read the text below and answer the questions with one or two words.**

Costa Rica is one of the most prosperous countries in Central America. There are high educational standards and a high life expectancy (about 74 years for men and 79 years for women). Agriculture employs 19% of the people. Costa Rica's natural resources include its forests, but it lacks minerals apart from some bauxite and manganese. Manufacturing is increasing. The United States is Costa Rica's main trading partner.

1 How long, on average, does a Costa Rican woman live? ....

2 What proportion of Costa Ricans are farmers? ....

3 Which natural resources does Costa Rica have few of? ....

4 Which economic activity is growing in Costa Rica? ....

5 Which country does Costa Rica do most business with? ....

TRUE/FALSE TASK

7 **Read the text and decide if the statements below are true (T) or false (F).**

Since the 1950s Spain has changed from a poor country, dependent on agriculture, to a fairly prosperous industrial nation. By 2001 agriculture employed 6% of the people, as compared with industry at 18% and services, including tourism, at 76%. Arable and grazing land make up about two thirds of Spain, while forest covers most of the rest of the land. Major crops include barley, citrus fruits, grapes, olives and wheat. Apart from some high-grade iron ore in the north, Spain lacks mineral resources, but it has many manufacturing industries. Products include cars, chemicals, clothing, electronics, processed food, metal goods, steel and textiles.

1 In 2001 the majority of people in Spain were employed in manufacturing. ....

2 Agricultural land covers a bigger area than forest in Spain. ....

3 Spain is rich in mineral resources. ....

4 Spain manufactures both clothing and cloth. ....

ACADEMIC VOCABULARY

8 **Choose a word from the box to complete the sentences. NB There are two extra words.**

| range include focus access |
| workforce income |

1 Agriculture in Sri Lanka employs about one third of the ....

2 In some areas of the world people have no .... to clean water.

3 Singapore's manufacturing industries .... scientific instruments and ships.

4 Estimates of the number of languages in the world .... from 3,000 to 6,000.

4 ▶ Family values

Focus on listening *Preparation for listening; completing sentences; recognising cues*

▶ **Preparation**

In the second section of the IELTS test you hear one speaker giving information about a social topic. Before you listen, you are told what the topic of the talk will be. Thinking about the topic of a talk before you hear it makes the talk easier to understand.

1 a) **Think about the topic of family history. How many generations of your own family do you know something about?**

- your parents' generation
- your grandparents' generation
- generations earlier than your grandparents

b) **How did you get information about the history of your family? Tick those which apply to you.**

- talking to relatives
- reading old letters or diaries
- looking at photographs
- other ....

EXAM PRACTICE
▶ Sentence completion task

One of the tasks you might meet in any section of the IELTS Listening paper is completing sentences. You have to write one, two, or three words (the instructions will tell you what the maximum number is). Before you listen you hear an introduction. For example:

You will hear a man giving a talk to some people who want to find out about their family history.

2 a) **Look at these five incomplete sentences. Think about grammar. What kind of word or phrase is missing from each sentence? How exact can you be (e.g. noun, verb, number)?**

1 The speaker is familiar with Woodham because his .... used to live there.

2 After about ten minutes the audience can .... if they want to.

3 First of all, researchers should write down things they .... about their family.

4 The next thing researchers should do is contact their ....

5 Researchers should prepare a ....

b) 🎧 Listen to the introduction to a talk about family history and fill in the gaps. Write no more than three words for each answer.

> **TIP** In this type of task the answers have to fit the sentences grammatically, as well as in meaning. If the answer you first think of doesn't fit, it is probably wrong. This can help you, because there are two clues (meaning and grammar) instead of just one.

c) Check your answers. Are the grammar and spelling correct?

d) 🎧 Listen again and check your answers.

HELP

In the IELTS test you will only have the chance to listen once, but to help you now you can hear the recording again.

As you only hear the recordings once in an IELTS test, it's important that you can recognise the places where the answers are going to occur. Usually there are cues in the recording. The cues contain words which are the same, or have a similar meaning to words on the question paper.

3 a) **Look again at the first part of sentences 1 and 2 from exercise 2a) and then at the underlined parts of the audio script below.**

    1 The speaker is familiar with Woodham because …
    2 After about ten minutes the audience can …

Good evening everyone. I'm very glad to be here in <u>Woodham</u>. It's a lovely village, and <u>I know it very well</u> because my own grandmother lived here when I was a boy. But that's not why I'm here tonight. I happen to be the secretary of the Family History Society, and I understand you are all interested in discovering the history of your own family. So this evening I'm going to try and help you get started. And I'm sure you're going to find the whole process very exciting. So … I'll talk first <u>for about ten minutes</u> about the steps you need to follow, <u>and then</u> I'll stop and you can ask questions, if you have any. Is that OK?

The underlined bits are cues, because they mean the same as the first parts of the incomplete sentences. When you hear them, you know that you are about to hear the words that you have to write to complete the sentences.

b) **Underline the cues in the audio script below for sentences 3–5.**

    3 First of all, researchers should …
    4 The next thing researchers should to is contact….
    5 Researchers should prepare…

Right. Now the very first thing you need to do for your research is to take a sheet of paper and write down everything you already know about yourself, your parents, your grandparents and so on. Make a list of dates and places of birth and marriage and death, as well as where people lived, whether they did military service in the case of men, what their jobs were and so on. And then, when you've finished doing that, get in touch with any of your relatives who might be able to fill in some of the gaps in your information. Ask if you can talk to them. And before you see them, make a list of questions. Right? As well as the more obvious ones, like 'When was grandfather born?' or 'Did great-uncle Eric have any brothers or sisters?' try to find out details like 'What places did you visit when you were growing up?'

TIP In this type of task the words missing from the sentences are always words which are in the recording, so you won't have to make any grammatical changes, such as singular to plural, or present simple to past simple.

TIP In the IELTS test there are pauses in the recording at various places. Use these pauses to check your answers and to look ahead at the next group of questions.

4   a) Look at the instructions for the listening task below. What is the maximum number of words you should write for each gap?

b) What kind of word(s) (e.g. verb, noun) do you think you will need for each gap?

c) 🎧 Follow the instructions on the recording, listen to the rest of the talk about family history and complete the sentences.

Questions 1–8
Complete the sentences below.
*Write **NO MORE THAN TWO WORDS** for each answer.*

Advice about researching family history

1   It is better to use .... for recording what people say.

2   At the beginning of each recording, say the date, ... , and person's name.

3   Apart from people's memories, you can get information from various ....

4   Obituaries appear in newspapers, and they announce a person's ....

5   Ancestor Charts are like ....

6   Ancestor Charts can be obtained from ....

7   It is best to use .... to fill in the Ancestor Charts.

8   A nickname is a .... name that your friends and family call you.

---

5   🎧 Listen again and check your answers for:

- number of words
- grammar
- spelling

Focus on vocabulary 1 *Family*

1   a) Read about Turki and his family.

My name is Turki and I am 22 years old. I am engaged to be married to Fatima next year. My family is a typical nuclear family. I live with my father, Hamed, my mother, Meera, and my brother, Salem. Five years ago, my sister, Reema, got married and left home. She now has two daughters. My brother-in-law is called Ahmed and my two little nieces are Alia and Noora.

b) Write the names on Turki's family tree below.

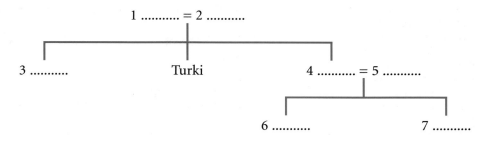

1 .... = 2 ....

3 ....   Turki   4 .... = 5 ....

6 ....   7 ....

2   a) Complete this paragraph about Alvaro Perez, using the information in his family tree.

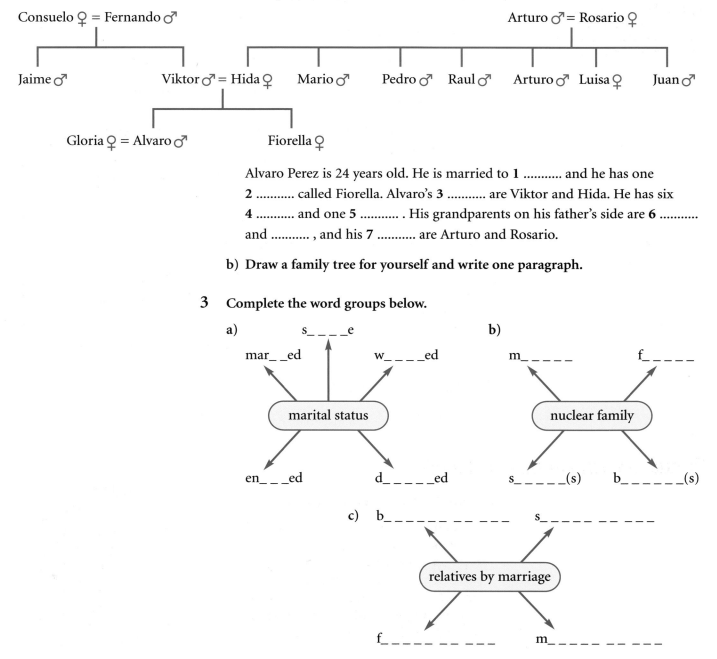

Consuelo ♀ = Fernando ♂   Arturo ♂ = Rosario ♀

Jaime ♂   Viktor ♂ = Hida ♀   Mario ♂   Pedro ♂ Raul ♂   Arturo ♂ Luisa ♀   Juan ♂

Gloria ♀ = Alvaro ♂   Fiorella ♀

Alvaro Perez is 24 years old. He is married to **1** .... and he has one
2 .... called Fiorella. Alvaro's **3** .... are Viktor and Hida. He has six
4 .... and one **5** .... His grandparents on his father's side are **6** ....
and .... , and his **7** .... are Arturo and Rosario.

b) Draw a family tree for yourself and write one paragraph.

3 Complete the word groups below.

a)   s_ _ _ _e

mar_ _ed   w_ _ _ _ed

marital status

en_ _ _ed   d_ _ _ _ _ed

b)

m_ _ _ _ _   f_ _ _ _ _

nuclear family

s_ _ _ _ _(s)   b_ _ _ _ _ _(s)

c)   b_ _ _ _ _ _ _ _ _ _   s_ _ _ _ _ _ _ _ _ _

relatives by marriage

f_ _ _ _ _ _ _ _ _   m_ _ _ _ _ _ _ _ _

Focus on grammar *Articles*

Focus on IELTS Foundation,
p.44, KLB p.141

TIP The best way to learn the use of articles is to read a lot. Through extensive reading you will become familiar with the rules without having to think about them.

1 Complete the following rules with a/an, the or – (zero article).

1 With superlatives, we normally use ......
2 When we talk about something for the first time, we normally use ......
3 For months, we normally use ......
4 For lakes, mountains, countries, names, streets and cities, we normally use ......
5 For oceans, we normally use ......
6 For something already mentioned, we normally use ......
7 For something which is one of many, we normally use ......
8 With plural and uncountable nouns, we normally use ......

2 Complete the text below about family structures by writing a/an, the or – (zero article) in the spaces.

Family structures in India and the USA

Families in **1** ...... India and **2** ...... USA have different structures. Traditional Indian households are multi-generational and sons or daughters are required to take care of their elderly parents. **3** ...... oldest male is the head of the household, but **4** ...... oldest woman also has authority over the other women in the household. However, **5** ...... traditional Indian family structure is now changing.

In North America, households usually consist of only parents and children. Grandparents usually live in **6** ...... separate house, often some distance away. In many households, both **7** ...... husband and wife work, and so they each have **8** ...... income. At **9** ...... certain age many North American children go away to **10** ...... college, or simply leave home, and are less likely to take care of their elderly parents.

Focus on vocabulary 2 *Quantity; language of change*

► Quantity

TIP Look out for these basic words, notice how they are used and which other words frequently occur with them.

There is a small set of nouns and verbs which occur very frequently in descriptions of quantity, whatever the topic. You may hear these words in the Listening test, especially Parts 3 and 4. They are also particularly useful for the IELTS Writing test.

figure(s); *number(s)*; *proportion(s)*; *rate(s)*

These words are all used to refer to quantities, but they differ in the way they are used:

- We use figure(s) to refer to (sets of) specific numbers, e.g. *The figures for 2007 show an increase in spending.*
- We use number(s) to refer to non-specific amounts, e.g. *The number of people using public transport has fallen.*
- We use proportion(s) to express the relationship between a part and a whole. Percentages are one of the most common types of proportion. For example, 40% means 40 out of every 100, e.g. *A small proportion of the students, around 5%, own their own home.*
- We use rate(s) to express the speed at which something happens, e.g. *Unemployment is increasing at a very high rate.*

1 **Complete the following sentences, using one of the words above.**

1 .... of grey seals are still falling.

2 Farmers in the region keep only a small .... of cows, because the tsetse fly causes cattle disease.

3 Having a high .... of part-time staff in a company can create problems for managers.

4 Mass production of radios was difficult because of the large .... of parts involved.

5 .... for London indicate that an extra eighty doctors are required.

6 Plants which live in shade have a much lower growth .... than those which live in unshaded areas.

7 .... recorded over a number of years show that the water level of the lake is falling.

8 Literacy levels went up, but by the 1990s the .... of improvement had slowed.

9 A child's reading ability might be related to the .... of books in the home.

10 The number of people living in towns has increased, but the overall .... has fallen.

▶ Dictionary work

> **da·ta** AC S1 W1 /ˈdeɪtə, ˈdɑːtə/ *n* [plural, U]
> **1** information or facts: *the data is displayed on a graph.*

data

Data is a general word for information, but is usually used in formal, especially academic contexts. It is a plural noun, but it is often used like an uncountable noun too, so it is used with both singular and plural verbs.

Examples

- *Data from two separate studies were analysed and compared.*
- *There is insufficient data to draw firm conclusions.*

Below are some of the most common phrases containing the word *data*.

> data base (or database)   data analysis   data collection   data processing

2   **Answer these questions and then use your dictionary to check the answers.**

1   Which two phrases are similar in meaning?
2   Which phrase is used to describe a type of computer programme?
3   Which three phrases describe an activity?
4   Which of the activities would a researcher do first?

3   **Read the words in the box below and answer the following questions.**

> rise   grow   decline   decrease   fluctuate   fall   increase

NB The word *number(s)* can be used with any of these words, e.g. *The number of workers decreased.*

The word *price(s)* is used with *rise, increase/decrease* and *fall*, but not with grow or decline e.g. *The price of petrol rose last year* NOT ~~The price of petrol grew ...~~

None of the words can be used with *figure(s)*.

1   List the one(s) which can used as nouns as well as verbs.
2   Divide the words into 3 groups, according to their meanings. Then match each of these symbols to one of the groups.

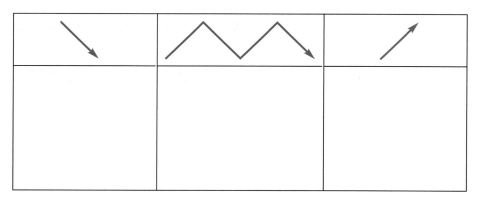

Focus on writing *Task 1: Key Skills*

▶ Understanding and
describing data
Focus on IELTS Foundation, p.40

▶ Numbers and proportions

▶ Pie charts

In Task 1 of the IELTS Writing module, you may be asked to interpret and describe data presented in graph form. There are three basic types of graph: pie charts, bar charts and line graphs.

Sometimes graphs and charts give information about proportions rather than numbers. It is important that you understand the difference between numbers and proportions and use the right language in each case because they are different types of data.

Pie charts are usually used to highlight differences in proportion at any one point in time.

The various portions, or sections, of a pie always add up to a total of 100%.

1 a) Look at this pie chart and answer the questions below.

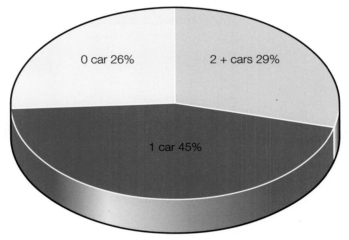

Car ownership in UK households: 2004

0 car 26% 2 + cars 29% 1 car 45%

1 How many portions/sections are shown?
2 What does each portion/section represent?
   A cars
   B people
   C households

b) Answer these questions about the data.

1 What proportion of households have no car?
2 How many cars do most households have?

▶ Bar charts

Bar charts can also highlight differences in proportion, but they may present data concerning selected groups rather than all groups.

2 a) **Look at the bar chart below about the proportions of people in different age groups in Botswana and in China.**

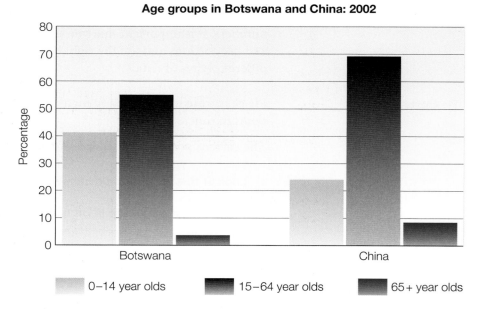

China is a much bigger area than Botswana, and has a much bigger population size. We may not know exact figures, but it is likely that the numbers of children under 15 are much higher in China than in Botswana. But this does not mean that the proportion is higher too.

1 Which country had a higher proportion of 0–14-year-olds in 2002?
2 Which country had a higher proportion of 15–64-year-olds in 2002?

b) **Complete the sentences below.**

1 In 2002 more than 40% of people in .... were 14 or under.

2 In 2002 the proportion of people over 65 was bigger in .... than ....

3 In China in 2002, nearly 70% of people were between .... and .... years old.

4 In 2002 the proportion of people over 65 in Botswana was approximately .... the proportion of those over 65 in China.

▶ Line graphs

Line graphs are usually used to highlight trends over a period of time.

3 Complete the paragraph below, using data from the graph.

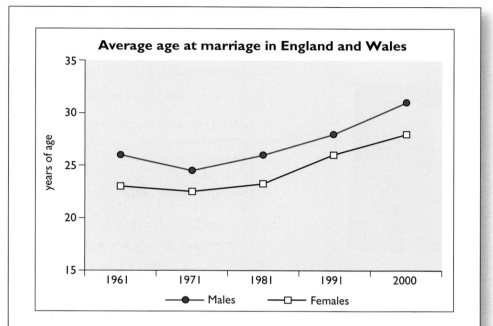

Average age at marriage in England and Wales

Between 1961 and 2000 the average age of marriage for both men and women in England and Wales 1 .... by approximately 2 .... years. In 1961 the age at which men generally married was 3 .... , but in 2000 it was 31. Women usually married at 4 .... in 1961, but in 2000 they married at 28.

Between 1961 and 1971 the average age of marriage for both men and women fell slightly. However, since 5 .... it has risen continuously. The biggest rise was between 6 .... and 7 ....

5 ► A sporting chance

Focus on grammar *Present perfect*

Focus on IELTS Foundation, p.54, KLB p.151

► Time words and phrases

1 **Which of the following sports activities have you done? Write a complete sentence for each activity using the correct form of the verb in brackets.**

I have (I've)… OR I have never (I've never)…

1 (attend) an international sports competition.
2 (join) a sports club.
3 (play) baseball.
4 (see) a Formula 1 race.
5 (meet) a famous sports person.
6 (do) yoga.
7 (work) out in a gym.
8 (take) part in a running race.

We use the present perfect to show that there is a strong link between the past and the present. We use the past simple for completed actions.

Time words often found with the past simple are:

a) **ago** e.g. *five minutes ago, thirty years ago*
b) **questions with when** e.g. *When did you see the match?*
c) **specific times in the past** e.g. *yesterday, in the last part of last century, during the 1920s*

Time words often found with the present perfect are:

a) **phrases which show an action or state which began in the past** and which is **still in progress** e.g. *I've lived in England <u>all my life</u>; I've been to the gym three times <u>this week</u>; I've run the marathon every year <u>for the last 20 years</u>; I've played hockey <u>since 1978</u>.*
b) **already, yet** (= before now) e.g. *I've <u>already</u> applied to join the running club.*
c) **ever** (= any time in the past) e.g. *Have you <u>ever</u> watched a football match?*
d) **never** (= not any time in the past) e.g. *I've <u>never</u> played basketball.*

2 **Complete the following sentences with the correct form of the verb in brackets.**

1 The popularity of yoga .... (increase) during the 1990s.
2 .... (ever see) a marathon from start to finish?
3 The university team .... (never reached) the semi-finals.
4 African athletes .... (dominate) long-distance running since the 1970s.
5 I .... (win) several minor events but never a major one.
6 I .... (manage) to get to the gym last night.
7 The team's performance .... (improve) recently.
8 Sorry I'm so late – I .... (just have) a seminar with my tutor.
9 I .... (never seen) an international sports competition.
10 Participation in team sports .... (decline) significantly in the last part of 20th century.

3 Correct the ten errors (<u>underlined</u>) in the text below. They may be verb form or time word errors.

Most people **0** <u>heard</u> *have heard of* triathlons but **1** <u>did you ever watch a biathlon</u>? The biathlon **2** <u>has begun</u> in the 1700s in Scandinavia as a military exercise but it has only been an official sport **3** <u>since</u> around 50 years. There are several versions of the biathlon but the basic idea **4** <u>has been</u> that the athletes must complete a cross-country skiing race with target shooting in the middle. Some of the races are 10 km while others are as long as 30 km!

The 20 km race **5** <u>is</u> an Olympic sport **6** <u>for</u> 1960. However, at that time the sport **7** <u>is</u> only for men. Women **8** <u>haven't been able to</u> compete until 1992.

Recently, television programmes **9** <u>introduce</u> many people to the sport for the first time. In fact, it **10** <u>has now been</u> one of the most popular winter sporting events on television in Europe.

Focus on listening 1 *Note completion; classification*

In Section 1 of the Listening module you will hear two people speaking about an everyday, non-academic topic, e.g. a customer talking to a sports centre receptionist. During these exchanges, one speaker often spells out difficult words.

SKILLS PRACTICE
▶ Recognising letters

1 🎧 Listen to the letters and put them in the correct column according to their vowel sound. One letter has been given in each column as an example.

/ei/	/iː/	/e/	/ai/
a	b	f	i

TIP The most common words spelt out in the IELTS listening test are people's names, addresses, postcodes and websites. They will often include double letters, so listen carefully for these. The exam often targets names which are quite unusual or spelt in an unexpected way so listen carefully right to the end.

2 🎧 Listen to the spelling of the following names, addresses, websites and postcodes and write them down. Examples of common spelling 'cues' are given. These tell you when you will hear a word spelt out.

1 _ _ _ _ _ _
2 _ _ _ _ _ _ _ _
3 _ _ _ _ _ _ _ _ _ Road
4 _ _ _ _ _
5 _ _ _ _ _ _ _ _

▶ Preparation

Before each part of the Listening module, you hear a short introduction. This tells you who is speaking and what the situation is. This introduction is not written on the exam paper so you have to listen carefully to it.

3 🎧 Look at the questions and listen to the introduction to the task below.

a) Who are the two speakers?
b) Are they speaking on the phone or face-to-face?
c) What topic are they speaking about?

▶ Form completion

TIP Look carefully at the instructions to see how many words are the maximum for each task.

TIP When answering questions where the answer is a number, write down figures rather than the number in words. It saves time, which is very important in the listening module.

EXAM PRACTICE
▶ Section I

TIP In the audio script there are cues which tell you when you are about to hear the answer to a question. For example, question I requires the caller's surname and the cue is a clear question: 'Can you spell your surname?'

For Section 1 of the IELTS Listening module, you **usually** only write ONE word for each answer. Be careful, you **sometimes** need to write two or three words. Each word must be correctly spelt for you to get a mark. If you write more words than the limit, it probably means your answer is wrong. Also there is more chance that you will spell something incorrectly if you write additional words.

4 Look at the answer sheet below, including the written instructions at the top.

a) In this case, what is the maximum number of words you should write for each answer?
b) Which questions do you think will require you to copy down spelling?

Questions 1–4
Complete the notes below.
*Write **NO MORE THAN ONE WORD AND/OR A NUMBER** for each answer.*

Santon Sports Club

Name: Alex **1** ....
Occupation: **2** ....
Postcode: **3** ....
Found out about the club from a **4** ....

5 🎧 Listen to the conversation and write down the answers to questions 1–4.

▶ Classification

Another common task type for IELTS Listening is Classification, where you have to match items to a set of general categories. In the task below, you have to match the facilities to the time period: weekend, daytime or evening.

6 🎧 Listen to the conversation and answer questions 5–8.

Questions 5–8

When would Alex like to use different facilities?

A weekend   **B** daytime   **C** evening

Write the correct letter, A, B or C next to questions 5–8

5 gym   ......
6 outdoor pool   ......
7 badminton court ......
8 steam room   ......

Look at the audio script for this section and check your answers. Classification questions often involve parallel expressions. For example, Alex wants to use the gym in the evenings but he does not use the word 'evenings'. Instead he says 'after about 7 p.m., when I finish work'.

7   Look through the audio script and find the parallel expression which helps you get the correct classification for each question. Fill in the table with the parallel expression(s) in the audio script. The first has been done for you as an example.

Classifications	Parallel expression in the audio script
evening	*that'll be after about 7 p.m., when I finish work.*
daytime	
weekend	

Focus on vocabulary 1 *Parallel expressions*

1   Match the word with its parallel expression. Try doing this without your dictionary.

Word	Parallel expression
1 competition	a) sports field
2 season	b) skill/capacity
3 record	c) tiring
4 pitch (noun)	d) take part in
5 health	e) period in the year when a particular sport is played
6 strenuous	f) top score/highest achievement
7 participate	g) contest
8 ability	h) physical condition

2   Complete the following sentences using the words in the left-hand column above.

1   I was really disappointed when my local football team lost the last match of the ....

2   I'm training for the London marathon. I love running but I'll never beat the world ....!

3   Last week, I played such a .... game of tennis that I was worried about my .... afterwards!

4   The team captain really wants to win the hockey competition next week but I'll be happy just to ....

5   I'd love to improve my swimming ....

Focus on writing 1 *Task 1: Describing line graphs*

SKILLS PRACTICE

Because one important use of the present perfect is to describe how things have changed over a period leading up to the present day, we often use the present perfect when we are asked to write a description of information given in a line graph in Task 1 of the IELTS Writing module.

You can only use the present perfect if the graph takes you up to the present day. If, for example, the last piece of data is for 2000 then your description must be in the past simple, because it deals with a time period which has finished.

1 a) **Look at the writing task below.**

> *The chart below shows the percentage of young people taking part in different outdoor sports from 1975 to the present day in the South West of England.*
>
> *Summarise the information by selecting and reporting the main features and make comparisons where relevant.*
>
> You should write at least 150 words.

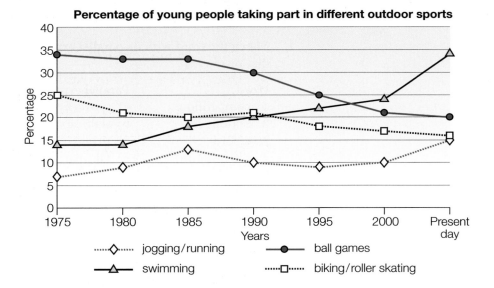

Percentage of young people taking part in different outdoor sports

......◇...... jogging/running   ——●—— ball games
——△—— swimming   ......□...... biking/roller skating

b) **Look carefully at the graph. Complete the following sentences.**

1 The time period shown in the graph is from .... to ....

2 The subject of the chart is .... The unit of measurement in the graph is ....

3 The levels of participation in .... and .... have gone down.

4 By contrast, the level of participation in .... has gone up.

5 The level of participation in .... has fluctuated.

TIP Note that the number of words in this sample answer is 160. Always write at least 150 words but do not go much over this figure as you will not get any extra marks and you will use up time which you can better spend on doing Task 2.

2 Read the sample answer below and complete the six missing words. They are all connected with the language of change (see Unit 4 p.46 for help).

The graph shows that over the past 30 years in the South West of England there has been a **1** d _ _ _ _ _ _ in the percentage of young people who take part in certain outdoor sports. However, not all outdoor sports have become less popular.

Over the period, the most significant **2** r _ _ _ _ _ _ _ _ has been in the percentage of young people who play ball games – this has fallen by almost 15%, from 34 to 20%, with the biggest **3** d _ _ _ _ _ _ since 1990. There has also been a **4** d _ _ _ of 9% in the percentage of young people who ride bikes and roller skate, from 25 to 16%.

However, there has been a steady **5** r _ _ _ in the percentage of young swimmers. In 1975 it was the third most popular sport and now it is the most popular. The percentage of young people who jog has **6** f _ _ _ _ _ _ _ _ _ over the period – 13% in 1985, falling to 9% in 1995 and then rising again to 15% in the present day. (160 words)

3 Underline all the verbs in the present perfect in the sample answer.

4 Highlight the sentence which has one verb in the past simple and one verb in the present simple. Why are these verb forms used in this sentence?

5 Look at the following writing task.

a) Which sports have had an increase in popularity?
b) Which sport has had a decrease in popularity?
c) Which sport has fluctuated in popularity?

The chart below shows the number of members taking part in different sports activities at Santon Sports Club from 1995 to the present day.

Summarise the information by selecting and reporting the main features, and make comparisons where relevant.

You should write at least 150 words.

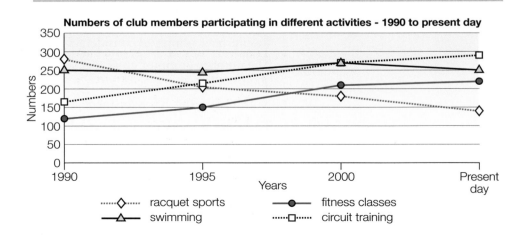

Numbers of club members participating in different activities - 1990 to present day

6 Look at the writing task on p.55. You are going to write your answer for this task. Choose the most suitable ending for each sentence below.

1 This graph shows …
… different sports available at a club.
… that there have been significant changes in the popularity of various sports between 1990 and the present day.

2 The number of people who swim …
… has gone up and down.
… has fluctuated.

3 Racquet sports …
… are not as popular as they were in 1990.
… are very popular.

4 Today, more members participate in circuit training than …
… in swimming.
… in any other activity at the club.

EXAM PRACTICE
▶ Task I

7 Write your answer to the writing task. Check your answer carefully

Focus on vocabulary 2 *Sports and prepositions*

1 Complete the following table with any sports that you know. Use the sample answer on p.55 to help you.

Play …	Do …	Go …
e.g. *basketball*	e.g. *ballet*	e.g. *swimming*

2 Complete the sentences with a preposition from the box. Sometimes it is possible to use two different prepositions.

from	*to*	*since*	*in*	*between*	*over*	*by*	*of*

1 Results have improved considerably ………. the past 30 years.

2 The number of motor cross spectators rose significantly ………. 1990 and 2000.

3 Nothing like this has happened ………. the Tokyo Olympics in 1964.

4 There has been a drop in ticket sales ………. approximately 30% during the last decade.

5 ………. 1960 ………. 2000 the number of different sports taught in schools doubled.

6 Ticket prices rose ………. 4% in 2005.

Focus on listening 2 *Multiple choice; two correct options*

In Section 4 of the Listening module, you will hear one person talking about an academic topic. They may be a student or a lecturer. Often they are talking about a project they have been working on.

SKILLS PRACTICE

1 **Look at the task sheet below.**

1 For questions 1–4, how many answers do you choose from each list?
2 For questions 5–7, how many words can you write in each space?

2 🎧 **Listen to the introduction and answer the following questions.**

1 Who is speaking? Is she a student or a teacher?
2 What is the subject of her project?

3 🎧 **Listen to the recording and answer questions 1–7.**

EXAM PRACTICE
▶ Section 4

HELP

For this exercise, you may listen to the recording twice to help you. However, in the real IELTS test you will only hear it once.

Questions 1–4
Choose TWO letters A–E.

Questions 1–2

What TWO reasons does Sadie give for choosing the focus for her project?

A She was failing as an athlete herself.
B She was asked by a fellow student to investigate the topic.
C She was advised to do so by her tutor.
D She saw links with her essay topic.
E She could use the results to help female athletes.

Questions 3–4

What TWO things surprised Sadie before starting her own research?

A that women are slower because they have less muscle
B that female hormones make women put on weight
C that men and women burn 'fuel' at the same rate
D that height is a key factor in running speed
E that women use more energy in a race than men

Questions 5–7
Complete the notes.
*Write **NO MORE THAN TWO WORDS** for each answer*

First experiment
• divided athletes' **5** .... by their height
Second experiment
• made race equally difficult for men and women by putting weights on men's **6** ....
Third experiment
• tested elasticity by measuring how high men and women **7** ....

---

4 Find where the answers occur in the audio script.

Focus on writing 2 *Task 2: Presenting arguments*

SKILLS PRACTICE

For this type of IELTS Writing task you are given two different points of view. You must discuss them both before reaching your own conclusion.

1 **Look at the following writing task. Two different points of view are presented.**

1 What is the first point of view? Circle the correct letter.
   A Governments should spend more money on sport.
   B Governments should support ordinary people doing sports.

2 What is the second point of view? Circle the correct letter.
   A It is better to invest in excellent sports people.
   B Top athletes only win if you invest a lot in them.

> Write about the following topic.
>
> *Some people believe it is better for governments to spend any available money for sports on providing facilities for the general population. Others believe that instead they should invest in training top athletes to win major competitions.*
>
> *Discuss both points of view and give your own opinion.*
>
> Give reasons for your answer and include any relevant examples from your own knowledge and experience.
>
> You should write at least 250 words.

2 **Look at the following list of arguments. Decide which support the first point of view and which support the second point of view.**

1 doing sport can prevent people from becoming overweight
2 supporting sportspeople can make people feel proud of their country
3 taking part in sports activities, particularly team games, can help children learn to be more co-operative
4 famous sportspeople can be good role models for the population as a whole
5 spending money to help athletes win means that people feel that winning is the only important thing
6 having successful athletes can help your country become well-known

3 **Read the sample answer on p.59 and answer these questions.**

1 What is the purpose of the first paragraph? Circle the correct letter.
   A for the writer to summarise her arguments about the issue.
   B to explain why governments must choose between two different types of sports people to invest in.
   C to explain the general benefits of participating in sports.

2 What is the purpose of the first sentence in paragraphs 2 and 3?
3 Which point of view does the writer agree with? Where does she state this?
4 Look at exercise 2. Where is each point covered in the sample answer?

Governments often do not have a huge amount of money to spend on sports development in their country. They have to make a decision about the most useful projects on which to spend their money.

There are many arguments in favour of the idea that it is good for a government to spend money on supporting the training of people who have already achieved success and who are likely to achieve more. <u>Firstly</u>, having successful sportspeople gives a country a sense of pride. People feel good about their country and about themselves. In addition, having a famous sportsperson from a particular place can help make that country better known in the wider world. Finally, successful national athletes are good role models for the young. Perhaps they will go on to become successful sportspeople themselves.

<u>However</u>, there are drawbacks to spending money only on outstanding athletes. It can give the impression that sport is all about winning whereas in fact, co-operation, trying hard and learning how to lose well are just as important. For these reasons, many people feel it is better for governments to spend money on ordinary sports projects, which try to encourage everyone to do some form of sport, even if they never achieve much success. This can help reduce levels of health problems such as being overweight, and get children off the streets, doing something useful instead of getting into trouble.

I personally believe that it is a much better use of money to help everyone to participate in sports because this leads to a healthier population with a more balanced view of life and it also shows a sensible attitude to achievement. (276 words)

▶ Signposting

To make your text easier to read, it is important to use 'signposting' words which tell the reader what's coming next. Two examples are underlined above.

4   Read the sample answer again. Look for words and phrases which give 'signposts' to the reader.

EXAM PRACTICE
▶ Task 2

5   Look at the following task.

a) What are the two points of view?
b) In two columns, write down a list of arguments for the two points of view.
c) After this, decide what your own opinion is.
d) Write your answer, using 'signposts' to help your reader.

> Write about the following topic.
>
> **Some people believe that it is good for a country to host a major sports competition. Others think it causes many problems for the country.**
>
> **Discuss both points of view and give your own opinion.**
>
> Give reasons for your answer and include any relevant examples from your own knowledge and experience.
>
> You should write at least 250 words.

6 ► Animal rights and wrongs

Focus on reading *Section headings; locating information*

EXAM PRACTICE
► Section headings

> **TIP** Reading the whole text quickly before attempting any of the tasks will help you to do them more easily. Don't try to save time by starting the tasks and reading the text in small chunks.

One IELTS Reading task is to match headings to sections of the text. (See also Unit 1.) There is one appropriate heading for each section, but there are some additional headings which do not match any of the sections.

1 a) Look at the text called *Polar Bears*, p.61. Read the text quickly, to get a general understanding. Try to guess, or ignore, individual words that you don't know.

   b) Look at the list of section headings below. If necessary, use your dictionary to check words you aren't sure about.

   Reproduction   Diet
   The fur trade   Habitat and distribution
   Physical characteristics Chances of survival

   > **TIP** Even the unsuitable heading(s) may contain words which are the same or similar to words used in the text. But unlike the suitable headings, they don't match the topic of the whole section.

2 Do the exam task below.

> **HELP**
> In the IELTS Reading task there is more than one unused heading. To help you, there is only one here.

> *Questions 1–5*
> *The Reading passage called 'Polar Bears' has five sections, A–E. Choose the correct heading for each section from the list of headings below.*
>
> **List of Headings**
> 1 Reproduction
> 2 The fur trade
> 3 Physical characteristics
> 4 Diet
> 5 Habitat and distribution
> 6 Chances of survival
>
> | Section | Heading |
> |---------|---------|
> | A | .... |
> | B | .... |
> | C | .... |
> | D | .... |
> | E | .... |

Polar Bears

A

The polar bear is the largest land-living carnivore. Adult males can measure more than 2.70 metres in length and weigh between 350 and 650 kilograms. The bear's body and neck are long and the head is
5 narrow and long, with small rounded ears.

The polar bear's coat, which covers it completely except for the nose and footpads, is superbly adapted to Arctic environments. Along with a thick layer of body fat, the water-repellent coat
10 protects the bear from cold air and water. The fur is 95 per cent efficient in converting the sun's rays into usable heat. Surprisingly, the fur has no white pigment; it is the reflection of the sun that causes the fur to appear white.

B

15 Polar bear populations can be found in northern Canada, Greenland, Norway and Russia, and there have been reports that polar bear tracks have been found as far north as the North Pole. The five-million-square-mile range of the polar bear circles
20 the Arctic, and contains stretches of open water where its primary food – seals – are easily caught.

Polar bears live on the annual Arctic sea ice, which provides a platform from which they can hunt. But as the edge of the ice moves further
25 north during summer, bears must either follow it, or become stranded on land until the fall.

C

Between late April and mid-July, polar bears hunt seals by breaking into their dens in the sea ice. The dens are not visible from above, but seeing
30 is less important than smelling to a polar bear. With their good sense of smell, polar bears can detect the breathing holes of seals in their dens beneath the snow and ice. Easy access to food in this period is critical, particularly for pregnant females. As the
35 southern edge of the arctic ice cap melts in summer, polar bears can become stranded on land. They then have to live off body fat stored from hunting in the spring and winter.

Polar bears also prey upon harp seals, as well as
40 young walruses and beluga whales, narwhal, fish and seabirds and their eggs.

D

Polar bears breed in late March, April and May. The males actively seek out females by following their tracks on sea ice. They remain with the female for a
45 short time, then leave in search of another female.

In winter, the female gives birth to twins, which stay warm in their mother's thick fur. She no longer feeds and instead lives off her stored fat throughout the winter. Her milk, high in fat content, enables the
50 cubs to keep warm and grow rapidly before leaving the dark den in March or April.

Short trips are made to and from the den for several days, as the cubs get used to the outside temperatures. Then the family leaves and makes its
55 way to the sea ice, where the mother feeds and protects her cubs. The family returns to the den the next winter and remains together during the following spring and summer.

E

With about 22,000 polar bears living in the wild,
60 the species is not currently endangered, but its future is far from certain.

In 1973 Canada, the United States, Denmark, Norway and the former USSR signed the International Agreement on the Conservation of
65 Polar Bears and their Habitat. This agreement restricts the hunting of polar bears and directs each nation to protect their habitats. However, it does not protect the bears against the biggest man-made threat: global warming.

70 As a result of global warming, sea ice in the Arctic is melting earlier and forming later each year. Ongoing research funded by the World Wildlife Fund (WWF) is finding that polar bears are left with less time on the ice to hunt for food. If current
75 warming trends continue, scientists believe that polar bears may disappear within 100 years.

TIP You need a general understanding to do this type of task, because headings relate to the overall meaning of sections, rather than the meaning of individual parts. Don't get distracted by minor details.

EXAM PRACTICE

▶ Locating information

Another IELTS task type involves finding in which sections or paragraphs of a text specific information is given. To do this you will have to scan the text.

If you have already read the whole text, you should be able to do this task quite quickly, because you will probably remember roughly which area of the text it came in.

HELP

To make things easier for you, the task is based on the same text that you have just read, although in the exam you are unlikely to find both a section heading task and an information task together.

TIP The list in the task sometimes contains exactly the same key words as the words in the text, but sometimes it uses other words with the same or a similar meaning instead.

---

3 a) Look at the exam task below. Before you start, look at the first item of information – *a list of countries which are home to the polar bear.*

To find this information, begin by scanning the text for places where the key word (countries) is mentioned, or words related to it.

b) How many places are there like this altogether? Which section(s) are they in? ....

c) Which of these references is *a list of countries which are home to the polar bear?* ....

d) Do the rest of the exam task below, following the same steps you followed above.

Questions 6–11
Polar Bears has five sections, A–E.
Which section contains the following information?
Write the correct letter, A–E.
NB *You may use any letter more than once.*

1 a list of countries which are home to the polar bear

2 measures intended to protect the polar bear

3 preparations made by female polar bears for the birth of their young

4 how the polar bear's coat produces body heat

5 a prediction of the decline of the polar bear

6 how the polar bear locates its prey

Example	*Answer*
1	Section B

2	....
3	....
4	....
5	....
6	....

Focus on vocabulary *Core vocabulary; wildlife; transitive and intransitive verbs*

▶ Form and meaning

1 a) Look at the base forms of six words used in the reading text. Are they used as nouns, verbs or adjectives here?

b) Match each word, as it is used in the text, to one of the meanings below.

1	*range* (section B, line 19)	noun	C
2	*critical* (section C, line 34)	....	....
3	*enable* (section D, line 49)	....	....
4	*restrict* (section E, line 66)	....	....
5	*fund* (section E, line 73)	....	....
6	*current* (section E, line 74)	....	....

A let
B essential for survival
C total area
D prevent
E happening now
F disapproving
G pay for
H limit

c) Use one of the six words in a) to complete these sentences. Change the form of the word if necessary.

1 Having shelter from winter winds is .... for many species of bird.
2 The EU .... the amount of fish which can be caught around its coastline.
3 River otters have a bigger .... than coastal otters.
4 Zoos .... children in cities to learn about wild animals.
5 .... reports suggest that the cheetah is extinct in Ghana.
6 The UN is .... a project to save the gorilla from extinction.

▶ Wildlife

Two words in the wordplan below do not belong to the group. They are crossed out.

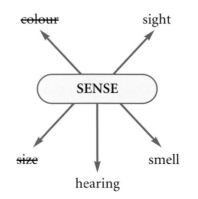

2 a) **Cross out the two words in each group which do not belong.**

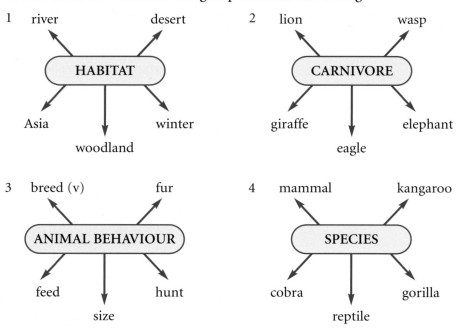

1   river   desert

HABITAT

Asia   winter

woodland

2   lion   wasp

CARNIVORE

giraffe   elephant

eagle

3   breed (v)   fur

ANIMAL BEHAVIOUR

feed   hunt

size

4   mammal   kangaroo

SPECIES

cobra   gorilla

reptile

b) **Study the sentences below and decide if they are true (T) or false (F).**

1   Humans are better adapted than crocodiles for swimming. ....

2   The ivory trade threatened the survival of the elephant. ....

3   At the present time, insects are the most endangered class of animals. ....

4   Despite international efforts to save it, the panda is a highly endangered species. ....

5   The giraffe's neck is adapted for leaf eating. ....

c) **Complete the following sentences using the words in the box below.**

> ~~endangered~~   predator   adaptations
> dangerous   hunting   adapt   prey

0   Tigers are *endangered* because people kill them for their skin.

1   Snakes can be very .... because they are poisonous.

2   Lions hunt zebras; lions are a kind of ....

3   Dolphins have clever .... to help them to stay underwater for a long time.

4   Owls are very good at .... mice.

5   Fish are often .... for crocodiles.

6   Animals must .... to their environment in order to survive.

▶ Transitive and
intransitive verbs

3 a) Look at these two sentences taken from the text above, about the way the female polar bear behaves when she is pregnant and after she has given birth.

  • *She no longer feeds* and instead lives off her stored fat throughout the winter.
  • *Then the family leaves and makes its way to the sea ice, where **the mother feeds and protects her cubs**.*

The word *feed* is used in two ways. In the first sentence, *feed* means the same as 'eat'. In the second sentence, *feed* means 'give food to'.

The word is used **intransitively** in the first sentence, and **transitively** in the second sentence. A transitive verb must be followed by a noun or noun phrase but an intransitive verb isn't. A few words, like *feed*, can be used in both ways. Most can only be used in one way. A good dictionary will tell you whether a verb can be used transitively, intransitively, or both. (Longman dictionaries use the symbols *I* and *T*.)

  b) Write *I* (for intransitive) or *T* (for transitive) next to the sentences below, according to how the underlined verb is used.

  0 …the water-repellent coat <u>protects</u> the bear   ..*T*..

  1 The five-million-square-mile range of the polar bear <u>circles</u>
     the Arctic.   ......
  2 Polar bears <u>live</u> on the annual Arctic sea ice.   ......
  3 Bears must <u>follow</u> the ice floes or become stranded on land.   ......
  4 Polar bears <u>hunt</u> seals on the sea ice.   ......
  5 Polar bears <u>prey</u> upon harp seals, as well as young walruses
     and beluga whales.   ......
  6 Polar bears <u>breed</u> in late March, April and May.   ......

Focus on grammar 1 *Comparison*

Focus on IELTS Foundation, p.66,
KLB p.142

1 Correct the ten errors in the table below. They are all in the comparative and superlative columns.

Adjective	Comparative form	Superlative form
big	biger	biggest
small	more small	most small
strange	strangest	stranger
heavy	heavier	heavyest
endangered	endangerer	more endangered
long	longger	longerest

2 a) **Complete the text below using the correct form of the adjectives and adverbs given. The symbols show whether the comparative should be more, less or the same.**

– (less)   + (more)   = (the same)

> **Moths and butterflies**
>
> Moths and butterflies belong to the same family and share a lot of features. However, there are some differences. Moths are **0** <u>less colourful than</u> butterflies (**– colourful**), and their bodies are **1** .... (**+ hairy**). When they are resting, moths lay their wings flat, but butterflies fold them together. Butterflies can hear, taste and see very well. Moths cannot see **2** .... butterflies (**= well**), but they are attracted to bright lights. Butterflies are **3** .... in daytime .... moths (**+ active**).
>
> Moths provide a very interesting example of adaptation. As industrial cities in Europe became blackened by smoke, light coloured moths were easily spotted by birds. For this reason there are now **4** .... dark-coloured moths .... light-coloured moths (**+ many**).

b) **Write a short paragraph comparing frogs and toads. Use the information in the table.**

Common frogs and toads of the UK		
	FROGS	TOADS
Size	Up to 8 cm	Up to 10 cm
Skin	– bumpy	+ bumpy
Back legs	+ long	– long
Touch	– moist	+ moist
Time spent in water	+ long	– long

Frogs and toads belong to the same group of amphibians and are very similar. However, there are some differences between them.

....

....

....

3 **Use the prompts below to write correct sentences with superlative forms.**

0   staying – groups – safe – way – animals – live
    Staying in groups is the safest way for animals to live.

1   locusts – one – harmful – insects
2   lions and tigers – large – members – cat family
3   giant panda – one – rare – mammals
4   elephant – heavy – animal – in the world
5   snow leopard – one – little – often seen animals

Focus on speaking *Part 1 practice, discussing animals; Part 2, the long turn*

EXAM PRACTICE
▶ Answering the examiner's questions

1 a) 🎧 Listen to these questions on the subject of animals.

b) Read the answers A–E below.

c) 🎧 Listen again, and choose the best answer from the list below for each question. Write the letters in the spaces. (NB There is one extra answer.)

A I really like the big cats, especially panthers. They're so beautiful and they remind me of my own cat!

B Most people like cats because they're easy to look after. But a lot of people in the countryside have a dog. Birds are popular too with people in big cities.

C About twelve years ago, when I was still at school. There was a school trip.

D I think the main reason why people keep pets is because they're like friends, especially for people who live by themselves.

E I don't at the moment. I had a rabbit but it died last year. I'd like to get another one.

Question: 1 ......   2 ......   3 ......   4 ......

d) 🎧 Listen again and practise answering the questions yourself.

▶ **The structure of the long turn**

In the second part of the IELTS Speaking test you have to talk by yourself for one – two minutes, on a subject chosen by the examiner. The examiner gives you a card with some instructions to help you.

The card looks like this:

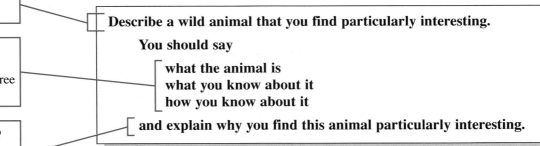

this line gives you the general topic	

these lines tell you what to describe. There are always three points to mention	**Describe a wild animal that you find particularly interesting.**
	You should say
	  what the animal is
	  what you know about it
	  how you know about it

this line asks you to give more details about your feelings or experiences	**and explain why you find this animal particularly interesting.**

The first sentence on the card is a summary of what you have to talk about. After that there are some details about the sub-topics you should mention.

2 How many sub-topics are there on this card and what are they?

> **TIP** There is always the same number of sub-topics on an IELTS Speaking card. You should take care to mention all of the sub-topics. If you check each time you practise, you will get used to the card layout.

► Note styles

3 **a)** Here are notes written by three different people in preparation for the speaking task on p.67 about a wild animal. Which important feature does each set of notes have?

A   Uses complete sentences.   ......
B   Uses numbering to plan a sequence.   ......
C   Uses a mindplan to link ideas.   ......

1
> Beaver
>
> 1) aquatic mammal, N. America and northern Europe, fur,
>   social groups, makes dams with trees, lives underwater
> 2) from TV and books
> 3) social, environment

2
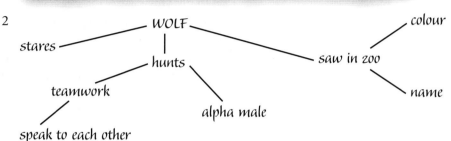

3
> The animal I find very interesting is the elephant. Elephants aren't found
> in the wild in this country – they're only found in Africa and Asia.
> They tend to live to

b) Write an advantage and a disadvantage of each of these note styles.

	Advantage(s)	Disadvantage(s)
Style 1	....	....
Style 2	....	....
Style 3	....	....

c) Which style do you prefer?

d) Do you think you could speak for one – two minutes in English without using notes? What might the advantages and disadvantages be?

e) Use the same card about a wild animal to prepare your own talk. Allow yourself one minute to make notes and then practise using the notes to give a talk.

Think about how useful your notes were.

4 🎧 Listen to three speakers doing the long turn. As you listen to each one, tick the card on p.67 as the speaker mentions each point on it.

TIP It might be useful to practise using different styles, until you are sure which one suits you the best.

Focus on grammar 2 *Review of present tenses*

Focus on IELTS Foundation, p.61,
KLB p.152

▶ Verb forms

1   Look again at the text called *Polar Bears*, p.61. The verb form which is used most of the time is the present simple. Which two of these uses of the present simple are found in the text? Circle the correct letter(s).

A   a regular action or event in the present
B   a scientific fact or a general truth
C   a mental or emotional state

▶ Mental states

2   Look at the extracts below from what the three speakers said for their long turn.

The present simple can be used to describe a mental or emotional state. Which of these verbs are examples of that use? Tick the correct sentence(s).

1   'The animal that I **want** to talk about is the beaver.'
2   'It **lives** in social groups.'
3   'I **think** they're very interesting, because they're social.'
4   'I **know** that it has to communicate with others.'
5   'They **hunt** in a team.'
6   'They **enjoy** having a mud bath.'

3   Complete the sentences below using either the present simple or progressive form of the verbs in brackets.

1   There is some evidence that otter numbers .... (increase) again.
2   Groups of elephants .... (communicate) over very long distances.
3   Stocks of many species of fish .... (decline) rapidly.
4   The Canada Goose .... (fly) with slow and regular wing beats.
5   The flamingo .... (have) an exceptionally long neck and legs.

Focus on listening *Recognising numbers*

SKILLS PRACTICE
Focus on IELTS Foundation, p.63

1   🎧 Look at these groups of numbers of different kinds. Listen and underline the number in each group that you hear.

1   4th; 14th; 40th
2   9th; 19th; 90th
3   12th; 12; 20th
4   35; 39; 93
5   17; 70; 77
6   2nd; 23rd; 22
7   182; 280; 802
8   503; 513; 305
9   54880; 54480; 54800
10   2010; 2100; 2001

2   Practise saying all the numbers above.

PRESENT PERFECT/PAST SIMPLE

1   Complete the texts below, using the correct form of the word in brackets. (Change the order of the words in the sentence if necessary.)

> In 1986 a committee **1** .... (decide) to redesign javelins to make them less dangerous. Since then, throwing distances **2** .... (become) considerably shorter, and there have been fewer accidents.

> Sports scientists now **3** .... (design) a vest for speed skaters with vibrating pads on the shoulders. These provide instant feedback on skaters' movements as they hurtle around the rink.

> Jorge Fernandez **4** .... (start) college three years ago. Since then he **5** .... (take) part in five college baseball tournaments, but his team **6** .... (not win) a major championship yet.

> Badminton is one of the world's most popular games, particularly in Asia. Together, China and Indonesia **7** .... (win) the majority of all International Badminton Federation events.

ARTICLES

2   Put an article (a/an or the) _where necessary_ in the spaces.

Birds are **1** .... fastest of all the animals. When the peregrine falcon is in **2** .... dive, it can reach **3** .... speeds of 350 kilometres per hour. Another bird, **4** .... Asian spine-tailed swift, can reach more than 160 kilometres per hour in level flight.

Amongst land animals **5** .... cheetah is **6** .... champion sprinter, while **7** .... fastest marine animal is **8** .... type of fish called a sailfish.

COMPARATIVES/SUPERLATIVES

3   Complete the sentences below, using the comparative or superlative form of the adjective given in brackets.

1   The three-toed sloth is .... of all mammals: it takes a whole day to travel 100 metres. (slow)

2   Most experts believe that chimpanzees and dolphins are .... animals. (intelligent)

3   Pets and zoo animals generally live .... wild animals. (long)

4   The crocodile's jaw is .... that of the alligator. (narrow)

5   The .... feature of birds is their feathers. (characteristic)

6   Certain species of spider are amongst .... of animals, because of their venom. (deadly)

LINKING EXPRESSIONS

4   Choose one of the words/phrases from the box for each space.

> _Secondly   In addition   However_
> _For example   Firstly_

Marriage

The rules concerning who a person can marry vary considerably from one society to another. Although all societies prohibit marriage between certain categories of relative, the categories themselves differ from one culture to another. **1** .... , in ancient Egypt marriages between brothers and sisters were permitted within the family of the pharaoh, in order to preserve the blood purity of the ruling dynasty. This was in marked contrast to the traditional family system of China, which prohibited marriage among a wide range of relatives, including distant cousins.

2 .... , there are different rules concerning the number of husbands or wives a person is allowed to have at any one time. **3** .... , there's _monogamy_, where a person only has one partner at a time. **4** .... , there's _polygamy_, where two or more partners are recognised socially. Polygamy can involve husbands having two or more wives (_polygyny_) or wives having two or more husbands (_polyandry_).

Polygamy is the most frequent form of marriage throughout the world, but monogamy is spreading. **5** .... , due to increases in divorce and re-marriage, the practice of having several partners consecutively is becoming more common. This is known as _serial monogamy_.

SENTENCE COMPLETION

5 **Use up to three words from the text about marriage to complete these sentences.**

1 Within the royal family of ancient Egypt, even .... were allowed to marry.

2 In China, relatives such as .... could not marry.

3 .... is the most common type of marriage worldwide.

4 A rise in divorce is causing an increase in ....

FAMILY VOCABULARY

6 **Answer the following questions.**

1 What relation are the following people to Nick?

A Lyn ....

B Kate ....

C Sue ....

D Bill ....

E Ben ....

2 What is Pete's marital status?

3 What is Alison's marital status?

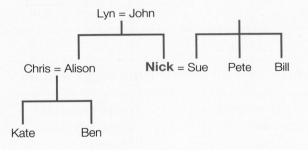

PIE CHARTS

7 **Answer the questions about the data in this pie chart.**

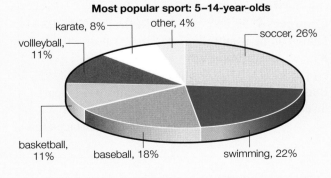

Most popular sport: 5–14-year-olds

karate, 8% — other, 4% — soccer, 26%
vollleyball, 11%
basketball, 11%
baseball, 18%
swimming, 22%

1 What proportion of children enjoyed karate more than other sports? ....

2 Which sport did the highest proportion of children like most? ....

3 Which two sports did equal proportions of children prefer? ....

4 Which sport did a higher proportion of children enjoy, swimming or baseball? ....

5 What proportion of children preferred something other than the top six sports? ....

LINE GRAPHS

8 **Answer the questions about the data in this line graph.**

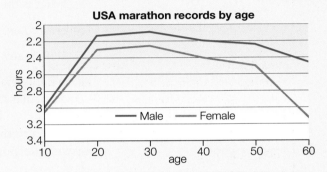

USA marathon records by age

hours / age — Male — Female

1 Between which ages did top running speeds rise most sharply? ....

2 Approximately what was the fastest time achieved by a woman? ....

3 At which age did women's top speed start to fall sharply? ....

4 At approximately which age did men's top speed level off? ....

5 What was the approximate difference between the top male and female times at age 60? ....

ANIMAL VOCABULARY

9 **Complete the text below using the words in the box. NB there is one extra word.**

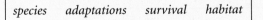

| *species* | *adaptations* | *survival* | *habitat* |

The Camel

Camels are very well adapted for their **1** .... For example, their toes are connected by a web of skin, so that their feet do not sink into sand. In addition, they have a hump to store water and fat, and they do not begin to sweat until the temperature reaches 40°C. These and other **2** .... ensure the camel's **3** .... in hot, dry environments.

7 ▶ Appropriate technology

Focus on listening 1 *Table completion*

In Section 3 of the Listening module, you listen to a conversation about an academic topic. There are two or more speakers who are often students and/or tutors. Table completion is a common task type in Section 3. The table is used to summarise information about two or more things under the same headings.

▶ Preparation

1 a) **Look at the exam task below and answer these questions.**

1 What is the general topic of the discussion? ....

2 How many objects are discussed? ....

3 How many aspects of these objects are discussed? ....

4 What is the maximum number of words for each answer in this particular task? ....

EXAM PRACTICE

▶ Table completion

b) 🎧 **Listen to the recording and answer questions 1–10.**

HELP

For this exercise, you may listen to the recording twice to help you. However, in the real IELTS test you will only hear it once.

Questions 1–10
Complete the table below.
*Write **NO MORE THAN ONE WORD** for each answer.*

Appropriate technology inventions			
Device	**How it works**	**Benefits**	**Extra design features**
Clockwork radio	• Powered by winding • Energy stored in a **1** .... • Gear box allows it to be released very **2** .... (highly efficient)	• Less expensive than radios using **3** .... • People not dependent on shops	• Special cell added, so you only wind it up when it is **4** ....
Solar box cooker	• Uses sun's light to cook food • Sunlight enters through a **5** .... lid • Converts light to longer wavelength so it is **6**	• Conserves **7** .... • Dung can be used for **8** .... (improves crops) • Reduces **9** .... diseases	• Reflector added to increase rays • Base of box **10** .... (retains more heat) • Lid inclined to increase surface area

▶ Transitions

The table format helps the listener because it often means that there are clear and predictable signals which tell you that the speakers are moving from one topic to another (transition). These correspond to moving from one cell of the table to another.

2 Read the audio script on p.168 and highlight the phrases and sentences which signal the transitions. The first one has been done for you.

▶ Answers/notes already given

Sometimes answers/notes are already given to you in the table and you do not have to fill in any gaps. For example in the first column, first row, you are given the first bullet point – *Powered by winding*. These example answers are very useful because they can help you to check your position in the table.

3 Read through the audio script on p.168 and underline the places where you hear information already given in the table.

Focus on grammar *Passive*

Focus on IELTS Foundation,
p.77, KLB p.148

> **TIP** The present passive is often used for IELTS Writing Task 1: Describing how things work or Describing processes (see p.74). The present perfect passive is particularly useful for IELTS Writing Task 1: Describing changes to places (see p.144).

1 Complete the following sentences using the passive form of the verb in the correct tense.

1 Solar box cookers .... originally .... (design) for use in rural areas.

2 The pendulum .... (invent) by Ibn Yunus.

3 The Internet .... (access) by millions of people around the world every day.

4 The museum .... (closed) for refurbishment since the beginning of the year.

5 Watering cans that can be carried on people's shoulders .... (used) for thousands of years throughout Asia.

▶ It + passive

> **TIP** In IELTS Writing Task 2 it is useful to use It + passive to support your points.

In IELTS Writing Task 2, you might want to talk about a common opinion or fact. For example, you might say, *Many people say that global warming is getting worse.* However, if you want to be more formal, it is good to use the structure *It + passive + clause: It is widely agreed that global warming is getting worse.*

Verbs which are often used in this way are:

agree	*believe*	*estimate*	*expect*	*feel*
know	*report*	*say*	*suppose*	*think*

2 a) **Correct the errors in these sentences.**

1 It is agree that seatbelts in cars save many lives.
2 It are said that more people work from home now than in the past.
3 It's knew that houses are more expensive than they were ten years ago.
4 They are expected that people will live longer in the future.

b) **Make sentences on the topic in brackets using the verbs in bold in the passive form. The first has been done as an example.**

0 **estimate** (population – double – last 40 years) *It is estimated that the world's population has doubled in the last 40 years.*

1 **report** (a vaccination – cancer – available – in ten years' time)

....

2 **know** (fleas on rats – carry – bubonic plague)

....

3 **say** (an actress – invent – mobile phone)

....

4 **believe** (over half – all schoolchildren – own – portable games console)

....

5 **expect** (the earth's temperature – rise by three degrees – by 2050)

....

6 **think** (organic produce – superior – to non-organic produce)

....

c) **Now make three of your own sentences using It + passive + clause, using the prompts below.**

0 It is thought that ...*You can watch any films you want* on the Internet. [the Internet]
It is thought that *you can find any information you want on the Internet.*

1 It is agreed that ...*We use the mobile phone in the class* [mobile phones]

2 It is felt that ...*You improve English slowly of British education* [education]

3 It is said that ...*You can't leave use the email* .... [email]

Focus on writing 1 *Task 1: Describing how something works*

SKILLS PRACTICE

Focus on IELTS Foundation,
p.165

1 a) **Read the instructions and look at the diagram for the writing task below. Answer these questions.**

1 Where do you find an air bag? ....

2 What is it used for? ....

3 What are the main parts of the device? ....

> *The diagram opposite shows how an air bag in a car works.*
>
> *Summarise the information by selecting and reporting the main features and make comparisons where relevant.*
>
> You should write at least 150 words.

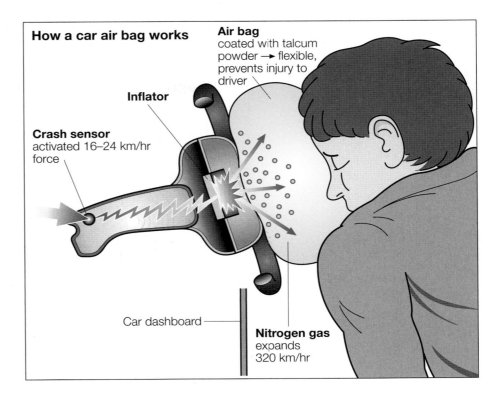

The diagram is labelled:

How a car air bag works

Air bag
coated with talcum powder → flexible, prevents injury to driver

Inflator

Crash sensor
activated 16–24 km/hr force

Car dashboard

Nitrogen gas
expands
320 km/hr

b) **Read the sample answer below. Fill in the gaps with words/phrases from the box.**

produces	*is fitted*	*inflates*	*is made of*
is activated	*is applied*	*mixes*	*expands*

TIP When we write a description of how something works, we often used the present passive form of the verb. However, it is unusual for all verbs in these texts to be in the passive form.

The diagram shows how an air bag **1** ...inflates... in a car to prevent injury when a car stops suddenly. The air bag device **2** ...expands... [is fitted] to the car steering wheel area and when a strong force **3** ...produces...? (for [applied] example, the car hits an object), the air bag is inflated. The air bag device consists of a long, thin crash sensor, an inflator switch and an air bag which **4** ...is made of... thin nylon coated with talcum powder to keep it flexible.

The device **5** ...is fitted... [activated] when a force of between 16 and 24 km per hour is applied. This switches on the inflator which **6** ...mixes... two chemicals. The reaction between these two chemicals **7** ...is activated [produce]... nitrogen gas, which **8** ...inflates... [expands] extremely rapidly, at over 320 km per hour.

c) **Look at the two paragraphs in the sample answer.**

1   Which paragraph describes functions and parts? ......
2   Which paragraph describes the process which occurs when the device is activated? ......

▶ Summing up

d) Which of the following sentences best finishes the sample answer on p.75?

    A This device is activated by an impact which causes the chemicals to react and blow up an air bag.

    B This reaction is sufficiently fast to make the bag come between the driver and passengers and the dashboard before they are thrown forward on to the dashboard.

    C Millions of people all over the world have been saved by this device.

e) The sample answer on p.75 includes several words and phrases which are often used to describe how something works. Look back over the sample answer and find words in it which mean the same as the words in column B. Use a dictionary if necessary.

A Words in text	B Synonym
1	mechanism/machine
2	comprise
3	trigger
4	exert
5	turn on
6	create/generate
7	enlarge
8	fast

EXAM PRACTICE

▶ Plan

2 Look at the task below and the plan of the essay. Then write your answer. You should spend around 20 minutes on this task.

- **Begin** with a brief introduction about what the thermos flask is used for.
- Start a **new paragraph** to describe the flask, e.g. size, materials, how the flask works.
- **Sum up** with one or two sentences about the flask.

The diagram opposite shows how a thermos flask works.

Summarise the information by selecting and reporting the main features and make comparisons where relevant.

You should write at least 150 words.

Thermos flask – maintains temperature – several hours

- Plastic cup – drink
- Some heat lost here
- Cap/plastic (usually)
- Metal/plastic
- Outer case
- Vacuum flask. Near vacuum => poor conductor. In glass envelope – silvered => less infrared radiation
- Insulated support

30 – 40cm

Hot liquid

Focus on listening 2 *Note completion*

SKILLS PRACTICE

> **TIP** When you look through the 'skeleton' notes, read the subheadings very carefully because they provide the structure of the talk.

A common task type for IELTS Listening is note completion. This is where you have to listen to the recording and fill in the gaps in a set of notes. It is particularly used for Section 4 where you listen to a talk, lecture or presentation in an academic setting. The task sheet is given in the form of 'skeleton' notes.

1 a) **Read through questions 1–6 in the exam task on p.78 and answer these questions. The task is divided into two sections.**

   A What do you have to listen for in questions 1–3? ....

   B What do you have to listen for in questions 4–6? ....

   C How many words can you write in each space? ....

   b) **What type of word(s) (e.g. verb, noun, adjective) could go in each space?**

   1 ....

   2 ....

   3 ....

   4 ....

   5 ....

   6 ....

Questions 1–6
Complete the notes below.
*Write **NO MORE THAN TWO WORDS** for each answer.*

Edible vaccines

Advantages

- Production is **1** ....
- Can last longer without being stored in a **2** ....
- Easy for vets to identify **3** .... animals

Disadvantages

- Difficult to control the dose
- Levels of vaccine in a plant vary according to its **4** ....
- Not sure how much of the protein is destroyed in the **5** .... of the animal
- Need to ensure plants don't contaminate **6** .... food

EXAM PRACTICE

c) 🎧 Listen and answer questions 1–6.

d) When you have done the task and checked your answers, look at the audio script and underline words which mean the same as:

- advantage
- disadvantage

Focus on vocabulary *Verbs to describe change*

Another type of task in the first part of the IELTS Writing module is to describe two plans, which show changes to one place over time. To do this, it is useful to know a range of verbs to describe change (also see Unit 4 p.46).

1 **The diagrams opposite show changes to one university campus between 1985 and the present day.**

Study the plans opposite and answer the following questions.

1 What does the first plan show? What does the second plan show?
2 Was there a lecture theatre in 1985?
3 Why do you think there are no car parks on the campus today?
4 Are there more or fewer trees on campus today than in 1985?

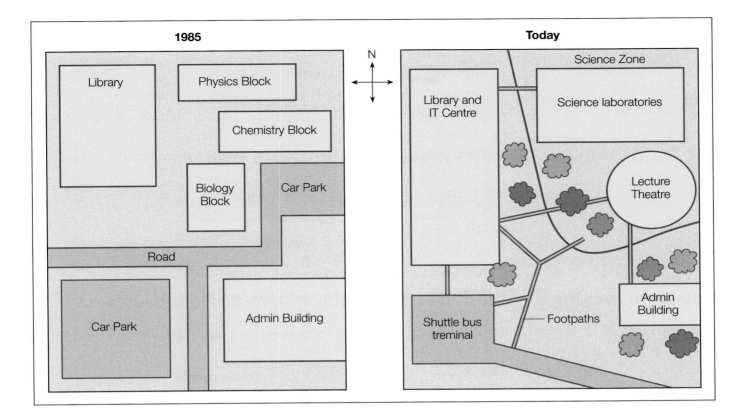

2 Look at the table below which classifies verbs of change. Complete the table using the words in the box. Some words may be used in more than one column.

Make the size bigger	Make the size smaller	Make the number bigger	Make the number smaller	Change or take away	Make better
extend	reduce	increase	reduce	replace (by)	improve

> enlarge   develop   add (to)   rise   grow   decrease
> decline   drop   fall   remove   convert (into)   increase

It is important to remember that we can't always use the same verbs with *size* as with *number*. *Size* refers to the area that something covers but *number* refers to how many there are of something.

3 Study the plans again and use the words in the table on p.79 to complete the sentences below.

1 The library has .... significantly.

2 The science blocks have been .... into one science zone.

3 The car park has been .... and .... by a shuttle bus terminal.

4 The number of footpaths has .... while the number of roads has ....

5 The size of the administration building has been ....

6 A new IT centre has been .... to the library.

NB See p.144 for a Writing task based on these plans.

Focus on writing 2 *Task 2: Describing advantages and disadvantages*

SKILLS PRACTICE

1 Read the Writing task below. Think about the positive and negative effects of mobile phones and make two lists.

Advantages: | Disadvantages:

....

....

....

....

....

....

You should spend about 40 minutes on this task.

Write about the following topic.

Mobile telephones have brought many benefits but they have also had negative effects.

Do the disadvantages of having mobile phones outweigh the advantages?

Give reasons for your answer and include any relevant examples from your own knowledge and experience.

You should write at least 250 words.

2   Think about the following questions to help you prepare your answer.

1   What do you find annoying about mobile phones? (e.g. in a cinema)
2   How might using mobile phones affect your health?
3   Do you think it's sensible to use a mobile phone while driving?
4   Have you ever had your mobile phone stolen?
5   Why do people travelling alone feel safer when they have a mobile phone?
6   How would life be different without mobile phones?

EXAM PRACTICE

3   Now prepare your answer. Organise your writing into four paragraphs. You may wish to use the useful expressions below in your answer.

1   <u>Introduction to the topic</u>
....
....

2   <u>Advantages</u>
There are several obvious benefits, such as ....
....
Another positive aspect is ....
....

3   <u>Disadvantages</u>
The impact has not all been positive ....
....
The most common criticism is ....
....
Another negative effect is ....
....
A final drawback is ....
....

4   <u>Summary and own opinion</u>
To sum up ....
....
In conclusion, I believe ....
....
The advantages/disadvantages outweigh the disadvantages/advantages
....
....

8 ▶ Communications

Focus on speaking 1 *Talking about personal preferences*

SKILLS PRACTICE
▶ Part I

In Part 1 of the IELTS Speaking module you might be asked about your personal preference for something. The structure of the question is usually *Do you like/prefer … or …?*

Questions like this can easily be misunderstood. Answering with *Yes* or *No* will be incorrect, because the person asking the question expects you to <u>choose between</u> two different things.

1 a) Look at the example below.

   Do you prefer listening to the news, or reading about it?

   Here are two possible ways of beginning your answer. Add any other beginnings you can think of.

I prefer listening to it.

I don't like either.

> **TIP** Replying correctly is the most important thing. However, you will get a better mark if you extend your answer and talk a bit more about the question. If you are asked about preferences, you can extend your answer by giving reasons or you can provide more details.

You might extend your answer to this question by saying:

I prefer listening to it. Then I can do other things at the same time, like the cooking.

OR

I don't like either. I usually watch the news on TV.

b) Think of some more ways that you could extend your answer to the question.

2 ∩ Listen to some more questions about personal preferences and practise giving extended answers. If possible, record yourself and then listen.

> **TIP** Remember, if the question isn't really relevant to you (for example, if you don't have a radio), *imagine* being someone else and then answer.

82

EXAM PRACTICE
► Part 2

3 a) Look at this card. What <u>four</u> things do you have to talk about?

   b) Prepare to talk, making sure that you cover all four of the sub-topics.
      Remember that in the exam you will have one minute to make notes.

> **Describe some exciting news that you heard or read about.**
>
> **You should say:**
>
> > **when you heard/read about the news**
> > **where you heard/read about it**
> > **what the news was**
>
> **and explain why you found the news exciting.**

   c) Practise talking about the topic for approximately two minutes. If possible,
      record yourself and then listen.

Focus on grammar *Permission, prohibition and obligation*

Focus on IELTS Foundation,
p.83, KLB p.146

PHOTOGRAPHY PROHIBITED

Safety Helmets
are provided
for your safety
and must be
worn

1 Below are some of the words which are used to express permission, prohibition
   and obligation. Which are verbs and which are adjectives? Write *V* (for verbs)
   or *A* (for adjectives) next to the words.

Ability/Permission		Obligation		Prohibition	
allow	....	*must*	....	*prohibit*	....
permit	....	*obligatory*	....	*forbid*	....
can	....	*compulsory*	....		
		necessary	....		
		have to	....		

The verbs *must* and *have to* share the same meaning but *must* only has one
form. When we are refering to the past, for example, we can't use *must*.

2 a) Complete the following sentences with a word or phrase from the list above
      in the correct form. There may be more than one correct answer for some
      sentences.

   0 Mobile phones *must/have to be* switched off in hospitals.

   1 In the early days of long-haul flights, passengers .... get off a
      plane when it refuelled.

   2 Within the next few years a bigger proportion of energy ....
      come from renewable sources.

   3 When I was a teenager, I was not .... to stay out late in the
      evenings.

   4 In most restaurants, smoking is ....

   5 At most schools in the UK, wearing a uniform is ....

   6 Many employees .... now work flexible hours.

In formal written English, rules are usually expressed impersonally (i.e. without reference to specific people). We do this by using the passive (see Unit 7 p.73).

b) **Where might you see sentences like these?**

1 Taking photographs **is strictly prohibited**.
2 Safety helmets **must be worn** in this area.
3 The use of dictionaries **is not allowed**.
4 The use of mobile phones **is not permitted** during takeoff and landing.

3 Look again at the list of words in question 1 on p.83. Which are the least formal and which are the most formal?

Focus on reading *True/False/Not Given; classification*

SKILLS PRACTICE
▶ Prediction

While you are preparing to do the IELTS test you should get as much practice as possible. Every time you read something in English it will help you if you think about the topic briefly before you start.

1 a) **You are going to read a text about the history of cinema. Before you begin, write down any words or phrases that come into your mind when you think about this topic.**

b) **Read the text below to get a general understanding.**

The early development of cinema in Britain

≫ THERE IS SOME DEBATE over when the first cinematic performance took place in Britain. Most people refer to 1896, when the first projected, moving photographs were
5 shown to a paying audience in London. This was an exhibition organised by the British representative of Louis and Auguste Lumiere, from France. The previous year the brothers had staged what is generally regarded as the
10 very first cinematic exhibition in the world involving projection and audience payment. However, it is important to note that many other inventors across Europe and the USA were almost ready to exhibit moving pictures
15 too. And in 1894, the first British 'kinetoscope[1]' had opened. This offered customers the chance to try Thomas Edison's coin-in-the-slot machine for viewing animated photographs.

Most people think of cinema as a means of
20 modern mass communication which was invented at some time in the past. However, while *film* and *projectors* were the result of invention, the *cinema* as a social institution evolved by chance.
25 People knew how to project images for centuries before the 1890s. The 'camera obscura', for example – a darkened room into which light passed through a small hole, or lens, producing an inverted picture on the wall
30 opposite – had been used in Italy as far back as the sixteenth century.

At the time of the Lumiere brothers' invention in 1895, critics, journalists and the early cinematographers disagreed considerably
35 among themselves about the use of the new machine: whether it should be for making

<< An old film accompanied by live music.

∨ Modern cinemas are large, social places.

archives, whether it was for teaching sciences such as surgery, or whether it was a new form of journalism and so on. In the end, however, it was the ability to tell stories which was responsible for the very rapid development of cinema as a mass medium. The growing popular-entertainment industry, which was motivated principally by money, recognised and developed this ability. By the end of 1896, only months after the first public performance of film in Britain, moving pictures were part of many music hall shows up and down the country. The pictures were accompanied by music and often by live, spoken commentary as well.

This expansion in exhibitions continued with great speed and profitability into the 1900s. After a short time films were shown in vacant shops, known as 'shop shows' or 'penny gaffs', and then after 1906 in custom-built premises called 'picture palaces', 'bijoux palaces' or 'majestics'. In 1909 the First Cinematographic Act was passed in parliament. Its main purpose was to regulate the size of cinemas, but it was also to introduce safety regulations concerning the number of people in the audience. In that year, estimates suggest that British production amounted to only about 20 per cent of films shown in British cinemas, and that 40 per cent were French, 30 per cent American and 10 per cent Italian.

By 1910 around 1,600 cinemas were in existence in Britain and by the outbreak of the First World War in 1914, this figure had risen to 4,000. The Cinema Commission estimated annual weekly attendances at cinemas before 1914 as seven to eight million. By the end of the war in 1918 British cinema exhibition had developed into a major industry, based on the extended fictional film. This had become an increasingly complex product: melodramas, comedies, westerns, travelogues and 'superspectaculars' were some of the early genres of popular 'silent' film. The films themselves were still largely produced abroad, increasingly in America. By 1914 Hollywood-produced American films accounted for over half the domestic market in Britain. This trend continued into the 1920s, but in 1927, the year of the first 'talkie[2]' film, government regulations were introduced to guarantee and reserve a proportion of the home market for domestic film production.

[1] An old machine used for watching moving pictures. Only one person could watch at a time.
[2] An old-fashioned word for a film with sound.

One of the tasks that you might meet in the IELTS Reading test involves comparing a list of statements with information in the reading text. Some of the statements are correct (True) and some are incorrect (False). Other statements are neither true, nor false, because the text does not provide enough information about them. These are called Not Given statements. You have to decide what kind of statement each one is.

Before you can make any decision you will have to scan the text to check. If you have already read the text for general understanding, you should find the search easier as you might remember roughly where the information was.

▶ Reading for detail

2 a) Look at the following statements. They all refer to information in the first three paragraphs.

1   The world's first cinematic show was free of charge.
2   People already knew how to project pictures in the sixteenth century.
3   Thomas Edison's kinetoscope was a very popular invention.

b) Look at the first statement above. Compare the statement with this extract from the text.

… the brothers had staged … the very first cinematic exhibition in the world involving projection and <u>*audience payment*</u>*.*

This means that the show was *not* free of charge, and the first statement is False.

c) To check the second statement, look at the third paragraph carefully.

You will see that the information here *does* correspond to the second statement. So this is True.

d) Finally, find the reference to the *kinetoscope* (at the end of the first paragraph).

You will see that we can't find out from this text whether it was popular or not. We can guess perhaps, but the text does not tell us. So the third statement is Not Given.

> **TIP** When you are doing T/F/NG tasks, don't use your own knowledge of the subject or your own opinions. Make a decision based only on what the text says, or doesn't say.

EXAM PRACTICE
▶ **T/F/NG**

> **TIP** The statements in this type of task always follow the same sequence as the information in the text.

3   Now do the exam task below.

Questions 4–8.
Do the following statements agree with the information given in *The early development of cinema in Britain?*
Write

TRUE	*if the statement agrees with the information*
FALSE	*if the statement contradicts the information*
NOT GIVEN	*if there is no information on this*

⇨

4   At the end of the 19th century, there were a lot of different opinions about the purpose of showing moving pictures.   ....

5   Cinema was slow to attract mass audiences.   ....

6   Moving pictures were sometimes shown in premises designed as shops.   ....

7   The first cinemas were dangerous because too many people were allowed inside.   ....

8   Between 1909 and 1914 the proportion of American films shown in Britain fell.   ....

EXAM PRACTICE
► Classification

Another task you might meet in the IELTS Reading module involves classifying names or objects or events, etc. *Classifying* means putting things into classes, or groups.

Doing classification tasks is similar in some ways to doing T/F/NG tasks. Both involve matching words in the question with words in the text, so you need to scan the text to find the right place before you can consider what to do next.

Sometimes the classes are different periods of time and you have to identify the period when certain events took place.

4   a)   **Do the exam task below, based on** *The early development of cinema in Britain.*

TIP In classification tasks the events, etc. to be classified are not in the same sequence as they are in the text.

Questions 9–13
Classify the following events as occurring between

A   1890 and 1899
B   1900 and 1910
C   1911 and 1920

*Write the correct letter, **A**, **B** or **C**.*

9   Moving pictures were first shown in specially designed buildings.   .B..

10   People could pay to use a machine showing moving pictures.   .A..

11   The majority of films shown in Britain were from Europe.   .A..

12   There were approximately 4,000 cinemas in Britain.   .C..

13   Moving picture shows were introduced in music halls.   ......

b)   **Before you check your answers, underline the places in the text where you found the answers. If any of your answers are wrong, this will help you to look for the reason.**

Focus on vocabulary *Adverbs of degree; academic vocabulary*

Focus on IELTS Foundation,
KLB p.140

1 a) **Look at these two sentences from the reading text about cinema in Britain:**

*The previous year, the brothers had staged what is **generally** regarded as the very first cinematic exhibition in the world. (lines 8–10)*

*The films themselves were still **largely** produced abroad. (lines 81–82)*

We use adverbs like *generally* and *largely* to show that a statement is true most of the time but not necessarily all of the time. The first example shows that <u>most people</u> believe that the exhibition referred to was the first in the world <u>but there is still some debate</u>. The second example shows that <u>most films</u> were produced abroad <u>but some films were produced in the UK</u>.

> **TIP** Knowing how to use adverbs of degree is very useful for the IELTS Writing module, particularly in Task 2, to help you express yourself more accurately.

b) **Underline the adverbs in this list that could replace *generally* and *largely* in the examples in 1a).**

> *sometimes, often, certainly, definitely, usually, mainly, truly, certainly, chiefly*

c) **Look at the position of the adverbs *generally* and *largely* in the two sentences.**

Adverbs like this usually appear after forms of the verb *be* and before other verbs. If the verb is passive, or has an auxiliary like *can*, the adverb usually comes in the middle of the verb phrase. (See also *Focus on IELTS Foundation*, p.19.)

Tick the sentences in which the adverb is in the right position.
Correct the sentences in which the adverb is in the wrong position.

1 People often prefer going to the cinema to watching films at home. ....
2 I check usually my emails every day. ....
3 The Internet definitely is very useful for research. ....
4 Celebrity-gossip magazines are mainly read by women. ....
5 People can learn certainly a lot by watching the news every day. ....

d) **Choose a suitable adverb from the list in b) to qualify these statements.**
Remember to check the position of the adverb.

1 British families with children have more than one television in the home.
2 Language develops more quickly in boys than girls.
3 National newspapers are better quality than they used to be.
4 Text messaging is preferred to letter writing by younger people.
5 Books which are classified as science fiction are more popular with men than with women.
6 Computers have had a very positive impact on education.

In academic texts of all kinds, but especially in texts from the social sciences, one very common word is *trend*.

2 a) **Look at this extract from the text about cinema.**

The films themselves were still largely produced abroad, and increasingly in America … This trend continued into the 1920s. (line 85)

b) **Which of the following words could replace *trend* in this sentence? Circle the correct letter.**

A pattern
B fall
C fluctuation

c) **A common collocation is *general trend*. Which other adjectives often appear before *trend*? Add to the wordplan below, using your dictionary if necessary.**

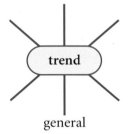

general

Another common word is *estimate*. The verb and the noun share the same spelling but they are pronounced slightly differently.

3 a) **Look at these two extracts from the text.**

In that year, estimates suggest that British production amounted to only 20 per cent of films shown in British cinemas … (lines 63–66)

The Cinema Commission estimated annual weekly attendances at cinemas … as seven to eight million. (lines 72–74)

b) **Which of these words means roughly the same as *estimated* in the second sentence? Circle the correct letter.**

A counted
B reported
C guessed

c) **Which two phrases are commonly used in English? Use your dictionary to help you and circle the correct letters.**

A rough estimate
B tame estimate
C conservative estimate
D untidy estimate

Focus on speaking 2 *Part 3; types of question; describing; comparing*

SKILLS PRACTICE

> **TIP** Remember, the examiner will not assess you on your opinions, only on how well you can express them.

In Part 3 of the IELTS Speaking test the examiner asks you about your ideas and opinions. The topic of the questions is connected to the topic of the long turn. The questions are less personal than the questions in Part 1.

The questions might begin in one of these ways:

Can you tell me about ... ?

What is/was ... like?

Do you think people should ... ?

What do you think can be done about ... ?

Which do you think is better, ... or ... ?

What do you think is the reason for ... ?

EXAM PRACTICE
▶ Part 3

Sometimes the examiner asks you to describe something.

1 **Look at these questions on the general topic of communication and think about how you might answer them.**

  1 What are newspapers like in your country?
  2 Tell me some of the rules about talking that children in your country learn, such as when they can talk and when they can't.
  3 What effects do you think using computers could have on children's writing skills?

2 🎧 **Listen to different people answering the questions and fill in the gaps below.**

Speaker 1

Erm, well, I suppose there are two basic kinds. Firstly, there are the more intellectual ones, the more serious ones. Then there's another kind which are not so serious, they are for – maybe less educated people. They have more articles **1** .... and things like that, for example. And they have more pictures. Also, the language they use tends to be simpler. So, I suppose that's more or less what newspapers are like in my country.

Speaker 2

Well, I used to be a teacher and one of the things we had to teach children was to make them **2** .... They were taught that it's rude to interrupt people, and that you should wait – you know, if you're a child in a classroom, you should put your hand up if **3** .... , to ask a question or to say something. I think children are also taught to use a certain volume when they're speaking, that it's rude **4** ...., to shout out. And then I suppose there are things about politeness – you know, saying 'Please', 'Thank you' – things like that.

Speaker 3

Well I think it must affect their handwriting skills – I mean neatness, and how easy it is for other people to read it. Because if children use the Internet a lot, they just **5** .... at holding a pen, and forming letters. And then there's the effect that emails have on writing – I mean, people don't usually **6** .... , or start and finish them like proper letters. So if children only send emails, their use of English might not be so good. They might not be very good at spelling, because if children use the computer's spell check, they **7** .... in the way that people do who don't use computers.

Sometimes the examiner asks you to compare two things.

3 a) ☞ **Listen to some more questions. What is the topic of each one and which two things are compared? Complete the notes.**

    1 Topic: *the way news is presented*   Comparison: *radio and TV*

    2 Topic: *interest in international news*   Comparison: ....

    3 Topic: ....   Comparison: ....

    4 Topic: ....   Comparison: ....

  b) ☞ **Listen to people answering the questions. Match each speaker to one of the questions above by writing the number of the question 1–4 next to the correct speaker.**

    Speaker A ....   Speaker B ....   Speaker C ....   Speaker D ....

  c) ☞ **Listen to the same questions again and practise answering them yourself. Record your answers if possible and then listen to them.**

9 ▶ Earth matters

Focus on listening 1 *Multiple choice; labelling a map*

▶ Preparation

1 Look at the exam questions below. What is the topic? What do you have to do for questions 1–3?

2 🎧 Listen to the introduction. What is the woman talking about?

EXAM PRACTICE
▶ Multiple-choice

3 🎧 Listen to the first part of the recording and answer questions 1–3.

> *Questions 1–3*
> *Choose the correct letter, A, B or C.*
>
> **Earth Matters Exhibition**
>
> **1** The main purpose of the exhibition is
>
>   **A** to educate people about environmental issues.
>   **B** to sell products to the general public.
>   **C** for businesses to sell to other businesses.
>
> **2** How often is the exhibition held?
>
>   **A** twice a year
>   **B** once a year
>   **C** once every two years
>
> **3** As well as the Town Hall, where can you buy tickets for the exhibition?
>
>   **A** at a bookshop
>   **B** at a health food shop
>   **C** at a local library

4 Look at first part of the audio script on p.170. Underline the parts which lead you to the answer for each question.

▶ Labelling a plan

5 a) Look at questions 4–6 and the plan opposite.

  1 What does the plan show?
  2 What do you have to do to answer these questions?

Several of the exhibits already have labels. Read these carefully. The speaker will use these names to give directions to the missing exhibits. Before you listen to this second part of the recording, think about the words we use to give directions.

b) 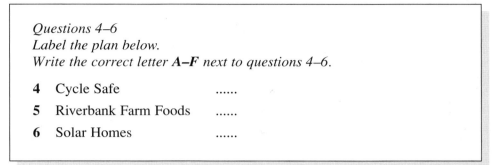 Listen to the second part of the recording and answer questions 4–6 below.

Questions 4–6
Label the plan below.
*Write the correct letter **A–F** next to questions 4–6.*

4 Cycle Safe ......

5 Riverbank Farm Foods ......

6 Solar Homes ......

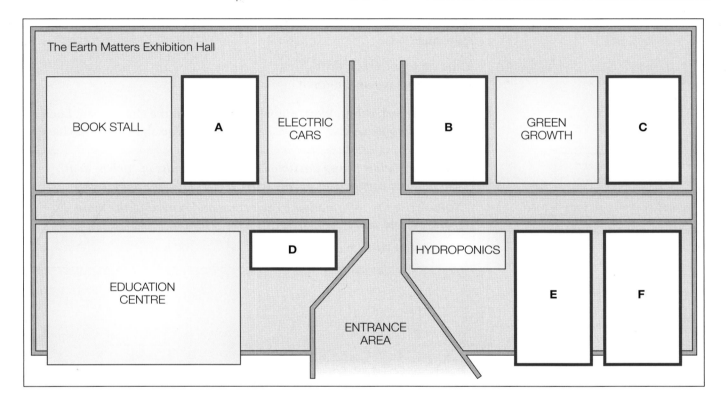

The Earth Matters Exhibition Hall

BOOK STALL | A | ELECTRIC CARS | B | GREEN GROWTH | C

EDUCATION CENTRE | D | HYDROPONICS | E | F

ENTRANCE AREA

6 a) Look at the second part of the audio script on p.170. Underline the phrases and sentences which lead you to answer each question. When you have done this, check your answers.

b) To help you learn and revise words relating to *Earth matters*, underline all the words and phrases in the audio script which you think might be useful for working with topics about the environment.

Focus on writing 1 *Task 1: flow charts*

SKILLS PRACTICE

For Task 1 in the IELTS Writing module you may be given a flow chart as visual input. Flow charts are designed to show clearly the stages in a process or a sequence of events. They often show cause and effect: how one thing (an event or events) can lead to other things happening.

To read a flow chart, follow the direction of the arrows. It is very important that you understand the different parts of the diagram to be able to answer the exam question.

The topic of the chart below is urban drift – why people move from the countryside to towns and what results from this move.

1 a) Before you read the task instructions, note down your own ideas on the following:

   • the causes of urban drift
   • what can happen as a result

   b) Look at the task below. Work out what the parts of the chart mean. Look at your notes from exercise 1 above. Are *your* ideas also shown in this chart?

> **TIP** You should spend about two minutes looking at the chart carefully before you start writing your answer.

> *The chart below shows possible causes and results of 'urban drift', where large numbers of people move from rural to urban areas.*
>
> *Summarise the information by selecting and reporting the main features, and make comparisons where relevant.*
>
> You should write at least 150 words.

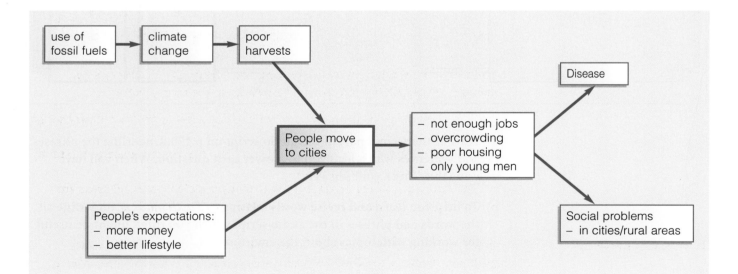

2   Look at the sample answer below.

....

....

....

....

There are two main groups of reasons for urban drift. Firstly, it can be caused by environmental problems. It is believed that burning fossil fuels leads to a change in climate, which often affects harvests. This means that the countryside can no longer feed such a big population. Secondly, people frequently move to cities because of their changing expectations. They may believe that they can have a better lifestyle in the city, with higher paid jobs.

However, when so many people move to the cities it is often the case that there are insufficient jobs and houses for them. As a result of this, large numbers of people tend to live together in slums. This can lead to disease and also a variety of social problems. In the cities there may be difficulties caused by too many young men living alone but also back in the countryside there are too few strong, healthy workers to work on the land and as a consequence, more people are driven to cities to seek work. (172 words)

3   **The answer does not have a suitable opening paragraph. Choose the best opening paragraph from A, B or C below. Circle the correct letter.**

A This chart indicates the reasons why people to move from the country to the city.

B The chart shows the problems which are often the consequence of too many people moving to and from cities.

C The flow chart shows the reasons why many people from rural areas are moving to cities and the problems which can result from this.

▶ Expressing possibility

In the writing task instructions it says that these are *possible* causes and problems. In the sample answer there are several words and phrases which indicate that the information is not definite but only possible, e.g. … *it can be* … (line 2).

4   **Underline the words or phrases in the sample answer which indicate that something is possible, or is only sometimes the case.**

Focus on grammar 1 *Expressing cause and effect*

Focus on IELTS Foundation, p.98

1 Look at the sentences (exercise 3) and the sample answer (exercise 2) on p.95. Underline the words and phrases which mean the same as:

- X causes Y
- Y is caused by X

2 Complete the following sentences with a suitable phrase.

1 Acid rain .... rain mixing with gases in the atmosphere.
2 Chemical waste in water .... the death of fish populations.
3 Smoke and fog mixing together .... smog.
4 Many people believe that lung problems .... increased air pollution.
5 Cutting down trees can .... severe soil erosion.

Focus on writing 2 *Task 2: Environmental problems and solutions*

In Task 2 of the IELTS Writing module a common topic is problems and solutions: listing problems in a particular area and then suggesting possible solutions.

SKILLS PRACTICE

▶ Understanding the question

1 Look at the task below.

1 What is the general subject?
2 What three areas of the environment do you have to cover?
3 What two main things must you cover for each area?

> Write about the following topic.
>
> *Many countries are experiencing serious problems with their environment, with pollution of their land, water and air.*
>
> *What are these problems and how might they be reduced?*
>
> Give reasons for your answer and include any relevant examples from your own knowledge and experience.
>
> You should write at least 250 words.

▶ Organising your ideas

In order to do this writing task you must first organise your ideas.

2 a) Look at the list of problems in column 1 of the table on p.97. Which problems are associated with land, which with sea and which with air? Use a dictionary if necessary. Tick the correct column. Some problems may have ticks in more than one column.

Problems	Land, sea or air (tick one or more column(s))		
	Land	Water	Air
• contaminated rivers • smog • soil erosion • acid rain • litter on the streets • floods • building in rural areas • toxic fumes • greenhouse gases • melting ice caps • land-fill sites full of rubbish • droughts • polluted atmosphere • global warming • deforestation			

b) **Match the problems above with possible solutions below. There may be more than one answer for each. Write the correct letters in the columns above.**

Possible solutions
a Turn off lights/appliances when they are no longer in use
b Use renewable forms of energy, e.g. wind or solar energy
c Use public transport more often
d Buy fuel-efficient cars
e Reduce waste and recycle rubbish
f Charge polluting factories high taxes
g Produce biodegradable objects, e.g. carrier bags
h Buy cars with less-polluting engines
i Refuse to give planning permission for new buildings
j Plant more trees

▶ Planning your answer

c) Go through the list and decide which you think you should include in an answer for the Writing task on p.96.

d) Look at the 'skeleton' sample answer below.

1 What is the topic of Paragraph 1?
2 What is the topic of Paragraph 2?
3 What is the topic of Paragraph 3?
4 What is the function of Paragraph 4?
5 How many main sections are there in each paragraph?

e) Complete the answer using ideas from the tables on p.97. Remember, you do not have to include all the points: you can just use what you think are the main issues.

First paragraph
Almost every country in the world has problems with the environment, affecting its land, air or water. I believe the main problems on land are

....

....

Perhaps the most helpful thing we can do to tackle these difficulties is to

....

....

....

....

Second paragraph
The ways in which air is affected are as follows. Firstly, ...

....

.... *I believe the best way to reduce these problems is by*

....

....

....

....

Third paragraph
The main effects of pollution and other environmental problems on water are

....

These can be dealt with by ....

....

....

....

....

Fourth paragraph – Conclusion
It is crucial that these measures are taken in order to ensure a healthy future for our planet.

Focus on listening 2 *Note completion; table completion*

IELTS Listening Section 3 sometimes involves a discussion between a student and a tutor. The task may require you to take notes on what the tutor advises the student to do. Because it is a personal tutorial the style is often fairly informal. However, the task is still based on an academic situation.

▶ Preparation

1 a) **Look at the task below.**

1 What do you have to do for questions 1–3? ....

2 What do you have to do for questions 4–10? ....

3 What is the maximum number of words/numbers you can use for each answer? ....

b) 🎧 **Listen to the introduction.**

1 Which two people are speaking? ....

2 What is the academic field or subject? ....

3 What specifically are they discussing? ....

EXAM PRACTICE
▶ Note completion,
table completion

2 a) 🎧 **Listen to the recording and answer questions 1–10.**

Questions 1–3
Complete the notes below.
*Write **NO MORE THAN TWO WORDS**
for each answer.*

Tutorial – Tutor's advice:

Areas for improvement in current work:

Need to write more about **1** .... pollution

Check for errors in section on **2** ....

Do more reading on what causes **3** ....

Questions 4–10
Complete the table below.
*Write **NO MORE THAN TWO WORDS OR A NUMBER** for each answer.*

Suggestions for further research

Topic	Research method	Deadline
The dumping of rubbish	**4** .... (10–20)	End of the **5** ....
Recycling of **6**	Questionnaires (larger numbers)	Beginning of **7** ....
Use of **8**	Questionnaires reviewing **9** .... • In library (go back 10 years)	**10** ....

b) Look at the audio script on p.171. Identify the parts of the audio script which lead you to answer each question.

In this audio script, the tutor is giving the student a lot of advice on his assignment. For example, she says:

- I would advise you to say quite a bit more on contamination of the river.
- …you need to develop that a bit more.

3 Underline the other phrases in the audio script where she is giving advice. Which two phrases indicate that she is giving strong advice?

Focus on vocabulary *Word formation*

1 a) Look at the table below. Fill in the gaps with the appropriate form.

Verb	Noun
advise	
	device
	description
refer	
present	
	education
complete	
	exhibition
discuss	
	production
	behaviour

b) Look at your completed table and check the answer key on p.160.

c) Underline the main stress in each word. If you aren't sure how the word is pronounced, use your dictionary to check.

d) Using a dictionary, try to answer these questions.

1 What is the difference in pronunciation between *devise* (verb) and *device* (noun)? (The pattern is the same for *advise* and *advice*)
2 A lot of the nouns have the ending *-tion*. Where is the main stress in all these words? Write down a rule about the pronunciation of words ending in *-tion*.

2 🎧 Listen to the words in the table and repeat.

Focus on grammar 2 *-ing v infinitive*

Focus on IELTS Foundation, p.102

Some verbs are followed by a word ending in *-ing*. Other verbs are followed by the *infinitive* with *to*.

Examples
- *We must **avoid using** powerful chemical cleaners.*
- *The activists **attempted to stop** the builders as they **tried to cut down** the trees.*

All prepositions are followed by the *-ing* form or a noun.

Example
- *We must reduce waste **by using** less packaging.*

Below are some of the most common verbs of both types.

1 **Complete the table with the words in the box.**

dislike   enjoy   hope   learn   manage   offer
ought   plan   promise   refuse   seem   try   want
attempt   be   can/can't afford   choose   dare
decide   encourage   expect   fail   finish   go on
imagine   keep   miss   risk   suggest

Verbs normally followed by the infinitive with *to*	Verbs normally followed by the *-ing* form
agree *appear* *arrange*	*avoid* *can't help*

2 **Six of the sentences below contain verb form errors. Find the errors and correct them.**

1 We risk to destroy the planet with our careless behaviour.
2 Many people refuse changing their lifestyle to help the environment.
3 Carbon monoxide emissions are reduced by using more efficient engines.
4 I can't imagine get rid of my car.
5 We must learn live with fewer luxuries.
6 They seemed solving the soil erosion problem by planting large numbers of trees.
7 We cannot expect to find many more reserves of fossil fuels.
8 We cannot go on to buy such big cars.

VOCABULARY

1 Complete the sentences using the words in the box.

> *presentation   advise   description*
> *complete   discuss*

1 It is very helpful to .... your ideas with a fellow student before starting to write an assignment.

2 Start research reports with a .... of the research methods you used.

3 I would .... you to read through your work thoroughly before submitting it.

4 Aim to .... your assignment at least one day before the deadline.

5 Students are often asked to give a short .... about their research findings to their tutor and other students.

2 Complete the wordplans below. (All the words come from Unit 9 and/or *Focus on IELTS Foundation* Unit 9)

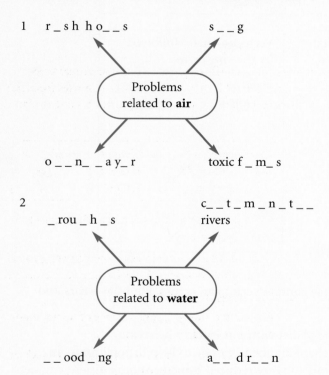

1 r_sh ho__s   s__g

Problems related to **air**

o__n__ay_r   toxic f_m_s

2   c__t_m_n_t__ rivers

_rou_h_s

Problems related to **water**

__ood_ng   a__dr__n

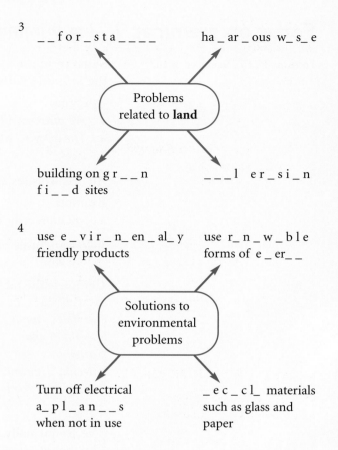

3 __for_sta____   ha_ar_ous w_s_e

Problems related to **land**

building on g r__n f i__d sites   ___l er_si_n

4 use e_vir_n_en_al_y friendly products   use r_n_w_ble forms of e_er__

Solutions to environmental problems

Turn off electrical a_pl_an__s when not in use   _ec_cl_ materials such as glass and paper

PASSIVE

3 Complete this paragraph, using the correct words from the brackets.

The bicycle taxi **1** .... (is used/uses) in places where it is difficult to **2** .... (be driven/drive) motorised vehicles, for example, on roads which have a lot of potholes. A traditional bicycle can easily **3** .... (be adapted/adapt): a wooden board seat **4** .... (is added/adds) to the top of the back wheel and the passenger **5** .... (is seated/sits) behind the 'taxi rider'. The atmosphere **6** .... (is polluted less/pollutes less) and journeys are actually faster!

PAST PASSIVE

4 Complete the following sentences using the past simple passive form of the verb in brackets. The first one has been done as an example.

0 The compass *was invented* (invent) by the ancient Chinese

1 The book *Small is Beautiful* .... (write) by E.J. Schumacher.

2 The ball-point pen .... (invent) by Laszlo Biro.

3 Vaccination .... (discover) in 1796.

4 The words 'The only way to discover the limits of the possible is to go beyond them into the impossible' .... (say) by Arthur C. Clarke.

5 The role of John Nash, the mathematician in the film *A Beautiful Mind*, ... (play) by Russell Crow.

OBLIGATION, PROHIBITION, PERMISSION

5 a) Rewrite the sentences as shown using the words in brackets, without changing the meaning.

1 a) The use of mobile phones is not permitted in the lecture theatre.
   b) You .... (not allow)

2 a) You have to wear ear protectors when you visit the factory.
   b) It .... (compulsory)

3 a) You mustn't use electronic devices when the aeroplane is taking off and landing.
   b) Passengers .... (not permit)

4 a) In this country it is compulsory for cars to have an annual pollution check.
   b) All our cars .... (must)

5 a) Children over the age of ten are permitted in the pool without an accompanying adult.
   b) Kids .... (can)

6 a) In the past, women in Britain weren't allowed to vote.
   b) Women .... (could not)

7 a) In the future, it will be compulsory to go outside your office if you want to smoke.
   b) Smokers .... (have to)

b) For each sentence you write (b), decide whether it is more formal or less formal than the first sentence (a).

-ING V INFINITIVE

6 Complete the sentences using a verb from the box in the correct form.

| drop | recycle | ~~write~~ | go | become |
| plant | stop | sell | | |

0 I finished *writing* my essay on global warming last night.

1 We ought .... as much paper as possible.

2 Someone keeps .... litter in the street near my house!

3 I've decided .... flying; it causes too much pollution.

4 The beach is too polluted to visit now and I miss .... there.

5 My company has promised .... more 'green'.

6 I've offered .... some new trees in my local park.

7 I'm planning .... my car and start using the train more.

CAUSE AND EFFECT

7 Are the underlined phrases in the sentences below appropriate? If they are not, choose phrases from the box to replace them. An example has been done for you.

is the consequence of	contribute to	result from
lead to	responsible for	because of	trigger
as a consequence of	as a result of	

0 Soil erosion can <u>lead to</u> people cutting down too many trees. *result from*

1 Contaminated rivers are often <u>the consequence of</u> pollution from nearby factories. ....

2 Cars <u>trigger</u> air pollution. ....

3 Recycling could <u>be a consequence of</u> saving many natural resources. ....

4 Building in rural areas could <u>result from</u> a lack of open spaces in the future. ....

5 It is thought that many things <u>contribute to</u> global warming. ....

6 Many sea animals are hurt <u>because of</u> the rubbish which ends up in our oceans. ....

10 ▶ Health check

Focus on reading *Sentence completion; summary completion*

SKILLS PRACTICE

1 You are going to read a text about disease. Before you look at the text, list any English words or phrases which you might expect to meet when you are reading about this topic.

2 Skim the text quickly without stopping at unknown words. Try to form a general understanding.

Preventing Disease

Until the 19th century there was little understanding of how diseases spread, but as our understanding increases, the more able we are to prevent it from happening. There are various methods of preventing disease. These range from very simple precautions taken by individuals in the home – washing the hands for example – to expensive international campaigns.

The importance of diet in maintaining health is increasingly recognised. Throughout history, for example, sailors on long voyages suffered from scurvy, a disease which causes bleeding gums and stiff limbs. In the mid-eighteenth century it was found that eating citrus fruits (oranges, limes, lemons, etc.) could cure these symptoms and ships began to carry supplies of limes. In the twentieth century it was discovered that citrus fruits are particularly rich in ascorbic acid, commonly known as vitamin C, and that it is the lack of this substance that causes scurvy.

The role of international organisations is also crucial in controlling disease. One example of this is smallpox. In 1980 the World Health Organisation declared that smallpox, an often fatal disease, was officially extinct. This was the result of a successful, worldwide vaccination programme. It was hoped that the same success would be achieved with malaria, a disease transmitted by the mosquito, but unexpected difficulties have prevented the success of this particular programme.

An older method of preventing disease from spreading between countries is quarantine, which comes from the Italian word *quarantine*, meaning forty days. The system dates from fifteenth-century Venice and refers to a period during which animals (and formerly humans) are kept in isolation[1], before being allowed to enter another country. This allows time for the symptoms of any disease to develop before it can be unknowingly transmitted. The UK has been successful in preventing rabies from entering its territory in this way. This serious illness is spread by animals, often wild animals such as foxes and rodents, but potentially also by domestic animals. Strict quarantine arrangements for all animals entering the UK have prevented the disease from becoming established there.

At a national level, risks to public health can be reduced by providing certain basic facilities. For example, adequate housing plays an important part, as overcrowded living conditions lead to the rapid spread of disease. Archaeologists examining primitive settlements have found millions of disease-carrying parasites and worms, which were passed easily from one person to another. Fresh water supplies and sewage systems are also necessary to prevent disease. Two thousand years ago the Romans realised the importance of these and the ancient ruins of Pompeii in Italy include fountains and toilet areas as well as drains. However, once installed it is essential that water and sewage systems are properly maintained. In London, for example, an outbreak of cholera in 1854 was traced to a faulty sewer pipe which was leaking into the supply of public drinking water. More recently, industrialisation has brought new problems of pollution and waste disposal, especially in the chemical and nuclear industries, and strict safety regulations are required to safeguard public health.

Much protection from disease is given to children through vaccinating them. Vaccines, which usually consist of bacteria or viruses that have been killed or weakened, are administered in the first year of a child's life. They can no longer cause disease, but they cause a defensive reaction in the body. Later, if the child is exposed to the same organisms, its body will be able to defend itself against them. One very successful vaccination programme was that which was developed against poliomyelitis[2]: just two drops of vaccine on the tongue can provide protection against that disease for up to ten years. In addition to childhood programmes, vaccination is available to international travellers, to prevent or reduce the risk of a wide range of illnesses.

Another measure which can help reduce the spread of disease is health education. Although a lot of this is done by doctors, nurses and health visitors, many other sources contain health information. Magazines, newspapers, television and the Internet carry increasing amounts of information and national campaigns to increase public awareness have been particularly successful. In Australia, for example, there is a high

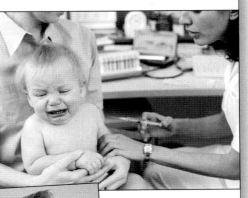

Clockwise from above: modern vaccination; everyday hygiene; London in the 1880s.

incidence of malignant melanoma, a skin cancer common in those exposed to strong sunlight. A media campaign has helped to save lives by providing information on early detection and on precautions that prevent melanoma from developing in the first place. In the USA the fictional cinema hero, *Superman*, has been used in a television campaign to encourage people to check their blood cholesterol level. A high level of cholesterol in the body may increase the risk of heart disease and eating less of certain types of fat can reduce it.

Finally, regular health checks can be given to detect various diseases, resulting in early treatment. For example, blood pressure can be measured to make sure that it is not dangerously high and blood tests can reveal the presence of many conditions, from anaemia to the presence of viruses. Although regular health checks cost a lot, they can save money in the long term by preventing diseases from developing, and thereby save the expense of treatments.

---

1 Alone, without contact with other animals
2 An infectious disease, which sometimes causes paralysis. Often referred to as 'polio'.

TIP Even if the maximum number of words is three, most of the answers may be just one or two words in length.

One of the tasks you might meet in the IELTS Reading module is completing sentences. After reading the whole text quickly, you will have to use a scanning strategy to find the exact parts that you want to look at more carefully.

The maximum number of words you can use is given in the instructions; it is usually three, but can sometimes be one or two.

In this task type, the words you have to use to complete the sentences must be taken from the text, exactly as they appear there.

3 **Use up to three words from the last paragraph of the text to complete this sentence.**

- The disadvantage of health checks is that initially they ………

The correct answer is *cost a lot*. Although the word *expense* is mentioned in the same paragraph, *expensive* does not appear. So even though it means the same thing, *are expensive* would be incorrect.

EXAM PRACTICE

▶ Sentence completion

> **TIP** In this task type, the sentences follow the same order as the references in the text.

> **HELP**
> In the IELTS test you are only told the maximum number of words to use. To make the task easier now, the number of words you need to use is indicated by the number of spaces.

4 Do the exam task below.

> *Questions 1–5*
> *Complete the sentences below with words taken from the reading passage.*
> Write **NO MORE THAN TWO WORDS** *for each answer.*
>
> **1** A dietary deficiency caused scurvy in ....
>
> **2** Thanks to an international vaccination programme, ... was eliminated.
>
> **3** The .... system for controlling disease was first used in Italy.
>
> **4** A damaged .... caused a cholera epidemic in London.
>
> **5** In Australia a .... has been effective in reducing skin cancer.

▶ Summary completion

Another task is completing a summary of the reading text by choosing from a list of words. The words are usually (but not always) nouns.

It is best to read the whole summary quickly, before attempting the questions. Then you have to follow steps similar to the ones above, for completing sentences.

5 Do the exam task below, based on the same text.

> **HELP**
> In the IELTS test there are usually several extra words which do not fit anywhere. To make this task easier now, there is only one extra word.

> **TIP** In summary completion tasks you only use each word once. When you have used one of the words, cross it out.

> *Questions 6–10*
> *Complete the summary below using words from the box.*
>
> There are various ways of preventing or reducing disease. Firstly, a good **6** .... can help prevent diseases like scurvy. Secondly, suitable **7** .... , with clean water and well-maintained sewage pipes, can be effective in stopping any diseases from spreading. Thirdly, children can be given a **8** .... to help them fight diseases such as polio. In addition, the mass media can be used to run health **9** .... programmes. In Australia, malignant melanoma was reduced in this way. Lastly, diseases can be treated in the early stages if people are given regular **10** .... These can be expensive, but they save money later.
>
> | | | | |
> |---|---|---|---|
> | education | diet | vaccination | housing |
> | quarantine | checks | | |

Focus on vocabulary 1 *Academic vocabulary*

1 a) **Look at two of the dictionary entries for the words below. Choose the definition (A or B) that matches the way each word is used in *Preventing Disease*.**

1 *role* (line 30)

A the character played by an actor in a play or film
B the way in which someone or something is involved in an activity or situation and how much influence they have on it

2 *part* (line 70)

A involvement in something
B one of the separate pieces that something such as a machine or piece of equipment is made of

3 *range* (line 116)

A a number of people or things that are all different, but are all of the same general type
B a group of mountains or hills, usually in a line

4 *measure* (line 118)

A an amount or unit in a measuring system
B an action, especially an official one, that is intended to deal with a particular problem

b) **Which of the following words could be used instead of *method* (line 44)?**

type way cause

c) **Choose one of these words to fill the gaps in the sentences below.**

role measure(s) range method(s)

1 Surgeons are constantly developing new .... of performing surgery.

2 A number of .... have been taken to prevent the spread of avian flu.

3 The government has announced a .... of reforms to the health service.

4 People are generally aware of the .... of exercise in promoting health.

5 The government will introduce new .... to improve care of the elderly.

6 Schools have a major .... to play in providing health information.

7 The drug is effective against a wide .... of bacteria.

8 Scientists have not yet found a satisfactory .... of controlling malaria.

▶ Whereas/While

When two quantities are compared using figures, we can mark the comparison using *whereas* or *while*.

Whereas is generally used when the difference is stressed, and *while* is generally used for more neutral comparisons.

2 a) **Look at the table and the sentence pairs below.**

Health Expenditure in 2002	
Country	**Health expenditure as a percentage of GDP (Gross Domestic Product)**
Switzerland	11.2
Canada	9.6
Denmark	8.8
New Zealand	8.5
Ireland	7.3
Mexico	6.1
Slovac Republic	5.7

Examples:

- In 2002, Switzerland spent much more on health than Mexico.
- *Switzerland spent 11.2% of its GDP on health, whereas Mexico spent 6.1%.*

- Canada and Denmark both spent around the same on health.
- *Canada spent 9.6% of its GDP on health, while Denmark spent 8.8%.*

b) **Read the following sentences and choose *while* or *whereas* to complete the second sentence of each pair.**

1 The Slovac Republic spent significantly less on health than Ireland.
The Slovac Republic spent 5.7% of its GDP on health, *while/whereas* Ireland spent 7.3%.

2 Denmark and New Zealand both spent around 9% on health.
Denmark spent 8.8 %, *while/whereas* New Zealand spent 8.5%.

3 Switzerland and Canada both spent more than the other countries in the table.
Switzerland spent 11.2%, *while/whereas* Canada spent 9.6%.

4 Canada spent a lot more than Ireland on health.
Canada spent 9.6% on health, *while/whereas* Ireland spent 7.3%.

► Collocations

TIP When you record information about new words, for example in a vocabulary notebook, you should include information about collocations.

Apart from rules of grammar and meaning, there are other reasons for the use of particular words in English. One of these is convention (custom).

This conventional relationship between words is called *collocation*. For example, the word *part*, in the sense in which it is used in the text *Preventing Disease* (lines 69–70), collocates with the verb *play*.

3 Add any adjectives to the wordplans below which collocate with the words in the centre. Use your own knowledge and/or a dictionary.

► Topic vocabulary

4 Add any words from the text, or that you know, to the word family below.

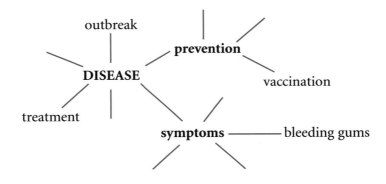

Focus on speaking 1 *Expressing negative attitudes; fluency and accuracy*

SKILLS PRACTICE

When English speakers say something they regard as negative they often begin with a phrase like *I'm afraid …* or *To be honest …* or *Unfortunately …* .

NB When speakers use these expressions, it tells us how they feel about what they are saying; it does not necessarily mean that we feel the same.

In Part 1 of the IELTS Speaking module the examiner asks personal questions based on a particular topic, such as health. Look at these answers to the question *Do you do regular exercise?*

Speaker A
No, not really. I don't like sport.

Speaker B
I'm afraid I don't. I don't have much spare time and I'm very lazy!

We can tell from these replies that Speaker B feels that a lack of exercise is a negative thing. Speaker A doesn't necessarily share this view.

1 a) **Read these questions and practise giving answers which show a negative attitude. Use one of the phrases on p.109.**

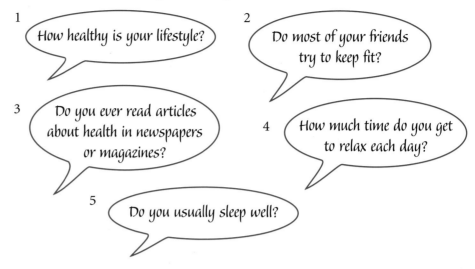

1 *How healthy is your lifestyle?*

2 *Do most of your friends try to keep fit?*

3 *Do you ever read articles about health in newspapers or magazines?*

4 *How much time do you get to relax each day?*

5 *Do you usually sleep well?*

b) 🎧 **Listen to five speakers giving a negative answer to the questions. Match the answer each one gives to one of the questions. The first one has been done as an example.**

Speaker A   *question 4*

Speaker B   ....

Speaker C   ....

Speaker D   ....

Speaker E   ....

▶ **Fluency and accuracy**

One of the things that the examiner will pay attention to in all three parts of the IELTS Speaking module is the flow of your speech. Speech which flows quite smoothly and quickly, without a lot of pauses, is called fluent speech.

It can be difficult to be accurate and fluent at the same time. If you try too hard to speak correctly, your fluency will probably decrease.

TIP When you are practising for the test, try to forget your classroom habits. Concentrate on what you are saying and not how you are saying it.

In the Speaking module it is better to focus on fluency rather than accuracy. Even when you make mistakes in your grammar or vocabulary, the examiner will probably understand what you are trying to say. But if you say too little, because you are trying hard to avoid mistakes, it may be difficult to understand you. Also, you cannot earn marks unless you give evidence of your speaking ability.

2 a) 🎧 **Listen to some more personal questions about health. Concentrate on understanding the question.**

b) 🎧 **Listen again to the same questions and give a personal answer. Concentrate on fluency by answering promptly and giving extended answers without long pauses. If you don't understand the question, practise asking for help.**
Record yourself if possible and check your own speech for fluency.

EXAM PRACTICE
▶ Part 2

3 a) Read the Part 2 exam task and spend one minute preparing to speak.

b) Practise doing the task. Concentrate on speaking <u>fluently</u> and <u>fully</u>.

> **Describe your favourite way of relaxing.**
>
> **You should say**
>
> > **what you do to relax**
> > **where you do it**
> > **how often you do it**
>
> **and explain why you enjoy this way**
> **of relaxing.**

c) 🎧 Listen to another speaker doing the same
task. As you listen, tick the sub-topics as the speaker deals with each one.

Focus on vocabulary 2 *Prepositions*

TIP When you record
any new words, don't just
make a note of their
meaning. Add information
about how the words can
be used, e.g. which
prepositions are linked to
them.

Some nouns, verbs and
adjectives are closely linked to
particular prepositions (they
are usually followed by them).
Your dictionary will tell you
what the preposition is in each case.

> **im·prove·ment** W2 /ɪmˈpruːvmənt/ *n*
> **1** [C,U] the act of improving something or the state of being
> improved **[+in/on/to]** *There were significant improvements*
> *in antenatal care following the opening of the new hospital.*

1 Write the correct prepositions in the spaces below. You will use some of the
prepositions more than once. Use your dictionary to check your answers.

> *against*   *from*   *in*   *of*   *on*   *to*

There are various methods **1** .... preventing disease. Firstly, eating a balanced
diet helps. It is now known that eating foods which are rich **2** .... certain
nutrients can help to prevent illness. For example, in the 1930s a lot of people in
the United States suffered **3** .... rickets, a disease caused by a lack **4** ....
vitamin D. The problem was solved when they drank more milk containing this.
On the other hand, cutting down **5** .... certain foods, such as animal fats, can
help to prevent disease too.

It is also important to prevent diseases **6** .... spreading. One way of doing
this is to isolate people or animals which might be carrying a disease. This
procedure has been successful **7** .... controlling the spread of BSE, a disease
of cattle which can infect humans. Another way is to provide good housing and
sewage systems. Poor facilities can lead **8** .... major outbreaks of disease.

Thirdly, the administration of vaccines, which consist **9** .... weakened viruses
or bacteria, gives children protection **10** .... certain diseases. Some diseases
have been entirely eliminated as a result **11** .... international vaccination
programmes.

Finally, disease can be reduced by providing information **12** .... the subject.

Focus on grammar *Countability*

Focus on IELTS Foundation, p.105, KLB p.144

1 Look at the sentences below. Underline the correct word in italics. One has been done as an example.

0 People of <u>all</u>/*every* ages benefit from regular exercise.

1 Even smoking *a few/ few* cigarettes a day is bad for health.

2 Children in some parts of the world have too *few/little* exercise.

3 The government has increased the health budget *every/any* year since 2001.

4 There are *any/many* different types of inherited disease.

5 *Every/All* new drugs are carefully tested before they are licensed for use.

6 Some diseases affect men in particular, but others affect *both/any* men and women equally.

2 Complete the text below about nutrition. Use each of the words in the box once.

each	all	both	any	many

Nutrition

To be healthy and active, humans need two things: energy and nutrients. They obtain **1** .... of these from food. When a baby is born, its mother's milk provides the energy and **2** .... the nutrients it needs. However, as the child gets older, it needs food from **3** .... different sources. The exact amount of **4** .... different nutrient a person needs depends on many factors, such as age, sex and size. The amount of energy a person uses depends on his or her level of activity. The body stores as fat **5** .... energy which is not used, so it is important to balance intake and output.

Focus on speaking 2 *Agreeing/disagreeing; giving reasons*

In Part 3 of the IELTS Speaking test the examiner asks you about your opinions.

You might be asked whether you agree or disagree with a belief or a statement.

SKILLS PRACTICE
▶ Part 3

1 a) Look at this example and a list of possible ways to begin a reply.

It's often said that hard work is good for people's health. Do you agree?

'Yes, I agree …'

'Yes, definitely …'

'Yes, I think that's right …'

'I'm not sure whether I agree or not …'

'It's possible …'

'No, not really …'

'No, I don't agree actually …'

'No, I disagree with that …'

b) How would you begin your answer to the question? How would you expand your answer?

c) 🎧 Listen to some more questions on the topic of health and practise answering. Record yourself if possible and then listen.

d) 🎧 Listen to other speakers answering the same questions. As you listen, decide how far you agree or disagree with the speaker. Mark a place on the line.

←————————————————————————→
strongly agree   strongly disagree

Another type of question might ask you to suggest reasons for a situation.

2 a) Look at this example and a list of possible ways to begin a reply.

Health problems often vary from country to country. Why do you think that might be?

I think that's probably because ...

The reason for that is probably ...

I expect it's because ...

I can think of several reasons. Firstly, ...

b) Practise using these phrases to begin answering the question.

c) 🎧 Listen to some more questions about health and practise answering. Record yourself if possible and then listen.

d) 🎧 Listen to other speakers answering the same questions. As you listen, decide how far you agree or disagree with the speaker. Mark a place on the line.

←————————————————————————→
strongly agree   strongly disagree

11 ▶ Happiness

Focus on writing 1 *Task 1: Interpreting pie charts*

As mentioned in Unit 4 (p.47), a common form of presenting information in IELTS Writing module Task 1 is in pie charts. These are circles divided into sections (the 'slices' of a pie) which show percentages.

SKILLS PRACTICE
▶ Interpreting data

1 Read the exam task below and answer the following questions.

1 What is the general topic of the pie charts?
2 How was the information in the charts obtained?
3 Which two groups of people were involved in the survey?
4 Which four main things make women happy?
5 Which four main things make men happy?
6 Which things are similar between the two groups?
7 Which things are different?
8 What does *other factors* mean?

The charts below show the results of a survey about what men and women say makes them most happy.

Summarise the information by selecting and reporting the main features and make comparisons where relevant.

You should write at least 150 words.

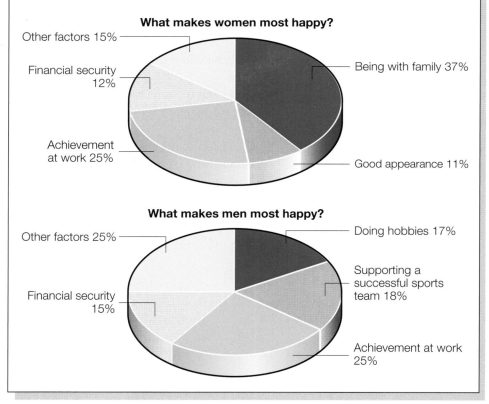

What makes women most happy?

Other factors 15%
Financial security 12%
Achievement at work 25%
Being with family 37%
Good appearance 11%

What makes men most happy?

Other factors 25%
Financial security 15%
Doing hobbies 17%
Supporting a successful sports team 18%
Achievement at work 25%

▶ Interpreting the data

TIP We can use either present simple tense or past simple tense when describing data in pie charts. Whichever tense you choose, remember to be consistent throughout your whole answer.

2 **Look at the sample answer below. What is the purpose of the different paragraphs? Choose from the list below.**

1 The first paragraph …
2 The second paragraph …
3 The third paragraph …

A … describes important similarities between the two groups.
B … summarises important general patterns shown in the charts.
C … describes important differences between the two groups.

3 **Which word/words in the sample answer mean approximately the same as:**

a) percentage
b) say
c) feel
d) important/obvious

TIP In these tasks it is helpful to quote some exact figures. However, do not simply list all the figures: only use them when you want to support a particular point.

There are a number of similarities between what men and women say makes them most happy. There are also several striking differences.

Firstly, significant percentages of both men and women mention the same two factors: achievement at work and financial security. Exactly the same proportion of men and women (25%) feel that doing well at work brings them most happiness. However, a slightly lower percentage of women (12%) than men (15%) identify financial security as the most important factor in making them happy.

Turning now to the major differences, many women regard being with family as extremely important: 37% of them state this brings them most happiness, which is the largest percentage of all the factors mentioned by this group. Also a significant minority of women (11%) mention that having a good appearance makes them happiest. Neither of these two factors is mentioned by men. Instead, 17% of men report that doing hobbies is important and 18% feel most happy when their sports team is doing well. (167 words)

EXAM PRACTICE

▶ Writing your answer

4 Look at the following task, which is based on the same survey mentioned in the task on p.114 and answer the questions below.

1 Which two groups of people are mentioned in these data?
2 What are the main similarities between the two groups?
3 What are the main differences between the two groups?

5 Write your own answer to the task below. Organise your answer in three separate paragraphs as in the sample answer on p.115.

The charts below show the results of a survey about what people of different age groups say makes them most happy.

Summarise the information by selecting and reporting the main features and make comparisons where relevant.

You should write at least 150 words.

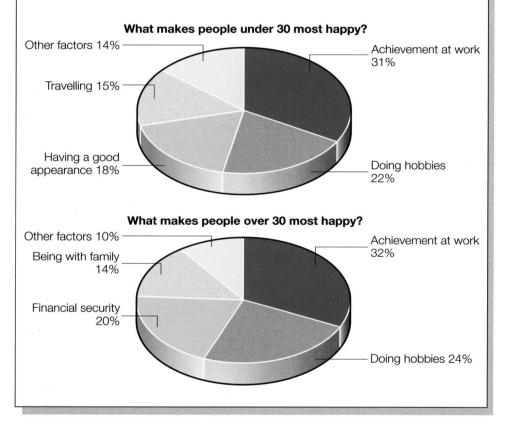

What makes people under 30 most happy?

Other factors 14%
Achievement at work 31%
Travelling 15%
Having a good appearance 18%
Doing hobbies 22%

What makes people over 30 most happy?

Other factors 10%
Being with family 14%
Achievement at work 32%
Financial security 20%
Doing hobbies 24%

Focus on listening 1 *Multiple choice; flow charts*

SKILLS PRACTICE
▶ Understanding the context

1 a) 🎧 **Listen to the introduction and the opening part of the recording.**

   1 Who is speaking?
   2 Who are listening to her?

   b) **Think about this topic. Write down any English words and phrases that you know connected with this topic.**

   ....

   ....

   ....

   ....

2 **Look at the exam task below. Read questions 1–4. Make sure you understand all the questions and all the options.**

EXAM PRACTICE
▶ Multiple choice

3 🎧 **Listen to the first part of the recording. Answer questions 1–4.**

Questions 1–4
*Choose the correct letter, **A**, **B** or **C**.*

1 What does Amy enjoy most about her work?

   A the social contact
   B the freedom of choice
   C the creative aspects

2 Why did Amy start her business?

   A a supermarket asked her to
   B she was inspired by a friend
   C she felt existing products were poor

3 Amy will take on more staff if

   A she decides to sell at a local farm shop.
   B her income reaches more than £7,000 a month.
   C she gets too tired to do so much work.

4 If Amy decides to sell on the Internet, she will have to

   A expand her work premises.
   B do more advertising.
   C use different ingredients.

---

4 a) Read the instructions for the second part of the recording and questions 5–10. These questions are presented in the form of a flow chart. A flow chart is used to show a process or a sequence of actions or events.

b) Answer the questions below.

1 Which process is being described in this task?
2 How many main stages are there?
3 What is the maximum number of words you can write for each answer?
4 What do the initials *SBA* stand for?

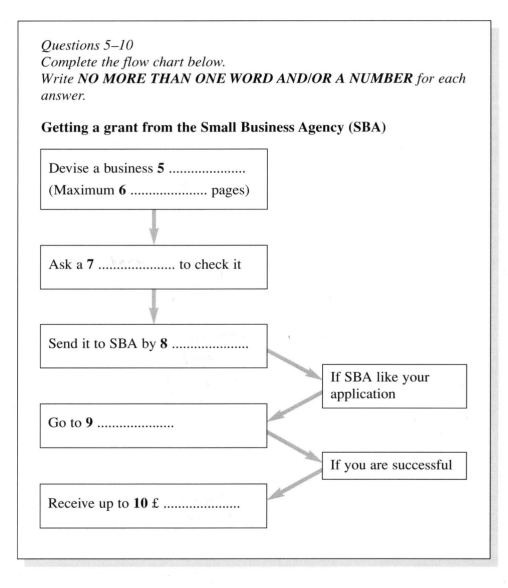

Questions 5–10
Complete the flow chart below.
Write **NO MORE THAN ONE WORD AND/OR A NUMBER** *for each answer.*

Getting a grant from the Small Business Agency (SBA)

Devise a business **5** ....
(Maximum **6** .... pages)

⬇

Ask a **7** .... to check it

⬇

Send it to SBA by **8** ....

If SBA like your application

Go to **9** ....

If you are successful

Receive up to **10** £ ....

5 🎧 Listen to the second part of the recording and answer questions 5–10.

6 When you have answered the questions, read the audio script on p.173. Underline the parts which lead you to answer each question.

Focus on grammar *Present tenses with future reference*

Focus on IELTS Foundation, p.118, KLB p.143

1 a) Look at the following extract from the audio script for the listening task on p.118, where Amy is talking about the stages of the process of getting a grant.

> ...*So when the SBA receives your grant application, they'll judge whether your business idea is interesting, that is, likely to benefit from their grant. If they think it's good, they'll invite you to interview...*

b) Underline the two examples of using the present tense to refer to the future. Why does Amy use this form?

2 Look at the following diagrams. They show different possibilities in the future. Write two sentences based on each one. The first has been done as an example.

0

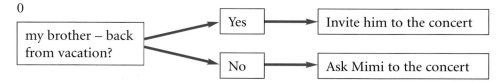

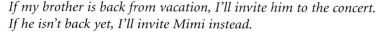

| | Yes | Invite him to the concert |
| my brother – back from vacation? | No | Ask Mimi to the concert |

If my brother is back from vacation, I'll invite him to the concert.
If he isn't back yet, I'll invite Mimi instead.

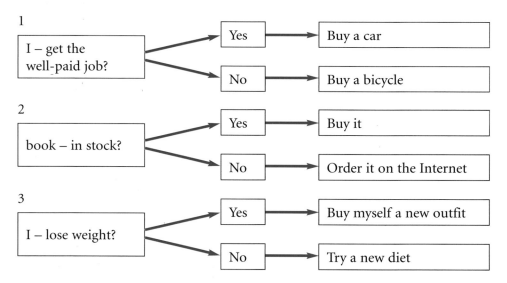

1

| | Yes | Buy a car |
| I – get the well-paid job? | No | Buy a bicycle |

2

| | Yes | Buy it |
| book – in stock? | No | Order it on the Internet |

3

| | Yes | Buy myself a new outfit |
| I – lose weight? | No | Try a new diet |

3 Complete the following sentences using your own ideas.

1 If my team wins the championship, ...

2 I promise I'll buy you a .... if ....

3 If I keep trying, ...

4 The business will do well if ....

5 I'll have a big party if ....

Focus on writing 2 *Task 2: Presenting an opinion*

Look at the following IELTS Writing Task 2. This type of task asks you to read a statement. You have to state whether you agree or disagree with this opinion. Of course, you may only partly agree with it. You must explain your point of view and give reasons for it.

> **'Wealth does not necessarily guarantee happiness.'**
>
> **To what extent do you agree or disagree with this statement?**
>
> **Give reasons for your answer and include any relevant examples from your own knowledge or experience.**
>
> Write at least 250 words.

1 Make a list of the arguments to support the opinion in the quotation. Below some clues are given in brackets. Use the clues to make one or more full sentences (the first is done as an example). Then add some of your own ideas.

> *Having a lot of money makes people miserable.*
>
> • *(no reason to try) E.g. When people have a lot of money, there is no reason for them to work hard and get on in life because it will make no difference to their lives. Life will become very boring and meaningless.*
>
> • *(they have no real friends)*
>
> • *(they worry they will lose it)*
>
> • *......*
>
> • *......*

2 Now list the arguments against the opinion. Again, use the clues in brackets to help you, if you wish.

> *Having lots of money makes people happy.*
>
> • *(they do not have to worry about money)*
>
> • *(they can do exciting activities)*
>
> • *(they can learn new skills)*
>
> • *......*
>
> • *......*

3 To what extent do you agree with the quotation? Mark your position (X) on the line below.

| 1 | 2 | 3 | 4 | 5 |

I completely agree   *I completely disagree*

4 Read the sample answer on p.162. Look at the following list of stages in the answer. Put them in the correct order.

a) Give reasons for your opinion.
b) Introduce the topic and, if necessary, define key words.
c) State your opinion.
d) Summarise your point of view.

5 What position on the 'opinion line' do you think the writer has?

6 Write your own answer to this task.

Focus on listening 2 *Multiple choice; multiple answers*

For questions 2–7 in Section 4 of the IELTS Listening module on p.122 you must choose three options from a list of seven. This task type is often used when the speaker lists several reasons, characteristics or factors.

SKILLS PRACTICE

1 🎧 Listen to the introduction to the talk.

1 Who is speaking?
2 What is the topic?

2 a) Read all the questions carefully.

1 What do you have to listen for in questions 2–4?
2 What do you have to listen for in questions 5–7?

b) Write down a few things that make you and your friends and family happy.

You	Friends and family
....	....
....	....
....	....
....	....

c) Read the options A–G for questions 2–4. Are any of your ideas mentioned?

EXAM PRACTICE

▶ Multiple choice, multiple answers

3 ◠ Now listen to the recording and answer questions 1–10.

Well-being research

Question 1
Choose the correct letter A, B or C

Carl chose well-being for his project because

A   it is an issue which many people worry about.
B   he and his relatives are generally very happy.
C   it can be looked at from several different angles.

Questions 2–4
*Choose **THREE** letters A–G*

Which THREE characteristics did the researchers identify in happy people?

A   having a strong interest in their work
B   recognising what they are good at
C   achieving something exceptional
D   being interested in the outside world
E   having lots of close family ties
F   valuing the good luck they have
G   being very popular with other people

Questions 5–7
*Choose **THREE** letters A–G*

Which THREE things should be avoided if you want to be happy?

A   thinking about past mistakes
B   spending a lot of time alone
C   blaming other people for bad situations
D   getting angry about world events
E   working hard to make a lot of money
F   being too competitive with other people
G   taking part in rough games and sports

Questions 8–10
Choose the correct letter A, B or C

8   What is the main criticism about *well-being research*?

   A   It ignores the reason why people become unhappy.
   B   It is not saying anything new or original.
   C   It cannot define what happiness really is.

9   What does Carl think is the main benefit of *well-being research*?

   A   It can help us understand how the brain works.
   B   It can help develop better medicines for depression.
   C   It encourages us to find new ways to help depression.

⇨

---

10 Carl talks about the 100-year-old woman in order to show that

    A keeping busy makes people live longer.

    B happiness contributes to a healthy life.

    C different things make different people happy.

Focus on vocabulary *Word families and expressions with self-*

1 **Eight of the sentences below (<u>including</u> the example given) contain a word form error. Underline the errors and correct them.**

  0 His new novel is <u>inspire</u>. *inspirational/inspiring*

  1 There is a really good advertise for a new type of coffee on television at the moment. ....

  2 I have to fill in a long applicant form for the job I want. ....

  3 My sister is a very optimism person. ....

  4 I have to make a long presentation at work tomorrow. ....

  5 Rich people aren't always happy. ....

  6 I saw a really interested film last night. ....

  7 She has always had a lot of lucky. ....

  8 Don't criticism me! ....

  9 I feel very depressing today. ....

▶ Expressions with *self-*

2 **Complete the sentences by choosing a suitable noun or adjective to combine with *self-*. You can use a dictionary to help you.**

conscious	study	control	portrait	help	reliant

  1 It takes a lot of self-.................... to keep calm when people criticise your work.

  2 I do a lot of water colour painting. I'm just about to start a self-.................... .

  3 We want our children to grow up to be more self-.................... . I feel our generation depended too much on other people.

  4 I think the reason I did so well in my exams was that I used the self-.................... centre a lot, before and after lessons.

  5 The community has set up several new self-.................... schemes designed to encourage people to tackle their own problems with minimal support from others.

  6 Adolescents are often very self-.................... , which makes them unwilling to do things like drama.

12 ▶ Buildings and structures

Focus on reading *Multiple choice; flow charts*

SKILLS PRACTICE
▶ **Preparation**

1   You are going to read a text called *Building in a Bag*. Think about the title, look at the picture and try to predict what the text will be about.

2   Write down any English words you already know connected with architecture and building construction.

3   a) Read the text and answer the following questions.

BUILDING in a Bag

Two young architectural engineers have designed a structure which will greatly assist the work of organisations working with refugees in emergency situations.
5 The structure is an inflatable[1] shelter made out of concrete, which can be erected quickly. It is nicknamed 'building in a bag', because it is delivered in the form of a sealed plastic sack. The sack consists of two parts: fabric which has
10 been coated with cement[2] and a plastic skin. The fabric is stuck to one surface of the plastic skin. Once the sack is in place, all that is necessary to erect the structure is the addition of water. The fabric absorbs the water and because the volume
15 of the sack itself controls the amount of water, there is no need for measurement. A chemical pack is then attached to a nozzle in the plastic skin. This releases a controlled volume of gas and inflates the structure. The shelter is left to dry out
20 and twelve hours later it is ready for use. Doors and windows are left without concrete cloth, so they can be cut out of the plastic inner once the cement has dried.

The shelter has been designed for ease of use.
25 The dry weight of the sack is only 230 kilograms and it can be lifted by eight men. It is light enough to be transported by a truck or light aircraft and it can be set up by a person without any training in under 40 minutes. The finished
30 structure has a curved outer surface, which gives it strength, and 16 square metres of floor space.

The 'building in a bag' has several advantages over two current methods of providing emergency shelter: tents and building kits. The cost of a
35 concrete shelter is estimated at $2,100, while the equivalent-sized building kit widely used in the UK costs about $7,700. The same-sized tent costs about $1,150, but soft-skinned tents provide only poor protection and last approximately two years.
40 Buildings kits are expensive and difficult to transport. The new concrete shelter incorporates the best aspects of both and in the medium- to long-term saves both effort and costs. The shelter has a design life of over ten years. It is almost as
45 easy to transport and erect as a tent, but is as long-lasting and secure as a portable building. It will provide quick accommodation, field offices and medical clinics that give much better protection in extreme climatic conditions. And as
50 the shelter can be delivered sterile[3], surgical procedures can be carried out inside the shelters from day one of any crisis.

Once the building has fulfilled its primary function as an emergency shelter, another use for
55 it can probably be found. However, it can be demolished easily, using basic tools, and the thin-walled structure has a very low mass, so leaves little material for disposal.

The engineers who designed the 'building in a
60 bag' arrived at the idea in an unusual way. Normally designers identify a need and then set to work to create solutions. However, in this case the two engineers worked the other way round. They had entered a competition to find new uses for

65 cement and they approached the task by thinking only in terms of the engineering properties of cement, and how to make best use of them. They were interested in egg shells, which are very thin but very strong, and they started by
70 experimenting with plaster, a material with similar properties to cement. By inflating plaster in a balloon they created a structure like a giant egg shell. They then moved on to using cloth coated with cement, which they inflated to
75 produce a curved surface. Finally, they arrived at a use for the process they had designed: inflatable emergency shelters.

After winning second prize in the cement competition, the two engineers obtained legal
80 protection for their concept. They then went on to win several awards and the prize money enabled them to travel to Uganda to do some field research. There they met representatives of various aid agencies, visited refugee camps and

85 demonstrated the shelter. They were also able to see for themselves how such camps operate. This opportunity was vital, because they were designing a product for use in settings previously outside their own experience.

90 The response to the 'building in a bag' amongst aid organisations in Uganda was very positive. For example, the programme head for Médicins Sans Frontières said that her organisation would have bought ten of the kits if they had been
95 immediately available. The organisations were impressed by the simplicity and economy of the idea. Fellow engineers also praised the design. According to one, the imaginative process by which the shelters are made 'deals with the key
100 issues of portability, ease of assembly, durability and cost. The applications of the shelter in the humanitarian field are immediate and obvious, but there are many other fields where this technology could be successfully employed.'

---

¹ has to be filled with air before use
² a grey powder that becomes hard when it is mixed with water
³ completely clean and free of bacteria

TIP Matching words is useful when you are scanning the text. After that you have to be careful, because the wrong options often contain words which are similar to/the same as the words in the text.

There are different types of multiple-choice tasks in the IELTS Reading module. One of them consists of questions (or incomplete sentences) with four options. Only one option is correct. Sometimes this multiple-choice task focuses on the overall meaning of a text (see Unit 3), and sometimes it focuses on details.

To do multiple-choice questions which focus on detail, first you have to scan the text to find the right place. Then you have to look carefully at what the text says.

b) **Look at the following example.**

Example
According to the writer, why is the 'building in a bag' more convenient than a conventional tent?

A It's easier to carry.   C It lasts longer.
B It's easier to put up.   D It costs less to produce.

c) **Scan the text to match the question to a phrase/sentence in the text. Which line(s) is it in?**

d) **Underline the words in the text which are a match for 'more convenient than a conventional tent'. The area of text which you have got to examine carefully lies around this point.**

Each of the options, A–D, contains words which have a match in that part of the text, so you can't find the answer by simply matching words. You have to examine the meaning of each option carefully and compare it to what the text says.

e) **Which option is correct? Why are the others wrong?**

4   Now do the exam task below.

NB Multiple-choice questions of this type follow the order of information in the text.

EXAM PRACTICE

▶ Multiple choice

HELP

These questions are all based on the second half of the text.

Questions 1–3
*Choose the correct option **A**, **B**, **C** or **D**.*

1   What first led the two engineers to design their building kit?

  A   They noticed that there was a need for better shelters.
  B   They were looking for new uses for cement.
  C   They were asked by aid agencies to supply a design.
  D   They discovered a new construction process by accident.

2   A trip to Uganda enabled the engineers to

  A   attract further investment.
  B   see their shelters in use.
  C   get information for their product design.
  D   obtain orders for their shelters.

3   How did another engineer evaluate the *building in a bag*?

  A   He thought the design met all the important criteria.
  B   He felt the idea was not a particularly new one.
  C   He claimed that some problems remained to be solved.
  D   He suggested that there were better uses for it than shelters.

Another type of multiple-choice task involves a longer list of options based on one specific topic. There is more than one correct option and you are told exactly how many to choose.

NB The options in this case do not usually follow the order of information in the text.

5   Do questions 4–5 below.

Questions 4–5
*Choose TWO letters, **A–E**.*
Which TWO of the following advantages of the *building in a bag* are mentioned?

  A   It can be erected in bad weather.
  B   It doesn't need cleaning before use as a hospital.
  C   It is more permanent than other portable structures.
  D   It has very thick walls.
  E   It is easy to dispose of after use.

EXAM PRACTICE

▶ Flow chart

Another task type in the IELTS Reading module is completing a flow chart. Flow charts appear in the form of a diagram and they show stages in a process. The information for this type of task often comes from one part of the text only.

The instructions will tell you what the maximum number of words is for each space. All the words that you use must come from the text: you cannot use your own words, even if these mean the same.

▶ Locating information

6 a) Look at the task below, based on the text *Building in a Bag*. Which paragraph contains the necessary information?

b) Which type of word(s) (noun, verb, etc.) can go in the spaces?

c) Do the exam task below.

> **TIP** Copy the word(s) exactly as they appear in the text. Only use words which already fit grammatically. Don't change words to make them fit (e.g. singular to plural, present to past).

Questions 6–9
Complete the flow chart below.
*Choose **NO MORE THAN TWO WORDS** from the passage for your answer.*

Erecting a concrete shelter

Put sack in place

↓

Add **6** ....

↓

Attach chemical pack to add **7** ....

↓

Allow to **8** ....

↓

Cut out **9** .... and ....

DELIVERY

HYDRATION

INFLATION

SETTING

Focus on grammar 1 *Passive*

Focus on IELTS Foundation,
KLB p.148

1 **a)** Look again at the third paragraph of the text and answer the question below.

> The shelter has been designed for ease of use. The dry weight of the sack is only 230 kilograms and it can be lifted by eight men. It is light enough to be transported by a truck or light aircraft and it can be set up by a person without any training in under 40 minutes. The finished structure has a curved outer surface, which gives it strength, and 16 square metres of floor space.

What/who is the main focus of this paragraph?

A the designers of the shelter
B the users of the shelter
C the shelter itself

Because the people who designed and use the shelter are not the main focus of the paragraph, the passive form of the verb is the one which is used most frequently here.

b) Underline all the passive forms in the paragraph.

c) Which of the passive verbs in the paragraph are in the present form?

d) Which of the passive verbs refer(s) to a *finished* process?

e) Complete the text below by filling in the spaces. Use the passive form of the verbs in the box.
An example has been done for you.

> | | | | | |
> |---|---|---|---|---|
> | *place* | *dig* | *hold* | ~~*lay*~~ | *install* |
> | *fill* | *erect* | *build* | *finish* | |

> **Construction of a Brick House**
> The foundations of the house ..*are laid*.......... using the architect's plans.
> Firstly, a narrow trench **1** ...., and then **2** .... with cement. The walls **3** .... on this firm base. When they reach shoulder height, a scaffolding **4** .... Openings for doors and windows **5** .... in place by wooden frames. When the walls **6** ...., the framework for the roof **7** .... on top. Finally, interior fittings such as pipes and wiring **8** ....

f) Check that you have used singular and plural forms as appropriate.

Focus on grammar 2 *Participle clauses*

Focus on IELTS Foundation, p.127 **1** **a) Look at these two sentence pairs.**

A • The *building in a bag* will revolutionise the work of aid agencies when they work with refugees in emergency situations.
   • The *building in a bag* will revolutionise the work of aid agencies *working with refugees in emergency situations.*

B • The shelter, which has been designed for ease of use, can be assembled in less than 40 minutes.
   • *Designed for ease of use,* the shelter can be assembled in less than 40 minutes.

The sentences in each pair have the same meaning, but the second sentences are shorter than the first. The phrases in *italics* have been reduced. These are known as participle clauses.

Notice the word order in these examples. In A, the reduced phrase appears after the noun it gives details about (*agencies*); in B, it appears before it (*shelter*). In this way, the main sentence is not broken up.

b) Rewrite these sentences so that they are shorter.

1 The new structure is an inflatable shelter, which is erected quickly on demand.

   ....
   ....

2 The structure has a curved outer surface, which gives it strength.

   ....
   ....

3 Aid agencies, which were impressed by the new design, expressed interest in buying the building kits.

   ....
   ....

4 The shelter, which incorporates the best aspects of similar structures, has won several awards.

   ....
   ....

5 The engineers won several awards, which enabled them to travel to Uganda for field research.

   ....
   ....

Focus on vocabulary *Materials and structures*

1   Which of these words is the odd-one-out and why?

> concrete   cement   sack   plaster   plastic

2   These words refer to stages in the life of a building structure. Which word refers to the first stage and which to the last?

> erect   design   demolish   construct

3   These adjectives can all be used to describe a building. Complete the table by adding the noun form of the words.

adjective	noun
durable	durability
imaginative	
portable	
strong	
simple	
secure	

4   Which two words in the table might be used to describe a building design too?

▶ Core vocabulary

5   Match the words below, as they are used in the text, to the definitions. NB Two of the words in the list are used in this text with a similar meaning, so they have the same definition here.

function (line 54)   characteristics

solution (line 62)   way of dealing with something

aspects (line 42)/ properties (line 66)   series of actions

concept (line 80)   practical uses

design (line 97)   use

process (line 98)   plan

applications (line 101)   idea

Focus on grammar 3 *If + past simple*

Focus on IELTS Foundation, p.132
KLB p.143

1 a) **Look carefully at these two sentences, written by different people, about the future.**

A *If all new buildings are designed to use solar power, global warming will be greatly reduced.*

B *If all new buildings were designed to use solar power, global warming would be greatly reduced.*

The two sentences are very similar. However, the people who wrote them have differing views. What is the difference between them?

If you want to talk or write about events or actions which you consider to be unlikely, you can use this grammatical structure:

Condition	Outcome
if/unless … + past simple verb form	… would + basic verb form

b) **Read these sentences and tick the ones describing an event which the writer thinks is unlikely.**

1 If architects listened more carefully to what people want, they would design better houses.
2 If plans for constructing a new road bridge go ahead, the traffic flow will improve.
3 Unless the construction industry can attract more trainees, there will be a serious shortage of skilled labour.
4 The need for office buildings will decrease if the IT revolution continues.
5 There would be less need for air conditioning if buildings were better ventilated.

c) **Match the sentence beginnings in A with the sentence endings in B.**

A	B
1 If building sites were better regulated,	costs would be reduced.
2 If wages in the construction industry were higher,	heating bills would be reduced.
3 If more cycle lanes were built in urban areas,	the price of houses would rise.
4 If the construction industry used more local materials,	there would be fewer accidents.
5 If buildings were better insulated,	there would be fewer traffic jams.

d) **Complete the sentences below.**

1 If there were fewer high-rise buildings in Shanghai, …
2 The housing shortage would be less serious …
3 Many coastal cities would be flooded …
4 If there were more parks in city centres, …
5 If urban roads were built underground, …

Focus on speaking 1 *Practice for Parts 1 and 2*

▶ Fluency

1 🎧 Listen to questions about the place where you live. Practise answering fluently (i.e. answer quickly and fully).

2 a) 🎧 Listen to one person doing this Part 2 speaking task.

Describe a public building that you like very much.

> **You should say**
>
>> **where the building is**
>> **what it looks like**
>> **what it's used for**
>
> **and explain why you like the building so much.**

---

b) Read what the man said and mark the four places where he begins each sub-topic described on the card.

A public building I really like is the old railway station in Kuala Lumpur. It's right in the centre of the city. It's a very striking building – it stands out from the others around it because of its architecture – it looks sort of middle-eastern. It has a lot of pillars and arches. But it's not a modern building – I think it's about a hundred years old. And of course, it's used for trains. It used to be the main station for the whole of Malaysia and there were trains passing through it to all parts of the country and to Singapore and Thailand as well. But now there's a new station, so the older station building is just used for local, commuter trains. But it's still a big tourist attraction too, so we get lots of visitors just coming to have a look at it. And … the reason why I like the building so much is … well I just like its appearance, it's a beautiful building I think. And it's also nice to have some historic buildings in a modern city – it gives variety.

c) Do the speaking task yourself. Record yourself if possible and then listen.

Focus on speaking 2 *Practice for Part 3; assessing and predicting*

In Part 3 of the IELTS Speaking test, the examiner might ask questions which require you to assess a situation, or predict future developments.

▶ Assessing

1 a) **Look at the question and some of the ways to begin a reply.**

Question
How important is it to provide public parks in inner city areas?

Replies: beginnings
1 'It's extremely important …'
2 'It can be important …'
3 'I don't think it's the most important thing …'
4 'It's not important at all …'

b) **Match the endings below with one of the beginnings.**

Replies: endings
A 'After all, there are lots of cities where there aren't any parks and people survive quite happily. They can always go out of the city at weekends or on holidays.'
B 'It depends on the situation. For example, in places where it's very difficult for people to get away from the city, because the city is very big, or because they can't afford transport, people do need a green area within their neighbourhood.'
C 'Other things are more important, like having a house and a job and a school for your children.'
D 'Everybody needs access to a nice green place where they can relax in the fresh air and meet other people. And parks help to control air pollution as well.'

c) ⌗ **Listen to some similar questions and practise answering. Record yourself if possible and then listen.**

d) ⌗ **Listen to some other speakers answering the same questions.**

▶ Predicting

2 a) ⌗ **Listen to someone answering this question and tick the developments which the speaker mentions.**

What kind of developments do you think there will be in architecture in the near future?

Likely developments:
Example more natural ventilation ✓

A bigger windows   D more communal areas
B individual wind turbines   E greater use of natural materials
C fewer high-rise buildings

b) ⌗ **Listen to some more questions about the future and practise answering. Record yourself if possible and then listen.**

c) ⌗ **Listen to some other speakers answering the same questions.**

VOCABULARY

1 a) Complete the sentences below using the words in the box. You may need to use some words more than once. If necessary, use the plural form.

| method   measure   range   role |

1 The government is taking .... to reduce energy consumption in all new buildings.

2 Traditional .... of house construction are often more environmentally-friendly than modern ones.

3 Several studies suggest that diet plays an important .... in maintaining good health.

4 In the 21st century, the .... of materials available for building construction is much wider than in the past.

5 Psychologists investigating the nature of happiness are unsure exactly what the .... of money is.

b) Are the following sentences true (T) or false (F)?

1 Bricks are more durable than wood.   ....

2 Camping equipment is designed to be portable.   ....

3 Tents are generally more secure than houses.   ....

4 The style of the Taj Mahal is very simple.   ....

5 Plastic is generally stronger than paper.   ....

PREPOSITIONS

2 Complete the sentences with the correct preposition.

1 City dwellers are more likely to suffer .... loneliness than people who live in villages.

2 A balanced diet consists .... protein, carbohydrate and fat.

3 Better housing often leads .... improvements in health.

4 People who live alone can often benefit .... keeping a pet.

5 Lack .... sunlight can cause bone deformity.

6 In some countries, increasing stress is the result .... work pressures.

NEGATIVE ATTITUDES

3 Match the questions (1–5) and replies (a–e) below.

1 Do you generally get enough sleep?

2 Do you go to work by car?

3 Do you have regular health checks?

4 Are you generally happy at work?

5 Have you got many hobbies?

a I'm afraid I don't. In fact I haven't seen a doctor for many years.

b I'm afraid I don't. I usually stay up late and then I feel tired in the mornings.

c I'm afraid not. I don't seem to have much time for leisure activities.

d I'm afraid I do. I used to walk, but I've got lazy.

e I'm afraid not. I'm looking for a new job with better pay and shorter hours.

WORD FORMATION

4 a) Look at the table. Fill in the gaps with the appropriate form.

Adjective	Noun
	excitement
financial	
	freedom
happy	
	interest
lucky	
	security
similar	
	society

b) Use words from the table above to complete these sentences.

1 A well-known writer once said that .... in marriage is largely a matter of luck.

2 Setting up your own business can be very exhausting but also very ....

3 Older people tend to value financial .... more than younger people do.

4 We seem to choose partners who come from .... social backgrounds to ourselves.

5 People often live longer when they are .... in current affairs.

IF + PAST TENSE + WOULD

5 Complete the statements below using the prompts given in brackets.

0   If everyone had access to clean water
.... (disease/reduce).
If everyone had access to clean water, *disease would be reduced.*

1   If working hours were reduced, ...
(family life/better).

2   People would probably do more exercise if
.... (watch/less TV).

3   Cities would be better places to live if
.... (fewer cars).

4   If roads were safer, ... (use
bicycles/more often).

5   Thousands of lives would be saved each year if
.... (scientists/develop/malaria
vaccine).

PASSIVE

6 Use the information in the flow chart to write a paragraph about emergency procedures. The first sentence has been done for you.

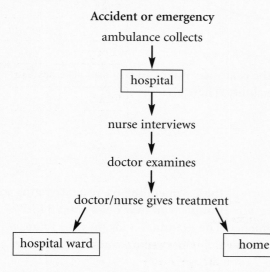

Accident or emergency

ambulance collects

hospital

nurse interviews

doctor examines

doctor/nurse gives treatment

hospital ward   home

In an emergency a patient is usually collected by an ambulance and taken to the nearest hospital. He/she is then ....

....

....

....

QUANTIFIERS

7 Are the following sentences true (T) or false (F)? Rewrite the false sentences, changing the words in italics and any others necessary.

1   Neither Zambia nor Zimbabwe lies on
the African coast.   ....

2   Neither Singapore nor Sri Lanka is an
island state.   ....

3   There haven't been any cases of smallpox
for several years.   ....

4   Most cities in Europe have an underground
train system.   ....

5   According to the UN charter, every child
has a right to security.   ....

6   There have been a few crises caused by
severe weather over the last decade.   ....

WHILE

8 Complete the sentences using *while*.

Motor vehicle exports 2000	
Country	Percentage of world total
Germany	20
USA	5

1   In 2000, Germany exported 20% of the world's
motor vehicles, while ...

Computer exports 2000	
Country	Percentage of world total
Singapore	11
Japan	8

2   In 2000, Singapore exported ...

Pharmaceutical products 2000	
Country	Percentage of world total
Switzerland	10
Belgium	6

3   In 2000, ...

135

► Assess your speaking

IELTS Bands

For each IELTS paper there are ten IELTS bands (grades), from 0 to 9. Half bands (4.5, 5.5, etc.) are also given. See p.5 for more information on the IELTS Bands.

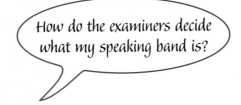

How do the examiners decide what my speaking band is?

During the IELTS Speaking test, the examiner listens to you and assesses four separate aspects of your speaking ability. These are:

- pronunciation
- fluency and organisation
- vocabulary
- grammar

You may get different grades for each of these, depending on your strengths and weaknesses in each particular area. For example, you may be at band 5 for pronunciation, but band 4.5 for fluency. The examiner adds up your scores for *fluency and organisation, vocabulary, grammar* and *pronunciation* to get your overall grade for speaking.

Opposite are some detailed descriptions of different bands specifically for *Speaking*. The IELTS examiner uses descriptions similar to these to decide what your ability level is.

SPEAKING TEST: DESCRIPTIONS OF BANDS 3–7

	Fluency and organisation	Vocabulary	Grammar	Pronunciation
3	• speaks with long pauses • is often unable to link simple sentences • says only simple things and is often unable to speak	• uses simple words to talk about him/herself • doesn't know enough words to talk about less familiar things	• only uses simple grammatical patterns and often makes mistakes • may rely on phrases or sentences which are memorised • makes a lot of mistakes except when using memorised phrases	
4	• usually pauses a lot • may speak slowly, with frequent repetition and self-correction • uses a small number of connectives, and sometimes makes mistakes with them	• is able to talk about common topics but has difficulty talking about unfamiliar topics and often uses the wrong word • rarely tries to paraphrase	• only produces simple grammatical patterns • makes a lot of mistakes and sometimes cannot be understood	• it is sometimes hard for the listener to understand what he/she says
5	• can usually keep talking, but uses repetition, self-correction and/or slow speech to keep going • may use certain connectives too much • can talk fluently about simple ideas, but has problems when talking about more complicated things	• knows enough words to talk about most topics • sometimes uses paraphrase successfully, but not always	• produces simple grammatical patterns quite accurately • can use some more complex grammatical patterns, but these usually contain mistakes and can cause comprehension problems for the listener	
6	• is able to speak for quite a long time, but sometimes pauses, or corrects him/herself • uses a range of connectives, pronouns, etc. but these are sometimes incorrect	• knows enough words to discuss a variety of topics, and make his/her meaning clear, but some words may not be appropriate in style • generally paraphrases successfully	• uses a mix of simple and complex structures • may make frequent mistakes with complex structures, though these rarely cause misunderstanding	• can always be understood, but sometimes the listener has to make an effort because words are mispronounced
7	• speaks for quite a long time without difficulty • uses a range of connectives, pronouns, etc. • might sometimes hesitate, repeat phrases, or re-start sentences	• knows enough words to discuss a variety of topics • uses some less common words • usually chooses words which are appropriate in style • uses paraphrase effectively	• uses a range of complex grammatical patterns • often produces correct sentences, but sometimes makes mistakes	

PRONUNCIATION

Few adults learn to speak in a foreign language exactly like a native speaker.

✓ Speakers with good pronunciation can be easily understood by other listeners, even when their accent isn't standard.

Tips for improving your pronunciation:

✓ Listen to spoken English (e.g. radio, TV, cinema).
✓ Record yourself speaking English as often as you can.
✓ Repeat phrases after the speaker in recordings. This will help with stress and intonation.

FLUENCY AND ORGANISATION

Fluency is about how well your speech flows.

✓ A fluent speaker talks at normal speed, without long pauses, frequent repetition or frequent correction.

Organisation is about how you plan and put your ideas in order.

✓ A well-organised speaker groups ideas together and uses words and phrases to *show* how the ideas are organised.

Tips for improving your fluency:

✓ Try to speak as often as possible with native speakers, and you can even talk to yourself in English!
✓ Record yourself speaking at length as often as you can.

VOCABULARY

✓ If you have a good *vocabulary* base, you can quickly choose words which are accurate in meaning, as well as appropriate in style (for example, formal or less formal). In addition, you will use phrases (groups of words) which are most commonly used by native speakers.

Tips for improving your vocabulary:

✓ Keep a vocabulary book and record words and phrases that can be used in a variety of academic contexts.
✓ Use a good monolingual dictionary. This will allow you to check how words are used.

GRAMMAR

Grammar is probably the aspect of language which teachers and learners are generally most conscious of.

✓ If you have good knowledge of grammar, you can express both simple and complex ideas quickly.

Tips for improving your grammar:

✓ Listen and read as much English as you can.
✓ Make a note of any key grammar points in a book so you can refer to them.

Examples of IELTS Speaking tests for you to assess

Here are some examples of learners doing an IELTS test. As you listen to them, think about the four different things which IELTS examiners assess. Try to do the assessment tasks shown with an arrow →.

PART 1

🎧 Listen to an examiner asking a candidate questions about reading (see Unit 1 Read all about it) during the first part of a Speaking test.

→ 🎧 Listen again and concentrate on the speaker's **pronunciation**. Put a tick in one of the boxes below, according to the number of mispronounced words you hear.

	none	a few	many
mispronounced words			

→ 🎧 Listen again and concentrate on the speaker's **fluency**. Put a tick in one of the boxes below, according to the number of pauses you hear.

	none	a few	many
pauses			

→ Now look at the audio script and consider the speaker's use of **vocabulary** and **grammar**.

NB On p.148 you can find a more detailed examiner's assessment of this example.

PART 2

🎧 Listen to a candidate talking about her favourite way of relaxing (see Unit 10 Health check) during the second part of an IELTS Speaking test.

→ Consider the candidate's **fluency.** How long does she speak *without help*? Tick one of the boxes.

more than one minute	about one minute	less than one minute

→ 🎧 Now listen again and consider the candidate's **pronunciation**. How many times does she say a word which you can't recognise? Tick one of the boxes.

never	once	more than once

NB On p.148 you can find a more detailed examiner's assessment of this example.

PART 3

🎧 Listen to an IELTS examiner asking a candidate two questions about relaxation (see Unit 10 Health check) during the third part of an IELTS Speaking test.

➔ Consider the candidate's **fluency.** What speed does he speak at? Tick one of the boxes.

normal	slow

Now read what the candidate said.

Question 1
There are, I think, lots of leisure activities. A traditional activity in my country … it's riding horses … and camel racing is very popular. … And the other thing is er falcon hunting and especially in the winter season … However … there are lots of other hobbies and activities which are popular… like quad bikes, fishing … Fishing is popular because we have a lot of coasts … my country is like an island so you can fish anywhere … so I think everybody does lots of activities …

Question 2
I think no, because … fifty to a hundred years ago … people used to work all day … Planting and working on the farm, and some people were fishing the whole day … to just bring the food to his family to eat … and there were no … facilities to move … I mean … to transport … just maybe horses … now they have cars and they have chairs to sit in, and I think it's more … more comfortable now … especially if a person works in a big company. You can have your food there or you can bring it in the cafeteria and can sit and talk with a friend … I think before it was difficult more than now.

➔ Consider the candidate's **organisation.** In his answer to the examiner's first question, which words/phrases does the candidate use to show the connection between his ideas? Write the words.

....

....

....

➔ Consider the candidate's **vocabulary.** How easily can he find appropriate words connected with the topic of relaxation? Tick one of the boxes.

he uses a variety of words	he uses only a few words

NB On p.149 you can find a more detailed examiner's assessment of this example.

► Assess your writing

In this section you will:
- Read about the way that IELTS candidates are assessed in the Writing module
- Read some tips on how to improve your written English
- Read some examples of candidates' answers for an IELTS Writing test and practise assessing them
- Read some comments from an IELTS Examiner about candidates' English
- Find out how you can prepare for an IELTS test
- Find out how you can best show your ability during an IELTS test

How do the examiners decide what my writing band is?

When you do the IELTS Writing test the examiner assesses four separate aspects of what you write:

- content
- organisation
- vocabulary
- grammar

As with speaking, the examiner adds up your separate band scores for *content, organisation, vocabulary* and *grammar* to get your overall band for writing.

On p.142 are some detailed descriptions of different bands for writing. The IELTS examiner uses descriptions similar to these to decide what your ability level is.

WRITING TEST: DESCRIPTIONS OF BANDS 3–7

	Content	Organisation	Vocabulary	Grammar
3	• is unable to do the given task, which may have been completely misunderstood • presents a few ideas which may be irrelevant or repetitive	• does not organise ideas clearly • uses only a few connectives and those may be inaccurate	• uses only a small set of words and makes mistakes of word-formation and/or spelling • errors may severely distort the message	• there are so many grammar and punctuation mistakes that the reader finds it difficult to understand
4	• tries to do the given task, but does not cover all the key features • the presentation may be inappropriate • details may be unclear, irrelevant, repetitive or inaccurate	• information and ideas are not organised clearly • uses some basic connectives, but these may be inaccurate or repetitive	• uses only basic words • sometimes repeats words and/or uses them inappropriately • makes mistakes of word-formation and/or spelling which may cause difficulty for the reader	• uses only a few, simple grammatical patterns • rarely uses complex grammatical patterns • there are more incorrect than correct sentences • punctuation is often wrong
5	• is generally able to do the given task, but the presentation may be inappropriate in places • may list details without providing a clear summary • may not provide figures to support the description	• in places the organisation is unclear • uses connectives, inaccurately, or over-uses them • writing may be repetitive because pronouns, etc. are under-used	• does not know a wide range of words, but knows just enough to do the given task • may make noticeable mistakes in spelling and/or word formation and these may cause difficulty for the reader	• uses only a limited range of grammatical patterns • sometimes tries to use more complex grammatical patterns • may make frequent mistakes of grammar or punctuation and these can cause some difficulty for the reader
6	• is able to do the given task • selects appropriate information for a summary • presents important features clearly but does not always give enough details • may make mistakes with details	• organises information and ideas clearly • sometimes makes mistakes with connectives • may not always use pronouns, etc. correctly	• usually uses the right words for the task • tries to use less common vocabulary but may make mistakes • makes some spelling and/or word-formation mistakes, but these don't cause misunderstanding	• uses a mixture of simple and complex grammatical patterns • makes some mistakes in grammar and punctuation, but they don't usually affect understanding
7	• is able to do the given task • presents a clear summary of trends, differences or stages • presents important features clearly but does not always give enough details	• organises information and ideas clearly • usually uses connectives, pronouns, etc. appropriately, although there may be some under-/over-use	• can write quite accurately about a variety of topics and sometimes uses less common words and phrases • generally chooses words of an appropriate style • may sometimes make mistakes in meaning, spelling and/or word formation	• uses a variety of complex grammatical patterns • often produces sentences without mistakes • may make a few errors of grammar or punctuation

CONTENT

The *content* of your writing is assessed according to how closely you've followed the instructions and how clear the focus is.

✓ If your writing has a clear focus, a reader will probably understand it quickly and feel satisfied that the information you've provided is relevant.

Tips for improving the content of your writing:

Task 1

✓ Remember to describe the information you see in the diagram and NOT the diagram itself. For example, you don't need to say what type of graph it is or what the title is.

✓ Select the most important features of the diagram and <u>give examples</u> with figures to support what you are saying.

✓ To practise understanding graphs and diagrams, look for examples around you, e.g. on TV, the Internet and in newspapers and try to understand what they are showing.

Task 2

✓ Read the question very carefully!

✓ Before you start writing, make a paragraph plan.

✓ Check that your answer covers all parts of the question.

ORGANISATION AND ACCURACY

Organisation is about the way that you arrange and present your ideas and help your reader to understand the connections between them.

✓ If your writing is well-planned and you provide helpful signposts, a reader will find it easier to understand.

Tips for organising your answer:

✓ Present your ideas in a clear and logical way.

✓ Learn how to use connectives such as *On the other hand*, *However*, etc.

✓ Make sure you leave time to check your writing and look out especially for your 'favourite' mistakes, including spelling and punctuation.

✓ Check that you haven't written too much or too little.

Spelling and *punctuation* are features which are additionally assessed in the writing test so don't forget to check them!

Examples of IELTS Writing tasks for you to assess

Try to do the assessment tasks shown with an arrow ➔.

TASK ONE

Read a candidate's answer to the following task about changes to a university campus (see Unit 7 Appropriate technology p.79).

> *The plans on p.79 show changes to one university campus between 1985 and the present day.*
>
> *Summarise the information by selecting and reporting the main features and make comparisons where relevant.*

The studing these days is one of the important thing and without the knowledge or studing it is impossible for the nation to progress.

So places of studing must be comfortable to provide good conditions for studing.

5 If you can note these is no comparing between the university campus in 1985 and the present day. For example, the library in 1985 was smaller than the library in the present day. Also the library in the present day has something extra which is the IT Centre. In 1985 the university campus had several pepreated blocks instance, physics Block, chemistry 10 Block and biology Block. However, in the present day all those Blocks bare merged in one block. The Admin Building in the present day is smaller than the Admin Building in 1985.

Now there are a lot of tree in the university campus in the present day which give the university a beautiful view.

15 In 1985 there was not shuttle bus terminal but now there is. Now there is lecture theatre. In the present day there are more roads than in 1985.

In the present day the university campus has not car park. Contrary in 1985 there was two car park. (199 words)

Think about the **content** of this summary.

➔ There are six paragraphs. Are all the paragraphs relevant to the task?
Yes/No (If no, give line number(s) of irrelevant paragraphs)

....

➔ Is there any information on the map which is missing from the summary?
Yes/No (If yes, what information is missing?)

....

....

➜ Think about the writer's **organisation.**
List the connectives (the words that link sentences) used by the writer:

....

....

➜ Think about the **vocabulary** and **grammar.** How easily can you understand what the writer wants to say? Tick one of the boxes:

I can understand everything	I can usually understand	There are a lot of parts that I don't understand

➜ Are all the words spelt correctly? Make a note of the writer's 'favourite' mistakes.

NB On p.150 you can find a more detailed examiner's assessment of this example.

TASK TWO

Read a candidate's answer to a task about mobile phones (see Unit 7 Appropriate technology p.80.)

Many people think that mobile phones have a benefits and many people think the mobile phones have a negatives.

The mobile phones is a very good invention, because it gives a lot of help for the people.

5 By mobile phones you can call to any one you want in any way in the world and any time you can call by just bress a butns ant too easy.

A lot of people can't go out without mobile phones. The mobile phones can take it anywhere with you.

The mobile phones are very important in my country because every weekend
10 we go to the desart, so some times we get lost or we have bancher and we need help, then the mobile phones gives a facilitys to get help from friends or the police.

The mobile phones are a good business to sell.

In my country who open a mobile phones have a good business.

15 However the mobile phones waste of money if you use it wrong. for exaple some times I use the mobile phone wrong like to talk along time then I get a very expensive bill, It waste of money and talking on the mobile its dangers speacily when you drive a car it maks an accidents, so becarful when you drive a car.

The mobile phones are nosey in the schools or in the cinemas or in the quite places.

20 The talking along on the mobile phones is not helthy because some of the mobiles can damge you ears.

➔ Think about the **content** of this essay. It doesn't deal with all parts of the task. Which part of the task *isn't* dealt with?

....

➔ Think about the **organisation** of the essay. Where does the writer move from describing advantages to describing disadvantages?

Line ......

➔ Tick any of these statements that you agree with:

There are too many paragraphs. ☐

There aren't enough paragraphs. ☐

The paragraphs help me to follow the writer's ideas. ☐

I don't find the paragraphs very helpful. ☐

➔ Think about the **vocabulary**. The writer uses 'mobile phones' in most sentences. Which word(s) could the writer have used instead?

....

Find three spelling mistakes.

....

....

....

➔ *Nosey* (line 19) is the wrong word. Suggest a word which the writer could have used here.

....

➔ Think about the **grammar.** Does the writer use a variety of sentence patterns? Tick one of the boxes:

there is a wide variety of patterns	there is quite a wide variety of patterns	only very simple sentences are used

➔ Sometimes the writer doesn't divide sentences in the correct places. Find one example of this.

Line ......

NB On p.151 you can find a more detailed examiner's assessment of this example.

Tips for improving your performance during the IELTS test

Some aspects of your speaking and writing ability can only improve over a long period. You will become more proficient by studying, by reading and listening to English and by practising. This is particularly the case with *grammar* and *vocabulary*, for example.

However, there are certain strategies that you can use at the time that you take the test, which will help you to achieve a better assessment on that particular occasion. It might make a difference of half or even one whole band.

SPEAKING

Don't worry too much about accuracy. Focus on *what* you are saying rather than *how* you are saying it.

Try to give full answers to the examiner's questions. You can extend your replies in various ways, such as giving examples, or giving reasons for things you say (Parts One and Three).

Organise what you want to say into clear parts and make it clear when you are moving from one part to another (Part Two).

WRITING

- *Read the task and the instructions very carefully. Focus closely on these when you write.*

- *Look carefully at the data (graph, chart or diagram) before you begin writing (Task One).*

- *Plan a structure for your writing and use paragraphs, etc. to make the structure clear to the reader.*

- *Use connectives to help your reader to follow the sequence of ideas or information.*

Examples of IELTS Speaking tests: detailed assessments by an examiner

PART ONE (p.139)

Fluency and organisation

✗ The speaker finds it difficult to answer the examiner's questions fluently. He often pauses, sometimes for a long time. As well as pausing, the speaker corrects himself frequently and re-starts his sentences. His answer to the final question is a good example of this.

✗ The candidate doesn't usually extend his replies to the examiner's questions without prompting. For example, his first reply to 'Do you like reading?' is simply 'Yes, I do.'

Vocabulary

✓ The speaker uses words quite accurately and doesn't make any obvious mistakes.

✗ However, the range of words he uses is small. In one place he suddenly stops what he is saying ('I read the history books, about …'), possibly because he can't remember the right words.

Grammar

✗ The writer uses simple structures, apart from in his answer to the final question.

✓ When he makes mistakes he is sometimes able to correct himself, for example 'When I am a child …' etc. It seems that he knows basic grammar, but can't use it quickly enough.

Pronunciation

✓ The speaker's pronunciation of words is quite close to standard pronunciation, and can be understood easily.

✗ The least standard aspect of his speech is the way he stresses syllables and words. For example, he gives equal emphasis to each syllable in a word, without reducing or combining any.

PART TWO (p.139)

Fluency and organisation

✗ The speaker makes long pauses and seems unable to talk for the minimum time (one minute). The examiner has to intervene and ask questions in order to get the candidate to say more. The quantity of language she produces is too small to judge her fluency and the problem affects assessment of vocabulary and grammar too.

Vocabulary

✗ The speaker uses only a very small number of words and repeats these.

Grammar

✗ The speaker has difficulty producing complete sentences and strings together words and phrases instead.

Pronunciation

✓ Apart from her pronunciation of 'pool', and 'hall' the speaker's pronunciation is quite clear.

✓ Although her word stress is not standard, because she gives equal weight to individual syllables, it's still possible to understand what she's saying.

PART THREE (p.140)

Fluency and organisation

✓ The speaker answers the examiner's questions fully, providing plenty of explanations and examples.

✓ He speaks at normal speed and he never pauses for a long time.

✓ He also repeats things:
'I think lots of leisure activities ...'
'So I think everybody does lots of activities'

✓ Regarding organisation, the speaker provides a variety of signals to help the listener understand what the link between his ideas is:
'lots of other hobbies and activities which are popular, <u>like</u> quad bikes, fishing'
'<u>fifty to a hundred years ago</u> people used ... <u>now</u> they have ...'
These are helpful for the listener.

Vocabulary

✓ The speaker's vocabulary is generally adequate for answering questions on this topic, and he seems to have easy access to suitable words, e.g. 'hobbies', 'hunting', 'fishing', 'facilities'.

✗ Occasionally he uses an inexact expression, presumably because he doesn't have access to the most suitable word:
'<u>planting</u> and working in the farm ...'
'there were no facilities to <u>move</u> ...'

✓ Despite some inexactness, the listener can easily understand what the speaker wants to say.

Grammar

✓ In general the speaker is able to use simple structures quite accurately. For example, in response to the second question he uses present and past verb forms correctly. Sometimes his grammar is perfect, e.g. 'my country is like an island so you can fish anywhere.'

✗ However, there is little evidence here that the speaker can express more complex ideas: the range of structures which he has access to is probably limited.

Pronunciation

✓ In general the speaker can be understood by a native English-speaker, even though his accent is non-standard. Perhaps the most obvious non-standard feature is his pronunciation of /r/.

✗ The /p/ in 'plants' or 'company' might also cause temporary problems for a listener, or certain long vowel sounds, e.g. in 'coasts', 'go' or 'around'.

✗ Only one word – 'comfortable' – had the wrong syllable stress.

✓ The way the speaker stresses words within sentences is not quite standard, but doesn't create any noticeable problems.

Examples of IELTS Writing tests: detailed assessments by an examiner

TASK ONE (p.144)

Content

✗ The writer's first two paragraphs are not relevant to the task and are unnecessary. As it is, the first sentence of his third paragraph, though it contains errors, is a suitable introduction for the essay.

✓ The essay is mainly complete, as it covers all the changes to the campus except the replacement of roads with footpaths.

✓ The writer summarises the changes to the science buildings well - 'in the present day all those blocks are merged in one block', but in other places he lists individual details rather than attempting to summarise.

Organisation

✓ The writer orders his information clearly and helpfully: he mentions each feature of the campus in turn, and describes what they are like in the early and then the later period.

✓ Apart from the first and second paragraphs, which should probably be merged, the paragraphing is helpful: the third deals with the topic of buildings, the fourth with the topic of greenery and the fifth with the topic of outdoor facilities.

✗ Pronouns are generally under-used. For example, 'the library in 1985 was smaller than the library in the present day. Also the library in the present day has something extra which is the IT Centre'. However, the writer generally makes good use of connectives to link ideas, e.g. 'in 1985'; 'now'; 'for example'; 'However'; 'Contrary'.

Vocabulary

✗ Most of the words that the writer uses already appear in the task rubric, so there isn't much evidence that he knows a range of vocabulary (apart from the use of 'merged', which is not a very common word).

✓ However, his use of words is mainly accurate. 'Contrary' is understandable, even though not completely correct.

✓ Spelling is mainly correct too and there is only one word – 'pepreated' - which is unrecognisable.

Grammar

✓ This writer's grammar is fairly accurate, but limited.

✓ Although the writer does make minor mistakes, the reader can always understand what he means. He can use comparative forms quite well – 'The Admin Building in the present day is smaller than the Admin Building in 1985' but he rarely uses subordinate clauses and the last paragraph in particular consists entirely of simple sentences.

TASK TWO (p.145)

Content

✗ The writer's first sentence simply repeats part of the task rubric, so might not be counted. This would leave the answer slightly under length, at only 233 words.

✓ Most of the writer's essay is relevant to the task.

✗ He doesn't express his own view about whether the advantages of mobile phones are greater than the disadvantages. So his answer to the question in the rubric is incomplete.

Organisation

✓ The writer orders his ideas clearly: first he lists the advantages and then he lists the disadvantages of mobile phones.

✗ However, the essay ends suddenly, without a conclusion.

✗ The paragraphs aren't generally helpful for the reader, because they don't show clearly which of the writer's ideas are connected. (In most places a new paragraph is used for each new sentence.) For example, the sentences following 'However' could be merged into one paragraph, as they are all about the same topic.

✗ The writer uses only two connectives – 'However' and 'for example'. His essay would have been improved if he had used more of these. Also, he doesn't use enough pronouns, which can help to show the links between ideas. For example, he constantly repeats the phrase 'mobile phones', instead of using 'they', 'them' or 'these'.

Vocabulary

✗ The writer generally knows enough basic words to do this task, but sometimes he uses expressions which are unusual, inexact or even wrong, e.g. 'expensive bill' and 'nosey'.

✗ Spelling mistakes cause difficulties for the reader which are serious at times: 'ant'; 'brass'; 'butns'; 'bancher'; 'speacily'; 'quite'.

Grammar

✗ The writer makes mistakes in most sentences, especially when he tries to use complex structures, such as, 'In my country who open a mobile phones have a good business.'

✓ However, grammatical mistakes are never so bad that they prevent the reader from understanding the meaning.

▶ Answer Keys

Focus on reading 1 page 8

1 1 1 hour   2 three
      3 950 words   4 the first
      5 understanding of English
2 a) libraries
   b) match two numbers
3 a) It's in Text 4
   b) There are three (two in Text 3 and one in Text 5).
4 1 ii   2 v   3 iii   4 i   5 iv

Focus on grammar page 10

1 1 one ('we know')
   2 two ('involves', 'include')
2 B (general facts)
3 a) 1 A   2 B   3 B   4 C   5 A   6 B
   b) 'produce' in sentence 5.
4 a) 1 plural   2 plural   3 singular
      4 plural   5 singular   6 singular
   b) 1 prefer   2 damage   3 believes
      4 wear   5 supplies   6 affects

Focus on vocabulary 1 page 11

1 c) 1 subject   2 fourth   3 dictionary
      4 first
   d) classification – classify
      reference – refer
2 a) Possible answers:
      LIBRARY MATERIALS books/
      CDs/articles/ journals
      REFERENCE BOOKS atlases/
      encyclopaedias/ dictionaries/
      thesauruses
   b) Possible answers:
      CLIMATE warm wet/cool wet/hot
      dry/cold dry
      SCHOOLS primary school/
      secondary school/college/
      university/teacher/lecturer
      ANIMALS dog/cat/horse/rabbit/
      pet/wild/tame
3 c) 1 involves   2 include   3 involves
      4 include   5 include   6 involves

Focus on speaking page 13

1 1 the first and third parts
   2 the second and third parts
2 a) 1 *enjoy reading*
      2 *usually read*
      3 *popular hobby*
      4 *read English books*
      5 *Did your parents*
   b) 1, 3 and 5

3 a) 1 b   2 f   3 e   4 d   5 a   6 c
4 a) 1 much time
      2 listening to the radio
      3 I was a child
      4 favourite hobby
      5 prefer music

Focus on reading 2 page 15

2 A iv   B ii   C v   D i   E vi   F iii
3 'able to read and write'
4 1 adjective
   2 'different' because there is 'but' between the two words
   3 'missed out' because 'main' is a positive word, like 'important' and we have established that we need a word that means something different from 'important', not similar
5 1 plural noun
   2 probably means something like 'members' or 'people who attended'
6 1 is   2 are   3 become   4 recognise
   5 agree   6 involves

Focus on vocabulary 2 page 17

1 1 verb   2 verb   3 adjective   4 verb
   5 adjective   6 verb
2 a) access (v)   b) focus on
   c) significant   d) range from …
   to …   e) lack   f) equivalent to
3 1 1 range from … to   2 significant
   3 focus on   4 lack   5 equivalent to

Focus on listening 1 page 18

1 B and D
2 1 C   2 A   3 A   4 B   5 C
3 A questions 2, 7, 9
   B questions 1, 5, 8
   C questions 3, 4, 6, 10
4 a) 1 C; 2 G; 3 L; 4 Q; 5 N; 6 O; 7 D;
      8 I; 9 P; 10 E
   b) Description 1 = Man C
      Description 2 = Man A
      Description 3 = Man B
   c)

Man	Name	Date of birth
A	James Mehan	18/6/1986
B	Anthony Queensford	3/12/1962
C	David Freeman	25/8/1932

Focus on grammar 1 page 20

1 1 All   2 Most   3 No   4 Few
   5 Most   6 Most   7 Most   8 Few
   9 Most   10 No
2 1 few   2 a few   3 a few   4 few
3 a) 1 exactly
      2 just under; almost
         around; approximately
      3 exactly; around
         exactly; approximately
         just under; just over
   b) Expenditure on public health in 2001 varied considerably. While the USA spent almost $5,000 per person, Australia spent just over half that amount. Both Norway and Luxembourg spent around $2,900, and Switzerland just over $3,300.
   c) 76% = just over three quarters
      29% = just under a third
      50% = exactly a half
      9,998 = nearly ten thousand
      497–503 = around five hundred

Focus on vocabulary page 21

1

Television	Radio	Newspaper
broadcast	broadcast	circulation
turn off	turn off	column
channel	station	headline
watch	listen	read
journalist	journalist	print
weather	weather	publish
forecast	forecast	tabloid
		broadsheet
		editor
		advertisement

2 1 journalist   2 weather forecast
   3 broadsheet; tabloid   4 circulation
   5 station   6 broadcasts

Focus on writing 1 page 22

1 a) 1 true   2 false   3 true   4 true
      5 true   6 true
   b) 1 Adults need less sleep than babies.
      2 There are fewer German speakers than Spanish speakers.
      3 Fewer women than men study science.
      4 Thailand exports more electrical goods than Germany.
      5 Nuclear power causes less environmental damage than fossil fuels.
2 a) *More/less* can be used. *Fewer* cannot be used because oil and gas are

uncountable nouns – *fewer* can only be used with plural, countable nouns. *Bigger/smaller* cannot be used as they are connected with size, not amount.

b) Suggested answers:
1 In 2004 we used considerably more oil than coal.
2 In 2004 we used much more oil than hydro energy.
3 In 2004 we used slightly less hydro energy than nuclear energy.
4 In 2004 we used slightly more coal than gas.
5 In 2004 we used far more oil than nuclear energy.
6 In 2004 we used much less gas than oil.

Focus on grammar 2 page 23
1 1 often and usually; seldom and rarely
2 always and never; often and seldom/rarely; usually and occasionally
3 Order (most often first) – always, usually, often, sometimes, occasionally, rarely/seldom, never
2 1 in the mornings   2 seldom
3 Generally   4 every day   5 never
6 frequently

Focus on writing 2 page 24
1 1 bar charts   2 B and C   3 A
4 A and C   5 B
2 **Chart A**
1 1 billion   2 just over
3 slightly fewer
Chart B
1 £50,000,000   2 far less than
3 considerably less
Chart C
1 F   2 T   3 T
3 1 slightly fewer   2 considerably fewer
3 around half   4 far smaller

Focus on listening 2 page 26
1 1 a man calling an adult education college about a course   2 five
2 1 two   2 on the phone
3 at a college/Kingsbury College
4 register for a course   5 the woman
3 1 Wright   2 18 to 25   3 accountant
4 11, Forest Road/Rd   5 992471
4 a) Possible answers:
6 probably need a noun or an adjective and noun   7 a date
8 a noun   9 a long number, possibly numbers and letters
10 a noun

b) 6 Mexican cookery   7 26th (of) March/ 26.03   8 (by) cheque
9 CZ943   10 wheelchair

Unit 3

Focus on grammar 1 page 28
1 b) 1 C   2 B   3 C   4 B
2 began, left, set up, founded, opened, continued
3 1 published   2 was   3 left
4 opened   5 set up   6 broke
7 did

Focus on reading page 30
1 a) Possible answers: fish; tropics; beach; tourists
2 C
3 Reason A – answer A
Reason B – answer B
Reason C – answer D
4 1 person/people
2 number/ amount   3 place
4 reason   5 number/amount
6 number/ amount   7 object or activity   8 reason   9 method
10 number/ amount
5 a) Answer C is the best answer. Answer B has four words, so it's too long. Answer A doesn't contain the most important noun in the phrase – 'rock'.
b) 2 over one hundred   3 25%
4 reef-based tourism   5 on foot
6 fishing equipment   7 cloth
6 b) 1 on the other hand
2 in addition   3 in fact
4 for example
c) 1 For example   2 In addition
3 On the other hand   4 In fact
d) 1 F   2 T   3 F   4 T   5 T   6 F

Focus on vocabulary page 34
1 a) 1 b)   2 c)   3 a)   4 e)   5 d)
b) (in any order)
1 selling/trading fish
2 processing fish
3 marketing fish
4 mending fishing gear
2 *generally* (line 30); *often* (line 36); *usually* (line 27)
3 1 applications   2 manager
3 employees   4 qualification
5 workers   6 promotion
7 retirement   8 writer
4 1 An *employer* hires and pays the *employee,* so the employer is the boss and the employee is the worker.

2 Resign   3 Make me redundant
4 Too old   5 An interview
5 1 1 e   2 a   3 b   4 c   5 d

Focus on speaking page 36
4 b) He gives a reason.
6 1 The man works in a restaurant and the woman works in an office.
3 Possible answers: journalist, artist, shop assistant, hairdresser, mechanic, plumber, electrician, actor, politician, doctor, nurse
7 a) 1 you have a   2 job well-paid
3 use English   4 Do you enjoy
5 How long

Progress Check 1 Units 1–3
1 1 groups   2 are trying
3 can't remember   4 are looking
5 want
2 1 produced   2 copied   3 took
4 invented   5 allowed   6 built
7 put   8 pressed
3 1 For example   2 In addition
3 However   4 In fact
4 1 fewer   2 fewer   3 more
4 the lowest   5 fewer sales than
5 C
6 1 79 years   2 19%   3 minerals
4 manufacturing
5 The United States
7 1 F   2 F   3 F   4 T
8 1 workforce   2 access   3 include
4 range

Unit 4

Focus on listening page 40
2 a) 1 noun; singular or plural
2 verb; root form/ infinitive without to
3 verb; root form/ infinitive without to
4 noun; singular or plural
5 noun, singular
b) 1 grandmother   2 ask questions
3 already know   4 relatives
5 list of questions
3 b) • very first thing you need to do for your research is to take a sheet of paper and write down everything…
• And then, when you've finished doing that, get in touch …
• And before you see them, make …
4 a) two

b) Possible answers:
1 noun, singular or plural
2 noun
3 noun, plural
4 noun, singular or plural
5 noun, probably plural
6 noun, singular or plural. Probably a place.
7 noun, singular or plural
8 adjective

c) 1 a tape   2 place   3 documents
4 death   5 maps   6 the Internet
7 pencil   8 short

Focus on vocabulary 1   page 42

1 b) 1 Hamed   2 Meera [1 and 2 in any order]   3 Salem   4 Reema
5 Ahmed   6 Alia
7 Noora [6 and 7 in any order]

2 a) 1 Gloria   2 sister   3 parents
4 uncles   5 aunt   6 Consuelo and Fernando   7 grandparents on his mother's side

3 a) single; widowed; engaged; married; divorced

b) mother; father; sister(s); brother(s)

c) brother-in-law; sister-in-law; father-in-law; mother-in-law

Focus on grammar   page 44

1 1 the   2 a   3 –   4 –   5 the
6 the   7 a   8 –

2 1 –   2 the   3 The   4 the   5 the
6 a   7 the   8 an   9 a   10 –

Focus on vocabulary 2   page 45

1 1 numbers   2 number
3 proportion   4 number   5 Figures
6 rate   7 Figures   8 rate
9 number   10 proportion

2 1 data analysis, data processing
2 data base/database
3 data analysis, data collection, data processing
4 data collection

3 1 rise, decline, decrease, fall, increase
2

rise; grow; increase

fluctuate

decline; decrease; fall

Focus on writing   page 47

1 a) 1 three   2 C (households)

b) 1 26%   2 one

---

2 a) 1 Botswana   2 China

b) 1 Botswana   2 China …
Botswana   3 15, 64   4 half

3 1 rose/ increased/ went up
2 5 / five   3 26 / twenty six
4 23 / twenty three   5 1971
6 1981   7 2000

Unit 5

Focus on grammar   page 50

1 1 I've (never) attended an international sports competition.
2 I've (never) joined a sports club.
3 I've (never) played baseball.
4 I've (never) seen a Formula 1 race.
5 I've (never) met a famous person.
6 I've (never) done yoga.
7 I've (never) worked out in a gym.
8 I've (never) taken part in a running race.

2 1 has increased
2 Have you ever seen   3 declined
4 have dominated   5 have won
6 I managed   7 has improved
8 I have just come   9 have never seen
10 has declined

3 1 have you ever watched   2 began
3 for   4 is   5 has been
6 since   7 was
8 weren't able to/couldn't
9 have introduced   10 is now

Focus on listening 1   page 51

1

/ei/	/ɪː/	/e/	/ai/
a	b	f	i
h	c	l	y
j	d	m	
k	e t	n x	
	g v	s z	
	p		

2 1 Carrow   2 Matthews
3 Fursdunne   4 BL6 4JE
5 Ericsson

3 a) A health club receptionist and a customer
b) On the phone
c) Joining the club

4 a) one (or a number)
b) Number 1 and Number 3

5 1 Cooze   2 Doctor   3 GT1 2BN
4 newspaper

6 5 C   6 B   7 A   8 A

7

Classifications	Parallel expression in the audio script
daytime	… don't want to be there when it gets very packed in the evenings. I think I'd only want to use the outdoor one and during the day, when I can get a bit of sun bathing in (Receptionist) And when the children are at school …
weekend	I'd like to book courts on Saturdays and Sundays when I can organise a game with friends. I'd probably only use it on Saturdays and the occasional Sunday …

Focus on vocabulary 1   page 53

1 1 g   2 e   3 f   4 a   5 h   6 c   7 d
8 b

2 1 season   2 record   3 strenuous, health   4 participate   5 ability

Focus on writing 1   page 54

1 b) 1 1975 to the present day
2 young people's participation in outdoor sports / percentage
3 ball games and biking/roller skating
4 swimming
5 jogging/running

2 1 decline   2 reduction   3 decrease
4 drop   5 rise   6 fluctuated

3 has been, have become, has been, has fallen, has (also) been, has been, has fluctuated

4 *In 1975 it was the third most popular sport and now it is the most popular.* In this sentence the past simple is used because the writer is describing the situation in one year in the past. The present simple is used to describe the situation now.

5 a) circuit training and fitness classes
b) racquet sports
c) swimming

6 1 This graph shows that there have been significant changes in the popularity of various sports between 1990 and the present day.
2 The number of people who swim has fluctuated.
3 Racquet sports are not as popular as they were in 1990.

4 Today, more members participate in circuit training than in any other activity at the club.

7 Sample answer

The graph shows that over the past 15 years some sports at the club have become more popular, while others have become less popular or have remained at virtually the same level.

There has been a steady rise in the numbers of club members regularly doing circuit training. In 1990 it was the third most popular activity but now it is the most popular with almost 300 using the gym regularly. Fitness classes have also grown in popularity – in 1990 about 130 participated but the number rose to 230 in the present year. The number going swimming has fluctuated over the period – 250 in 1990, falling and then rising by a small amount before falling back to 250 in the current year. Over the period, there has been a decline in numbers of club members taking part in racquet sports – this has fallen from almost 275 playing these sports in 1990 to approximately 140 in the present day, with the steepest decline occurring between 1990 and 1995. (167 words)

Focus on vocabulary 2 page 56

1 Possible answers:

Play...	Do...	Go...
e.g. basketball	e.g. ballet	e.g. swimming
hockey	yoga	jogging
tennis	karate	running
football		
rugby		
ball games		

2 1 over/in 2 between 3 since
   4 of 5 From ... to / Between.... and
   6 by

Focus on listening 2 page 57

1 1 two 2 one
2 1 A student.
   2 The differences between male and female performance in sport.
3 1 B 2 E (B/E in either order)
   3 C 4 E (C/E in either order)
   5 running time 6 shoulders
   7 jump

Focus on writing 2 page 58

1 1 B 2 A
2 For first point of view: 1, 3, 5
  For second point of view: 2, 4, 6
3 1 B
  2 To show the reader which point of view she is going to write about in each paragraph
  3 She agrees with the first point of view. Her opinion is in the last paragraph.
  4 See annotated sample answer below.

<u>Firstly</u>, having successful sportspeople gives a country a sense of pride. People feel good about their country and about themselves. <u>In addition</u>, having a famous sportsperson from a particular place can help make that country better known in the wider world. <u>Finally</u>, successful national athletes are good role models for the young. Perhaps they will go on to become successful sportspeople themselves.	2 6 4
<u>However</u>, there are drawbacks to spending money only on outstanding athletes. It can give the impression that sport is all about winning whereas in fact, co-operation, trying hard and learning how to lose well are just as important. <u>For these reasons</u>, many people feel it is better for governments to spend money on ordinary sports projects, which try to encourage everyone to do some form of sport, even if they never achieve much success. <u>This</u> can help reduce levels of health problems such as being overweight, and get children off the streets, doing something useful instead of getting into trouble.	5 3 1
I personally believe that it is a much better use of money to help everyone to participate in sports because this leads to a healthier population with a more balanced view of life and it <u>also</u> shows a sensible attitude to achievement. (276 words)	Her point of view

4 See annotated sample answer above.
5 a) The first point of view is that it is good for a country to host (i.e. have in their country) a major sports competition (e.g. the Olympics).

The second point of view is that hosting a major sports competition can cause problems for the country.
  b) Possible answers:
  First point of view:
  • Sports competitions bring lots of people (athletes, tourists, etc.) to the country. This can help the local economy and create new jobs.
  • The country will gain international recognition and local people might feel proud.
  • Lots of local people will enjoy watching the sports live, instead of on television.
  Second point of view:
  • Lots of people coming into a country can cause problems with things like transport.
  • Hotels and restaurants might put their prices up for the tourists, so local people won't be able to afford them
  • The government might put taxes up because it is expensive to run a major sports competition.

Unit 6

Focus on reading page 60

2 A 3 B 5 C 4 D 1 E 6
3 b) There are three altogether: one in B (line 16) and two in E (lines 62–63 and 71).
  c) B
  d) 1 B 2 E 3 D 4 A 5 E 6 C

Focus on vocabulary page 63

1 a) 1 noun 2 adjective 3 verb
     4 verb 5 verb 6 adjective
  b) 1 C 2 B 3 A 4 H 5 G
     6 E
  c) 1 critical 2 restricts 3 range
     4 enable 5 current 6 funding
2 a) 1 *winter* and *Asia*
     2 *elephant* and *giraffe*
     3 *fur* and *size*
     4 *mammal* and *reptile*
  b) 1 F 2 T 3 F 4 T 5 T
  c) 1 dangerous 2 predator
     3 adaptations 4 hunting
     5 prey 6 adapt
3 b) 1 T 2 I 3 T 4 T 5 T 6 I

Focus on grammar 1 page 65

1

Adjective	Comparative form	Superlative form
big	bigger	biggest
small	smaller	smallest
strange	stranger	strangest
heavy	heavier	heaviest
endangered	more endangered	most endangered
long	longer	longest

2 a) 1 hairier   2 as well as
   3 more active … than
   4 more … than

b) Sample answer

> **Common frogs and toads of the UK**
> Frogs and toads belong to the same group of amphibians, and are very similar. However, there are some differences between them. Frogs are generally smaller than toads. Toads have bumpier skin and shorter back legs. Frogs are less moist and spend a longer time in water than toads.

3 1 Locusts are one of the most harmful insects.
   2 Lions and tigers are the largest members of the cat family.
   3 The giant panda is one of the rarest mammals.
   4 The elephant is the heaviest animal in the world.
   5 The snow leopard is one of the least often seen animals.

Focus on speaking page 67

1 c) 1 B   2 E   3 A   4 C
2 There are four sub-topics – what the animal is; what you know about it; how you know about it; why you find the animal particularly interesting
3 a) 1 B   2 C   3 A
   b) Possible answers:
   Style 1 **Advantage(s)**
      Quick to produce
      Shows sequence
      Disadvantage(s)
      Doesn't help with grammar
   Style 2 **Advantage(s)**
      Quick to produce
      Easy to add new ideas
      Disadvantage(s)
      Doesn't show sequence
      Doesn't help with grammar

Style 3 **Advantage(s)**
   Can read the notes as they are
   Disadvantage(s)
   Takes a long time to produce
   Incomplete
d) Advantages: Your talk might be more fluent and natural if no notes are used.
   Disadvantages: You might forget to mention all the subtopics or you might repeat yourself.

Focus on grammar 2 page 69

1 A and B
2 1, 3, 4 and 6
3 1 are increasing   2 communicate
   3 are declining   4 flies   5 has

Focus on listening page 69

1 1 14th   2 9th   3 12th   4 39
   5 70   6 23rd   7 802   8 305
   9 54880   10 2001

Progress Check 2 Units 4–6

1 1 decided   2 have become
   3 have now designed   4 started
   5 has taken   6 has not won
   7 have won
2 1 the   2 a   3 -   4 the   5 the
   6 the   7 the   8 a
3 1 the slowest   2 the most intelligent
   3 longer than   4 narrower than
   5 most characteristic   6 the deadliest
4 1 For example   2 In addition
   3 Firstly   4 Secondly   5 However
5 1 brothers and sisters
   2 distant cousins
   3 Polygamy
   4 serial monogamy
6 1 A mother   B niece   C wife
   D brother-in-law   E nephew
   2 single
   3 married
7 1 8%   2 soccer
   3 volleyball and basketball
   4 swimming   5 4%
8 1 10–20 years   2 2.35 hours
   3 50 years   4 20 years
   5 0.6/0.7 hours
9 1 habitat   2 adaptations   3 survival

Unit 7

Focus on listening 1 page 72

1 a) 1 Appropriate technology inventions
   2 Two   3 Three   4 One
   b) 1 spring   2 slowly   3 batteries
   4 dark   5 plastic   6 trapped
   7 trees   8 fertiliser   9 lung
   10 raised
2 • So let's start with the clockwork radio and how it works.
   • Now the next section is, 'What are its benefits?'
   • And then in the developments column …
   • So we'll then move on to the solar box cooker. …And again, let's keep the description of the mechanism very simple.
   • And then where do we begin on the advantages?
   • And then we need to say something about the way cook boxes have been improved.
3 • ….it's powered, i.e. that it's wound up.
   • …people don't have to depend on buying anything in a store which in remote rural areas is really important.
   • … it uses sunlight to rather than conventional fuels to cook food.
   • ….a reflector is often added at angle to the lid to maximise the amount of light entering.
   • ….many of the new boxes have a sloping or inclined lid which increases the surface area to capture the sun's rays.

Focus on grammar page 73

1 1 were…designed   2 was invented
   3 is accessed   4 has been closed
   5 have been used
2 a) 1 It is **agreed** that seatbelts in cars save many lives.
   2 It **is** said that more people work from home now than in the past.
   3 It's **known** that houses are more expensive than they were ten years ago.
   4 **It is** expected that people will live longer in the future.
   b) 1 It is reported that a vaccination for cancer will be available in ten years' time.

2 It is known that fleas on rats carry bubonic plague.

3 It is said that an actress invented the mobile phone.

4 It is believed that over half of all schoolchildren own a portable games console.

5 It is expected that the earth's temperature will rise by three degrees by 2050.

6 It is thought that organic produce is superior to non-organic produce.

b) Possible answers:

1 It is agreed that mobile phones should be banned in schools.

2 It is felt that education should be free for every child.

3 It is said that every business in the world now uses email.

Focus on writing 1 page 74

1 a) 1 In a car.

2 To prevent injuries when a car stops suddenly.

3 A crash sensor, an inflator and an air bag.

b) 1 inflates   2 is fitted
3 is applied   4 is made of
5 is activated   6 mixes
7 produces   8 expands

c) 1 Paragraph 1   2 Paragraph 2

d) B

e) 1 device   2 consists of
3 is activated   4 is applied
5 switches on   6 produces
7 expands   8 rapid

2 **Sample answer**

The thermos flask is used to keep the liquids it contains at the same temperature. Its most common use is to keep hot drinks, for example coffee, hot but you can also use it to keep things like milk cold.

A thermos flask is a cylinder-shaped object between 30 and 40 cm high. On the inside is a flask made of glass. There is nearly no air inside this glass so it is a very poor conductor. In addition, the glass is silvered, which reduces infrared radiation. This vacuum flask is surrounded by another cylinder made of metal or plastic, which protects the fragile glass inside. On the top is a plug or cap, usually made of cork or plastic, which is covered by a plastic cup. This is taken off and used to drink the liquid from.

Some heat escapes from the cap but the special design of the thermos flask means that liquid maintains its temperature for several hours.
(161 words)

Focus on listening 2 page 77

1 a) 1 The advantages of using this edible vaccine.

2 The disadvantages of using this edible vaccine.

3 two

b) Suggested answers: 1 adjective
2 noun (singular)   3 adjective
4 noun   5 noun   6 adjective

c) 1 cheap/inexpensive   2 fridge
3 infected   4 growing conditions
5 stomach   6 human

d) advantage: plus factor, benefit
disadvantage: problem, drawback, shortcoming, negative aspect

Focus on vocabulary page 78

1 1 The university campus in 1985. The university campus in the present day.

2 No.

3 Because people use a shuttle bus service and walk instead.

4 There are many more trees now than there were in 1985.

2

Make the size bigger	Make the size smaller
extend enlarge develop grow increase	reduce

Make the number bigger	Make the number smaller
increase add (to) grow rise	reduce decrease decline drop fall

Change or take away	Make better
replace (by) remove convert (into)	improve develop

3 1 grown   2 converted
3 removed; replaced
4 decreased; increased
5 reduced   6 added

Focus on writing 2 page 80

1 Possible answers:
Advantages:
Easy to keep in touch with friends and family

Text messages are cheap and quick
Can call for help if lost or in danger
Parents can find their teenage children at any time
Urgent business doesn't have to wait
Disadvantages:
Expensive
Conversations aren't really private
You can't escape work
People often ring in places that should be quiet, like the library
They might be bad for your health

3 **Sample answer**

Mobile phones have certainly had an enormous impact on us. They have significantly changed the way we communicate with each other in both our personal and our professional lives. However, the impact has not all been positive.

By far the most common criticism of mobile phones is the fact that we are now expected to be available all times of the day and night, especially for work-related communication. Before mobile phones were invented, anyone who wanted to contact us had to wait until we were at work, which meant time spent away from the office was our own. Mobile phones mean that the separation between work and free time has disappeared. Another negative effect is that in places such as theatres, cinemas or public transport we often have to listen to the noise of infuriating ring tones and loud one-sided conversations. A final drawback is that these small but very expensive devices are easy targets for thieves. A great deal of street crime involves hand phones.

On the other hand, there are several obvious benefits from this invention. The most powerful argument in favour of mobile phones is that they can be used to call for help in the most inaccessible places, for example, when our car breaks down in a remote area. Another positive aspect of mobiles for business people is the fact that they can be available for potential customers at all times. Finally, mobile phones are extremely simple and convenient to use.

To sum up, I feel that although there are some clear drawbacks to mobile phones, their efficiency and portability has greatly improved our ability to communicate in both our professional and personal lives. In my opinion, the benefits of having mobile phones certainly offset the drawbacks. (291 words)

Unit 8

Focus on speaking 1 page 82

1 a) Possible answers:
Reading about it.
Both.
I like both.

3 a) 1 when you heard/read the news
2 where you heard/read the news
3 what the news was
4 why you found the news exciting

Focus on grammar page 83

1
Ability/ permission	Obligation	Prohibition
allow V	must V	prohibit V
permit V	obligatory A	forbid V
can V	compulsory A	
	necessary A	
	have to V	

2 a) 1 had to   2 will have to
3 allowed/permitted
4 forbidden/prohibited
5 compulsory/obligatory
6 can

b) Possible answers:
1 in a museum or cinema
2 at a building site
3 in an exam
4 on a plane

3 *Allow, can, must, have to* and *necessary* are the least formal.
Permit, obligatory, compulsory, prohibit and *forbid* are the most formal.

Focus on reading page 84

3 4 T 5 F 6 T 7 NG 8 F
4 a) 9 B 10 A 11 B 12 C 13 A
b) 9 After a short time films were removed from music halls and shown first in vacant shops, known as 'shop shows' or 'penny gaffs', and <u>after 1906 in custom-built premises called 'picture palaces', 'bijoux palaces' or 'majestics'.</u>
10 And <u>in 1894, the first British 'kinetoscope' had opened. This offered customers the chance to try Thomas Edison's patent, coin-in-the-slot machine for viewing animated photographs.</u>
11 <u>In 1909 the First Cinematographic Act … In that year, estimates suggest that British production amounted to only about 20 per cent of films shown in British cinemas, and that 40 per cent were French, 30 per cent American and 10 per cent Italian.</u>
12 By 1910 some 1,600 cinemas were in existences in Britain, and <u>by the outbreak of the First World War in 1914, this figure had risen to 4,000.</u>
13 By the end of 1896, <u>only months after the initial public performance of film in Britain, moving pictures were part of many music hall shows</u> up and down the country.

Focus on vocabulary page 88

1 b) <u>sometimes</u>, <u>often</u>, certainly, definitely, <u>usually</u>, <u>mainly</u>, truly, certainly, <u>chiefly</u>
c) 1 Correct
2 I usually check my emails every day.
3 The Internet is definitely very useful for research.
4 Correct
5 People can certainly learn a lot by watching the news every day.
d) Possible answers:
1 British families with children <u>sometimes</u> have more than one television in the home.
2 Language <u>usually</u> develops more quickly in boys than girls.
3 National newspapers are <u>largely</u> better quality than they used to be.
4 Text messaging is <u>chiefly</u> preferred to letter writing by younger people.
5 Books which are classified as science fiction are <u>often</u> more popular with men than with women.
6 Computers have <u>generally</u> had a very positive impact on education.

2 b) A
c) Suggested answers: current, recent, latest, upward, increasing
3 b) C
c) A and C are correct

Focus on speaking 2 page 90

2 1 about celebrities and crimes
2 wait their turn to speak
3 you want to speak
4 to speak too loudly
5 don't get enough practice
6 write full sentences in emails
7 don't have to memorise correct spelling

3 a) 2 Topic: *international news*
Comparison: *now/past*
3 Topic: *talking*
Comparison: *face–to–face/on the phone*
4 Topic: *the way people communicate*
Comparison: *men/women*
b) A 3 B 1 C 4 D 2

Unit 9

Focus on listening 1 page 92

1 Topic: The Earth Matters Exhibition
You have to: choose one correct answer from options A, B or C
2 An exhibition on environmental issues which she is organising
3 1 A 2 B 3 B
4 1 But the principal reason for running this fair is to raise awareness about what people can do to live a greener lifestyle.
2 …but at the moment we have it once a year, either in March or in September.
3 …but you can also get them from Green Apple Health Foods.
5 a) 1 The layout of the exhibition hall.
2 Write a letter (A-F) in the space beside the name of the exhibit.
b) 4 E 5 A 6 B
6 a) 4 The first is the Cycle Safe stall and it's very easy to find. After you've walked through the entrance area turn immediately right and walk past Hydroponics. It's right next door to that.
5 Riverbank Farm Foods. It's right opposite the Education Centre, between the Book Stall and the exhibit for electric cars.
6 Solar Homes exhibit, which is opposite Electric cars and behind the gardening exhibit called Green Growth.

Focus on writing 1 page 94

3 The best opening paragraph for this task is C because it mentions both causes and effects.

4 can be, It is believed, often, tend, can lead, there may be

Focus on grammar 1 page 96

1 X causes Y: leads to/ as a consequence
Y is caused by X: can result from/ is often the consequence of/ can be caused by/ as a result of this

2 1 ... is (can be) caused by / ... is (can be) a result of
2 ... causes / ... results in / ... leads to /... can cause
3 ... causes / ... results in / ... leads to / ... can cause
4 ... are caused by / ... result from / ... are the consequence of / can be caused by
5 ... lead to / ... cause ...

Focus on writing 2 page 96

1 1 Pollution
2 Land, water and air
3 Problems and possible solutions

2 a)

Problems	Land, sea or air (tick one or more columns)		
	Land	Water	Air
• contaminated rivers		/	/
• smog			/
• soil erosion	/		
• acid rain	(/)	(/)	/
• litter on the streets	/		
• floods	(/)	/	
• building on 'green field sites'	/		
• toxic fumes			/
• greenhouse gases			/
• melting ice caps	(/)	/	
• land-fill sites full of rubbish	/		
• droughts	(/)	/	
• polluted atmosphere			/
• global warming			/
• deforestation	/		

b)

Problems	Possible solutions
contaminated rivers	f
smog	b, c, d, h
soil erosion	j
acid rain	f
litter on the streets	e, g
floods	j, b
building on 'green field sites'	i
toxic fumes	b, c, d, f, h
greenhouse gases	b, c, d, f, h
melting ice caps	b
land-fill sites full of rubbish	e, g
droughts	b, c, d, f, h
polluted atmosphere	a, b, c, d, h
global warming	a, b, c, d, h, j
deforestation	i, j

d) 1 Introduction and pollution on land
2 Pollution of air
3 Pollution of water
4 The conclusion.
5 Two sections: problems and their solutions

e) **Sample answer**

Almost every country in the world has problems with the environment, affecting its land, air or water. I believe the main problems on land are caused by building too many houses, using up land for depositing rubbish and also the destruction of trees, which leads to soil erosion. Perhaps the most helpful thing we can do to tackle these difficulties is to try to persuade governments to stop building on certain areas so that there will be room for more trees. We should also try to use more 'biodegradable' materials so that they decay naturally and do not stay in the ground for thousands of years. We should also aim to plant more trees which will prevent soil erosion.

The ways in which air is affected are as follows. Firstly, by burning so many fossil fuels we pump large amounts of toxic gases into the atmosphere which leads to harmful climate change and the destruction of the protective ozone layer. I believe the best way to reduce these problems is by changing our transport policies: we should use more public transport or at least try to use more efficient fuels in cars.

The main effects of pollution and other environmental problems on water are the melting of the ice-caps because of global warming which leads to flooding. There is also contamination of rivers by harmful chemicals. These can be dealt with if global warming is reduced and also by such measures as taxing industries which repeatedly pollute our waterways.

It is crucial that these measures are taken in order to ensure a healthy future for our planet. (266 words)

Focus on listening 2 page 99

1 a) 1 Complete the notes
2 Complete the table
3 Two words or a number

b) 1 A student and his tutor
2 Environmental Science
3 The student's assignment

2 a) 1 river 2 toxic smoke 3 floods
4 interviews 5 month 6 paper
7 May 8 sprays 9 statistics
10 23rd June/ 23/6

b) 1 (Tutor) However, I would advise you to say quite a bit more on contamination of the river because it has been in the media so much.
2 (Tutor) ... there are quite a few mistakes in the part about toxic smoke. If I were you, I'd look carefully through that again.
3 (Tutor) And my final point is about reading. You've obviously done a lot on the causes and effects of acid rain but you only mentioned one book on the causes of floods. You ought to read a couple more.
4 (Tutor) That's often quite hard to organise. Why not go for interviews instead – 10 to 20 people should be enough. And because you talk to them one to one I think it's easier to extract your data.
5 Tutor: But I think you'll need to do that pretty soon. I suggest before the end of ....
Wazim: the week?
Tutor: No, the month should be fine
6 (Wazim) Well, related to that I thought I'd try to find out how people felt about recycling...in particular I wanted to focus on paper.
7 (Tutor) Sounds fine. But I think you should allow a much longer time for that – to prepare them and send them out, so I'd aim to get that done by the start of May.

8 (Wazim) Well, I suppose I could look at using sprays.. ...you know, whether people are following advice on this.

9 Wazim: So for the research method, I'd use questionnaires again.
Tutor: Why not. But I also think it'd be a good idea to look at the statistics on this in the library. They cover the last decade so you could look at how they've changed over that period.

10 (Wazim) I imagine I could do that pretty quickly. I'll aim to do that by 23rd June and I can follow up on it during the vacation if I need to get extra information.

3 • I would advise you to say …
• … you need to develop that …
• If I were you, I'd look carefully …
• You ought to add …
• Why not go for …
• … I think you'll need to do …
• I suggest …
• … I think you should allow …
• … so I'd aim to get that done …
• My advice is to focus …
• I think it'd be a good idea to …
• … you could look at…
Strong advice: *you need to* and *you'll need to*

Focus on vocabulary page 100

1 a)

Verb	Noun
advise	advice
devise	device
describe	description
refer	reference
present	presentation
educate	education
complete	completion
exhibit	exhibition
discuss	discussion
produce	production
behave	behaviour

c) ad**vise**, ad**vice**, de**vise**, de**vice**, de**scribe**, de**scrip**tion, re**fer**, **re**ference, pre**sent**, presen**ta**tion, **edu**cate, edu**ca**tion, com**plete**, com**ple**tion, ex**hib**it, exhi**bi**tion,

dis**cuss**, dis**cu**ssion, pro**duce**, pro**duc**tion, be**have**, be**ha**viour

d) 1 the *s* in the verb is pronounced /z/. The *c* in the noun is pronounced /s/
2 In words ending in -*tion*, the main stress goes on the syllable just before -*tion*.

Focus on grammar 2 page 101

1

Verbs normally followed by the infinitive with *to*		Verbs normally followed by the -*ing* form
agree	try	avoid
appear	want	can't help
arrange	attempt	dislike
hope	can/can't	enjoy
learn	afford	be
manage	choose	finish
offer	dare	go on
ought	decide	imagine
plan	encourage	keep
promise	expect	miss
refuse	fail	risk
seem		suggest

2 1 risk destroying 2 refuse to change
3 Correct 4 imagine getting rid of
5 learn to live 6 seemed to solve
7 Correct 8 go on buying

Progress Check 3 Units 7–9

1 1 discuss 2 description 3 advise
4 complete 5 presentation

2 1 smog toxic fumes ozone layer rush hours
2 contaminated rivers acid rain flooding droughts
3 hazardous waste soil erosion building on greenfield sites deforestation
4 use renewable forms of energy recycle materials such as glass and paper
turn off electrical appliances when not in use
use environmentally friendly products

3 1 is used 2 drive 3 be adapted
4 is added 5 either is possible
6 is less polluted

4 1 was written 2 was invented
3 was discovered 4 were said
5 was played

5 1 You are not allowed to use mobile phones/ your mobile phone in the lecture theatre. (Less formal)
2 It is compulsory to ear protectors when visiting the factory/ when you visit the factory. (More formal)

3 Passengers are not permitted to use electronic devices when the aeroplane is taking off and landing. (More formal)
4 All our cars must have an annual pollution check. (Less formal)
5 Kids over ten years old can go in the pool without an adult. (Less formal)
6 Women couldn't vote in Britain in the past. (Less formal)
7 Smokers will have to go outside their offices in the future. (Less formal)

6 1 to recycle 2 dropping 3 to stop
4 going 5 to become 6 to plant
7 to sell

7 1 Correct 2 contribute to
3 lead to/contribute to 4 lead to/ contribute to/be responsible for
5 Correct 6 Correct

Unit 10

Focus on reading page 104

4 1 sailors 2 smallpox 3 quarantine
4 sewage pipe 5 media campaign
5 6 diet 7 housing 8 vaccination
9 education 10 checks

Focus on vocabulary 1 page 107

1 a) 1 B 2 A 3 A 4 B
b) way
c) 1 methods 2 measures 3 range
4 role 5 measures 6 role
7 range 8 method

2 b) 1 whereas 2 while 3 while
4 whereas

3 Possible answers:
1 **role/part**: significant, big, considerable, major, crucial, important
2 **range**: broad, extensive, huge, wide

4 Possible answers:
prevention: vaccination, health education, fresh water supply, health screening
disease: cause, control, spread, treatment, diagnosis, outbreak, detection
symptoms: rash, bleeding gums, stiff limbs, fever

Focus on speaking 1 page 109

1 b) Speaker B – question 1
Speaker C – question 5
Speaker D – question 3
Speaker E – question 2

Focus on vocabulary 2 page 111

1 1 of 2 in 3 from 4 of 5 on
6 from 7 in 8 to 9 of
10 against 11 of 12 on

Focus on grammar page 112

1 1 a few 2 little 3 every 4 many
5 All 6 both
2 1 both 2 all 3 many 4 each
5 any

Unit 11

Focus on writing 1 page 114

1 1 Happiness
2 From a survey
3 Women and men
4 Women: Being with family; Good appearance; Achievement at work; Financial security
5 Men: Doing hobbies; Supporting successful sports team; Achievement at work; Financial security
6 Significant percentages of both women and men say *achievement at work* and *financial security* make them most happy.
7 Large percentages of women identify *being with family* and *good appearance* as making them most happy – no men identify these factors. Large percentages of men identify *doing hobbies* and *supporting successful sports team* as making them most happy. No women mention these factors.
8 This category groups together all the other things which small percentages of people mention make them most happy.
2 1 B 2 A 3 C
3 a) *percentage*: proportion
b) *say*: state, report, mention
c) *feel*: regard, identify,
d) *important/obvious*: significant, striking, major
4 1 People under 30 years old and people over 30 years old.
2 Both groups say *achievements at work* and *doing hobbies* make them happy.
3 The younger group mention *good appearance* and *travel* as important whereas the older group mention *financial security* and *being with family*.

5 Sample answer

There are several similarities between what younger and older people say makes them most happy. However, there are several striking differences.

Firstly, let us look at the similarities. It is noticeable that for both younger and older people, the highest percentage says that achievement at work brings them most happiness: 31% for the younger age group and 32% for the older group. Doing hobbies is also very important for both groups: the second largest percentage of both age groups mention doing hobbies as making them most happy.

Turning now to the differences, many younger people regard having a good appearance as extremely important: 18% of them state this brings them most happiness. This is followed by 15% who state that travel brings them happiness. Neither of these two factors is mentioned by older people. Instead, 20% of older people report that having financial security is most important to their happiness and 14% say they feel most happy when they are with their family. (163 words)

Focus on listening 1 page 117

1 a) 1 A woman who is giving a talk.
2 People who would like to run their own business.
b) Possible answers: employer, employee, self-employed, earn money, resign, retire, boss, manager, worker, workforce, staff, promotion, be made redundant, interview
3 1 B 2 C 3 C 4 A
4 b) 1 How to get a grant from the Small Business Agency
2 five 3 one
4 Small Business Agency
5 5 plan 6 2 **or** two
7 bank 8 post **or** mail
9 interview 10 20,000
6 1 I really value the fact that I'm my own boss and I can decide what I do, you know…
2 I was visiting a local supermarket and I looked at what was on offer in the ready-meals section – lots of low quality, unhealthy packs. And I thought, 'I could do so much better!'

3 I think the thing which will make me take on new staff is if I just feel too exhausted and stop enjoying what I'm doing.
4 I think I'll need a bigger kitchen and packing area, otherwise we'll get very cramped.
5 The first thing you have to do is to draw up a business plan.
6 it should just be up to two pages in length.
7 Your best bet is to go to your bank and get them to look through it.
8 Now they advise you not to do this by e-mail but by post.
9 If they think it's good, they'll invite you to interview.
10 And then the successful candidates can get a maximum of £20,000.

Focus on grammar 1 page 119

1 … *when the SBA receives your grant application, they'll judge …*
… *If they think it's good, they'll invite you to interview …*
Amy uses this form because she is describing the stages of a process which people might try in the future. It is not definite that everyone will be successful and go through all the stages of the process so she uses 'if'.
2 Possible answers:
1 If I get the well-paid job, I'll buy a car.
If I don't get the well-paid job, I'll buy a bicycle.
2 If the book is in stock, I'll buy it.
If the book isn't in stock, I'll order it on the Internet.
3 If I lose weight, I'll buy myself a new outfit.
If I don't lose weight, I'll try a new diet.
3 Possible answers:
1 If my team wins the championship, I'll be delighted!
2 I promise I'll buy you a car if you pass your driving test.
3 If I keep trying, I'm sure I can get a good job.
4 The business will do well if they advertise in the right places.
5 I'll have a big party if my parents go away this weekend.

Focus on writing 2 page 120

1 Possible answers:
Having a lot of money makes people miserable.
- The people they think are their friends might only want to be near them for their money.
- Rich people might become so worried about security that they can't relax, because they will always be worried that someone is trying to steal their money.

2 Possible answers:
Having lots of money makes people happy.
- Most people worry about paying the mortgage and bills every month; rich people don't have this stress.
- Instead of cheap holidays and weekend activities, people with money can do anything they want, like racing cars or parachuting.
- If they have lots of money, people can take more time off work (or even stop working!) and they can go to classes to learn skills like foreign languages, cooking, painting, etc.

4 b), c), a), d)

5 The writer is probably near to left end of the scale – 'I completely agree'.

6 **Sample answer**
Many people believe that money is the key to happiness and that the more money you have the happier you become. Other people feel that having a lot of money actually causes more problems than it solves.

I believe that as long as people have enough money for basic necessities such as food and a reasonable place to live, a great deal of surplus money tends to make life less rather than more content.

There are several reasons for this. First of all, if you have a great deal of money there is no real reason to go out to work or to strive for anything. Secondly, wealthy people tend to attract the wrong sort of people. After a while, the rich start to believe that the people around them are only after one thing: having a share in their money. This makes rich people distrustful even of those good and loyal people who are their genuine friends. Another result of having plenty of money is the fear of losing it. Rich people start to build high walls around themselves and invest in hi-tech security systems to keep out the rest of the world. They also become snobbish about whom they meet, always frightened that people without money are potential thieves or con artists.

For all these reasons I feel that having a great deal of money actually brings the opposite of happiness. It leads people to lose sight of the real sources of happiness, which often come from simple things like family life and friendship. Wealth prevents people from seeing the true value of things, only recognising what they cost. (278 words)

Focus on listening 2 page 121

1 1 a psychology student
2 his project (on 'well-being research' or what makes some people happier than others)

2 a) 1 For the characteristics which happy people have
2 For the things you should avoid if you want to be happy

3 1 C 2 B 3 D 4 F (2, 3 and 4 can be in any order) 5 A 6 C
7 F (5, 6 and 7 can be in any order)
8 B 9 C 10 C

Focus on vocabulary page 123

1 1 … good <u>advertisement</u> …
2 … long <u>application</u> form …
3 … very <u>optimistic</u> person.
4 Correct 5 Correct
6 … really <u>interesting</u> film …
7 … a lot of <u>luck</u>.
8 Don't <u>criticise</u> me!
9 I feel very <u>depressed</u> today.

2 1 self-control 2 self-portrait
3 self-reliant 4 self-study
5 self-help 6 self-conscious

Unit 12

Focus on reading page 124

3 d) The 'building in a bag' <u>has several advantages over two current methods of providing emergency shelter: tents</u> and building kits. (lines 32–33)

e) The correct answer is C
A and B are wrong, because the text says, 'It is almost as easy to transport and erect as a tent', so it's not eas<u>ier</u>.

D is wrong because the shelter costs about $2,100 and a tent about $1,150, so it's not cheaper.

4 1 B 2 C 3 A

5 4 B 5 E (4 and 5 in either order)

6 a) Paragraph 2
b) 6 noun 7 noun 8 verb 9 nouns
c) 6 water 7 gas 8 dry (out)
9 doors … windows

Focus on grammar 1 page 128

1 a) C
b) has been designed, can be lifted, be transported, can be set up
c) All except the verb in the first sentence.
d) The verb in the first sentence.
e) 1 is dug 2 (is) filled 3 are built
4 is erected 5 are held
6 are finished/have been finished
7 is placed 8 are installed

Focus on grammar 2 page 129

1 b) 1 The new structure is an inflatable shelter, erected quickly on demand.
2 The structure has a curved outer surface, giving it strength.
3 Impressed by the new design, aid agencies expressed interest in buying the building kits.
4 Incorporating the best aspects of similar structures, the shelter has won several awards.
5 The engineers won several awards, enabling them to travel to Uganda for field research.

Focus on vocabulary page 130

1 *sack* – it's not a building material.
2 *design* is first and *demolish* is last.
3

adjective	noun
durable	durability
imaginative	imagination
portable	portability
strong	strength
simple	simplicity
secure	security

4 imaginative, simple
5 function – use
solution – way of dealing …
aspects/properties – characteristics
concept – idea
design – plan
process – series of actions
applications – practical uses

Focus on grammar 3 page 131

1 a) The person who wrote sentence A thinks that it is likely that all new buildings will use solar power; the person who wrote sentence B thinks that it is unlikely.

b) 1 and 5 should be ticked.

c) 1 If building sites were better regulated, there would be fewer accidents.

2 If wages in the construction industry were higher, the price of houses would rise.

3 If more cycle lanes were built in urban areas, there would be fewer traffic jams.

4 If the construction industry used more local materials, costs would be reduced.

5 If buildings were better insulated, heating bills would be reduced.

d) Possible answers:

1 … there would be a housing shortage.

2 … if there were more high-rise buildings.

3 … if sea levels continued to rise at the current rate.

4 … the quality of life would be improved.

5 … cities would be much more attractive.

Focus on speaking 1 page 132

2 b) A public building I really like is the old railway station in Kuala Lumpur. // It's right in the centre of the city. // It's a very striking building … I think it's about a hundred years old. // And of course, it's used for trains. … lots of visitors just coming to have a look at it. // And … the reason why I like the building so much is …

Focus on speaking 2 page 133

1 b) 1 D 2 B 3 C 4 A

2 a) A, B, D

Progress Check 4 Units 10–12

1 a) 1 measures 2 methods 3 role 4 range 5 role

b) 1 T 2 T 3 F 4 F 5 T

2 1 from 2 of 3 to 4 from 5 of 6 of

3 1 b 2 d 3 a 4 e 5 c

4 a)

Adjective	Noun
exciting/excited	excitement
financial	*finance*
free	freedom
happy	*happiness*
interesting/interested	interest
lucky	*luck*
secure	security
similar	*similarity*
social/sociable	society

b) 1 happiness 2 exciting/ interesting. 3 security 4 similar 5 interested

5 1 If working hours were reduced, family life would be better.

2 People would probably do more exercise if they watched less TV.

3 Cities would be better places to live if there were fewer cars.

4 If roads were safer, people would use bicycles more often.

5 Thousands of lives would be saved each year if scientists developed a malaria vaccine.

6 Sample answer

In an emergency a patient is usually collected by an ambulance and taken to the nearest hospital. He/she is then interviewed by a nurse before a doctor examines him/her. After that, either the nurse or the doctor gives the patient the necessary treatment and, depending on what is wrong with the patient, he/she will either then go to a hospital ward or return home.

7 1 T 2 F – they are both island states 3 T 4 F – a lot of European cities don't have an underground train system. 5 T 6 T

8 1 In 2000, Germany exported 20% of the world's motor vehicles, while the USA exported 5%.

2 In 2000, Singapore exported 11% of the world's computers, while Japan exported 8%.

3 In 2000, Switzerland exported 10% of the world's pharmaceutical products, while Belgium exported 6%.

Assess your speaking

PART 1

Pronunciation: The candidate mispronounces a few words.

Fluency: The candidate pauses many times.

PART 2

Fluency: The candidate speaks for less than a minute without help.

Pronunciation: listeners may find it difficult to understand two words ('pool' and 'hall').

PART 3

Fluency: The candidate speaks at normal speed.

Organisation:
'And the other thing is …'
'However …'
'like …'

Vocabulary: The candidate uses a variety of words.

Assess your writing

TASK 1

Paragraphs: The first two paragraphs (line 1 and line 3) are irrelevant to the task.

Information: The candidate did not mention that the roads had been replaced by footpaths.

Organisation: For example, also, however, contrary

Vocabulary and grammar: We can always understand what the candidate wants to say.

Spelling: The candidate's 'favourite' mistake is 'studing' (which should be 'studying'). The only word we cannot understand at all is 'pepreated'.

TASK 2

Content: The candidate doesn't give his own opinion on the advantages and disadvantages of mobile phones.

Organisation: Line 15

Paragraphs: There are too many paragraphs and the paragraphs are not very helpful.

Vocabulary: Instead of writing 'mobile phones', the candidate could have used the pronoun 'they'.

Spelling mistakes: There are many mistakes, including *bress, butns, desart, facilitys, exaple, speacily, helthy Nosey* should be *noisy*.

Grammar: The candidate only uses very simple sentences.

An example of incorrect sentence division is in line 17.

# Audio script

Unit 1, Focus on speaking

EXERCISE 2

1 Do you enjoy reading?
2 What kind of things do you usually read?
3 Is reading a popular hobby in your country?
4 How often do you read English books?
5 Did your parents read to you when you were young?

Unit 1, Focus on speaking

EXERCISE 3

1 What do you enjoy reading most?
2 When did you first learn to read?
3 Do you usually buy books, or borrow them from the library?
4 Where do you usually read?
5 How often do you read newspapers?
6 Are books expensive where you live?

Unit 1, Focus on speaking

EXERCISE 4

1 A Do you enjoy reading?
   B Yes, I do, but I don't get much time these days.
2 A Do you enjoy reading?
   B Not really. I prefer listening to the radio.
3 A Do you enjoy reading?
   B Oh yes. I've always loved reading, ever since I was a child.
4 A Do you enjoy reading?
   B Yes. It's my favourite hobby!
5 A Do you enjoy reading?
   B No. I only read when I have to. I prefer music.

Unit 2, Focus on listening 1

EXERCISE 2

(M= Man, W = Woman)

1 M: How can I help you?
   W: I wonder if you could tell me how much membership costs?
   M: That depends which facilities you're likely to use. And also whether you want to use them in the evenings or in the daytime when we're less busy.
   W: Well, my main interest is swimming, but I'd like to use the gym occasionally and if you've got …
2 M: Excuse me madam … I wonder if you could spare a few minutes to answer some questions?
   W: Er, yes, I suppose so. As long as it doesn't take too long …
   M: It's just a few minutes. Thank you. I work for a sportswear company, and we're trying to find out what sort of …
3 W: Good morning, Mr Fletcher. What's the problem?
   M: Well, I'm finding it difficult to walk - my ankle's quite painful.
   W: Did you twist it or have an accident?
   M: Well, not as far as I know. I was just walking along and suddenly it started hurting …
   W: OK. If you'd just take your shoe off … Let's have a look at …

4 M: Hi. I'm calling about the advert you put in the Portsmouth Herald.
   W: For the bicycle, you mean?
   M: Yes. Have you sold it yet?
   W: No, not yet. Are you interested in it?
   M: I think so. Is it in reasonably good condition?
   W: Oh yes. Do you want to come and look at it? I think you'll be …
5 M: Pearsons.
   W: Oh hello. I've got a problem with my car – I've broken down actually. Could you come out and look at it?
   M: Right. I'll just take some details first if that's OK. Where are you?
   W: I'm in Central Avenue, just opposite the football ground.
   M: And what actually happened? Did it stop suddenly, or was there …

Unit 2, Focus on listening 1

EXERCISE 4a)

1 C 2 G 3 L 4 Q 5 N 6 O 7 D 8 I 9 P 10 E

Unit 2, Focus on listening 1

EXERCISE 4b)

1 This man is called David Freeman. That's D-A-V-I-D, David, F-R-Double E–M-A-N, Freeman. He was born on the 25th of August, 1932.
2 This man is called James Mehan. That's J-A-M-E-S, James, M-E-H-A-N, Mehan. He was born on the 18th of June, 1986.
3 This man is called Anthony Queensford. That's A-N-T-H-O-N-Y, Anthony, Q-U-E-E-N-S-F-O-R-D, Queensford. He was born on the 3rd of December, 1962.

Unit 2, Focus on listening 2

EXERCISE 1

You will hear a man calling an adult education college to enquire about a course.
First you have some time to look at questions 1 to 5.
You will see that there is an example which has been done for you. On this occasion only, the conversation relating to this will be played first.

Unit 2, Focus on listening 2

EXERCISE 2

(R = college receptionist, P = Peter)

You will hear a man calling an adult education college to enquire about a course.
First you have some time to look at questions 1 to 5.
You will see that there is an example which has been done for you. On this occasion only, the conversation relating to this will be played first.

R: Kingsbury College. Can I help you?
P: Oh hello. I'm ringing to find out about one of your courses.
R: Yes … Is that a daytime or an evening course?
P: Evening.

R: Right… I'll just get a few details from you if I may?
P: Fine.

The man is enquiring about an evening course, so an evening course has been written in the space.

Now we shall begin. You should answer the questions as you listen, because you will not hear the recording a second time. Listen carefully and answer questions 1 to 5.

Unit 2, Focus on listening 2

EXERCISE 3

(R = college receptionist, P = Peter)

R: Kingsbury College? Can I help you?
P: Oh hello. I'm ringing to find out about one of your courses
R: Yes … Is that a daytime or an evening course?
P: Evening.
R: Right … I'll just get a few details from you if I may?
P: Fine.
R: Could I have your full name first of all?
P: It's Peter Wright – that's W-R-I-G-H-T
R: OK … And I don't need to know your exact age, but can you tell me which of these age groups you belong to: 18 to 25, 26 to 35, 36 to 45, or over 45?
P: 18 to 25.
R: Fine. And do you have a job, or are you a full-time student?
P: I'm an accountant. I just do courses in my spare time, for interest.
R: OK. Right. And your address, Mr Wright?
P: It's 11, Forest Road …
R: F-O-R-E-S-T?
P: Yes.
R: Mmm. Is that in Kingsbury?
P: Yes, it is. I'm just down the road here.
R: And do you have a phone number?
P: It's double 9 2471. That's my home number – I haven't got a work number.
R: That's fine. We probably won't need it.

Unit 2, Focus on listening 2

EXERCISE 4b)

(R = college receptionist, P = Peter)

Before you hear the rest of the conversation, you have some time to look at questions 6 to 10.

Now listen and answer questions 6 to 10.

R: Now, you want to register for a course?
P: Yes – cookery.
R: Do you happen to know the exact title of the course? We've got Thai cookery on Wednesdays … or Mexican cookery on Fridays … or …
P: Mexican. I'd like to do both but I'm busy on Wednesdays.
R: OK. Well, you can always do the other one next term I suppose … Now do you know when it begins?
P: Is it the 26th of March?
R: That's right … And it's £45 in total, that's including the ingredients. How would you like to pay? Card, cash …?
P: Can I send a cheque?
R: You can, yes. As long as it arrives at least one week before the start of the course.
P: OK.

R: And I'll just give you a reference number – if you could make a note of it and write it on the back.
P: Yes?
R: It's CZ 943.
P: Yes, got that.
R: Good. Well, there's just one last question. Do you have any special requirements that I should make a note of?
P: Yes, there is one thing. I use a wheelchair.
R: Right. So you need to have access for that … OK. Don't worry, your room is on the ground floor, and I'll make sure there are no steps involved. We can always put a ramp in.
P: Thanks.
R: So, we look forward to seeing you on …

Unit 3, Focus on speaking

EXERCISE 1

How often do you do housework?
Which job do you least enjoy doing in the house?
Which job do you most enjoy doing in the house?
How much time do you spend doing housework?
Did you help with the housework when you were a child?

Unit 3, Focus on speaking

EXERCISE 2

(M= Man, W = Woman)

W: How often do you do housework?
M: I do a little bit every day, like washing dishes or making beds, but I do most jobs at the weekend.
W: Which job do you least enjoy doing in the house?
M: Cleaning the floors – they take such a long time and it's so boring.
W: Which job do you most enjoy doing in the house?
M: I like cooking – I've always been interested in food, and I like trying new recipes.
W: How much time do you spend doing housework?
M: Oh, I'm not really sure. Perhaps an hour every weekday and three hours at the weekend.
W: Did you help with the housework when you were a child?
M: No, never! My mother thought that housework was for girls, so I wasn't expected to do any.

Unit 3, Focus on speaking

EXERCISE 5

How often do you do housework?
Which job do you least enjoy doing in the house?
Which job do you most enjoy doing in the house?
How much time do you spend doing housework?
Did you help with the housework when you were a child?

Unit 3, Focus on speaking

EXERCISE 7

Do you have a job?
Is your job well-paid?
Do you use English in your work?
Do you enjoy your work?
How long have you done this job for?

Unit 4, Focus on listening

EXERCISE 2

You will hear a man giving a talk to some people who want to find out about their family history.

Man: Good evening everyone. I'm very glad to be here in Woodham. It's a lovely village and I know it very well because my grandmother lived here when I was a boy.

But that's not why I'm here tonight. I happen to be the secretary of the Family History Society and I understand that you are all interested in discovering the history of your own family. So this evening I'm going to try and help you to get started … And I'm sure you're going to find the whole process very exciting. So … I'll talk first for about ten minutes about the steps you need to follow and then I'll stop and you can ask questions, if you have any. Is that OK?

Right. Now the very first thing you need to do for your research is to take a sheet of paper and write down everything you already know about yourself, your parents, your grandparents and so on. Make a list of dates and places of birth and marriage and death, as well as where people lived, whether they did military service in the case of men, what their jobs were and so on. And then, when you've finished doing that, get in touch with any of your relatives who might be able to fill in some of the gaps in your information. Ask if you can talk to them. And before you see them, make a list of questions. Right? As well as the more obvious ones, like 'When was grandfather born?' or 'Did great-uncle Eric have any brothers or sisters?' try to find out details like 'What places did you visit when you were growing up?'

Unit 4, Focus on listening

EXERCISE 4

You are going to hear the rest of the talk about family history. Before you begin listening, you have 30 seconds to look at questions 1–4.

Man: So that's a few ideas about getting information. But what about methods of recording it? Of course you can just write down what family members say. But it's even better if you can use a tape, so that you can record them as they're talking. Then you don't have to worry too much about making mistakes, you'll always be able to listen to it again. But whatever method you do use to record information, remember that it's very important to make a note of exactly how you got it. So if you are using a tape, always start the recording by saying the date and the place, as well as the name of the person you're interviewing.

So … apart from people's memories, where else can you find information? Well there are all sorts of documents. And they can be extremely useful. People keep lots of kinds of documents in the home, like photos, or letters, or diaries, or birth certificates … And some people keep things from newspapers like obituaries. Obituaries are announcements of a person's death – and they usually contain a lot of detail about that individual, like address, occupation, date of death, as well as the names and ages of the widow or widower and the dead person's children. So be creative – look around your home, or the home of your relatives, for any items that might contain clues such as these about your family history. OK?

Before you listen to the rest of the talk, you have 30 seconds to look at questions 5–8.

Man: Now you'll find that you'll collect a lot of information, so you'll need to record it in an organised way. I'd recommend that you use an Ancestor Chart. Like this one here. Can you all see? Ancestor Charts act like maps … they link four or five generations in a family tree. So they're very convenient, and they don't cost anything. You can get as many as you like – you just download them free from the Internet. Then you fill them out as you go along, and for each individual you record all the key information next to their full name. It's very convenient …

Now at this point I'd just like to give you a couple of tips about filling in the Ancestor Sheet. First of all, I'd advise you to use pencil, at least until you have definite evidence for the information you're recording. Secondly, as well as recording official names, I mean given names, it's worth writing any nicknames down. You know – these are the short names that people call you when they know you very well. And you can show them by using quotation marks.

That's Ancestor Charts then. They really do save a lot of work … now, before I show you …

Unit 5, Focus on listening 1

EXERCISE 1

a b c d e f g h i j k l m n p s t v x y z

Unit 5, Focus on listening 1

EXERCISE 2

1 A: How do you spell your surname, please?
  B: It's C-A-R-R-O-W.
2 A: Matthews …
  B: Is that spelt M-A-T-H-E-W-S?
  A: No, it's actually M-A-double T-H-E-W-S.
3 A: How do you write the name of your street?
  B: It's F-U-R-S-D-U-N-N-E Road.
4 A: Do you remember your postcode?
  B: It's BL …
  A: Did you say VL?
  B: No, B for bed-L-6 4-J-E.
5 A: Does your name have a single S?
  B: Double … it's E-R-I-C-S-S-O-N.

Unit 5, Focus on listening 1

EXERCISE 3

You hear a man speaking to a receptionist on the telephone about joining a sports club.

Unit 5, Focus on listening 1

EXERCISE 5

(R = Sports club receptionist, A = Alex)

R: Good morning, Santon Sports Club.

A: Oh hello. I spoke to one of your colleagues last week about becoming a member of your club and I'd like to go ahead and join … if I can do it over the phone?

R: Absolutely. I'll start by taking a few details, if I may.

A: Of course.

R: What's your name?

A: It's Alex Cooze.

R: Can you spell your surname?

A: It's C-O-O-Z-E.

R: Lovely, I've got that. And are you a student or in employment?

A: Employed.

R: Thank you. And can I ask, what's your job?

A: I'm a doctor.

R: Right. Thanks. Now, we don't need to get your full address at this stage. But could I just take your postcode?

A: If I can remember it. I've only just moved. Oh yes. It's G-T-1

R: Right

A: and then 2-B-N.

R: Is that V-N?

A: No B-N.

R: Sorry. Now, one last question in this section. Can I just ask how you heard about us? Was it from a friend?

A: Actually I read about the club in a newspaper … it …

R: That's fine. Thank you very much.

Unit 5, Focus on listening 1

EXERCISE 6

(R = Sports club receptionist, A = Alex)

R: Now, we do offer different types of membership according to which facilities you want to use and when.

A: Yes, I gathered that but my schedule's a bit problematic. I mainly want to use the gym and that'll be after about 7 p.m., when I finish work.

R: Fine, right. And will you be interested in swimming?

A: I understand you have both an indoor and an outdoor pool?

R: That's right.

A: I'm not a fan of swimming actually and certainly don't want to be there when it gets very packed in the evenings. I think I'd only want to use the outdoor one and during the day, when I can get a bit of sunbathing in.

R: And when the children are at school, of course, so it's a bit quieter. A lot of our clients prefer that.

A: I can imagine!. And I might occasionally want to have a game of badminton …you know, and I suppose I'd like to book courts on Saturdays and Sundays when I can organise a game with friends.

R: Right. And would you be wanting to use our other club facilities such as the sauna, steam room or tanning bed? They're open all day until 9 p.m.

A: Well, I think I'd only want to use the steam room and probably after I've been doing heavy exercise.

R: So shall I put that down as evenings?

A: Sorry, no, I'd probably only use it on Saturdays and the occasional Sunday, you know, when I have more time to relax.

Unit 5, Focus on listening 2

EXERCISE 2

You will hear a third-year Sports Science student talking about a project on the differences between women and men in sports.

Unit 5, Focus on listening 2

EXERCISE 3

Sadie: Good morning. Today I'm going to talk about my end of year project. I wanted to find out why men and women tend to perform at different levels in particular sports. Let me start by explaining why I chose this subject. Now, as some of you may know, I'm an enthusiastic long-distance runner myself but I have never felt particularly worried about the fact that I usually finish several minutes behind my male counterparts. How it all started was when a first-year student approached me because he'd read an article about why women swimmers never compete successfully with men and wondered if I could look into the issue in regard to running. My tutor confirmed that a lot of interesting research had been done on this issue and also I knew that whatever I found out was likely to be useful in training programmes I run at a local girls' school.

So I started doing some preliminary reading and what I found out was a mixture of the expected and the unexpected. It didn't come as all that much of a surprise to learn that male runners have more muscle and women more fat. And this accounts for most of the difference in sports performance between men and women. This is normally caused by differences in hormones: a male hormone, testosterone, builds muscle whereas a female hormone, oestrogen, causes fat to accumulate. Of course, this was something that we learnt about very early on in Sports Science. But then I began reading about the nature of muscle and this is where I found something that did surprise me - men and women have exactly the same type of muscle fibres, which means that they are capable of 'fuel burning' at the same rate. I was also reading some very interesting research on differences between the average height of men and women. We all know, of course that men are much taller on average than women. But what this means is that women actually work much harder because they have to take a lot more strides to cover the same distance. I hadn't understood that before I read this research.

So I set up my own small-scale research project to investigate some of these points and a few others. I asked for men and women volunteers from the university running club and I timed their speed in a race. Then I worked out proportions by dividing a person's running time by their height. And what I found was that by this measure men were only slightly ahead of the women. For my second experiment, I put weights on the men's shoulders so that the men and women would have the same height to weight ratio. I found that under these conditions, the women actually ran faster than the men. In my last experiment, I decided to look at what is called 'elasticity' by measuring how high the men and women could jump. And I found that my male and female participants had equal levels …

Unit 6, Focus on speaking

EXERCISE 1

1 What are the most popular kinds of pet where you live?
2 Do you have a pet?
3 What is your favourite wild animal?
4 When was the last time you visited a zoo?

Unit 6, Focus on speaking

EXERCISE 4

1 The animal that I want to talk about is the beaver. It's a mammal and it lives around water. It lives in North America and northern Europe as well. It's a very attractive little animal – it's the size of a small dog, but quite fat. It's got thick, brown fur, which keeps it warm, and particularly when it swims around the water, because it spends a lot of time diving. What the beaver does is – it lives in social groups of several families, and it builds dams across streams to form lakes and ponds. So to make the dams it cuts down trees – it's got very sharp front teeth – and so it chops the trees down, branches, drags them down to the stream and blocks it. And then it makes its house in the dam. The entrance to the house is under water, and so they're very safe from any predators that might try to attack them.

 Unfortunately, I've only seen beavers on TV but … I think they're very interesting because they're social, and because they're good for the environment.

2 I find the wolf very interesting. I know that it has to communicate with others, and that they always hunt in packs. And the alpha male normally gets the first bite of what they kill. I've seen it in zoos. I find it particularly interesting because of the way it hunts and the way it travels in packs. The way that wolves actually talk to each other. They hunt in a team, and each one knows what to do. And I find it very interesting how they do it. I also find the way it looks at you very interesting … The way it just likes to stare at you. There's a wolf at Paignton Zoo, but I can't remember what type of wolf it was. It was a reddish colour, and its name meant something like 'fox on stilts' – it had very long, thin legs.

3 The animal I find interesting is the elephant. Elephants aren't found in the wild in this country, in fact they're only found in two places – Africa and Asia. There are two different kinds of elephant – the African and the Asian! They're now endangered because a lot of them were killed for their tusks to make ivory products. But ivory's now banned so that has hopefully stopped. Erm, they tend to live to about a hundred years and tend to stay in groups I think. And they enjoy having a mud bath and a swim in the river as well … I know about elephants from books and films. And I saw elephants in my childhood, when we were in Thailand. I've actually ridden on the top of one with somebody. I just find them particularly interesting because I think they're wise and quiet, and very … majestic creatures, I suppose.

Unit 6, Focus on listening

EXERCISE 1

1 fourteenth
2 ninth
3 twelfth
4 thirty nine
5 seventy
6 twenty third
7 eight hundred and two
8 three hundred and five
9 five four double-eight zero
10 two thousand and one

Unit 7, Focus on listening 1

EXERCISE 1

(*J = Joseph, A = Aline*)
You will hear two first-year engineering students discussing their project on devices which have been specially designed for use in developing countries.

J: Hi, Aline. Thanks for coming.
A: No problem. We've got our presentation coming up on Tuesday so we need to get everything prepared now.
J: Yeah. So we're agreed that we're going to concentrate on these two devices which have particularly helped people in developing countries.
A: Yes and we'll present the information in the form of a table so it'll be really clear for non-specialists. We'll have three columns, you know, using the headings we discussed in the last seminar.
J: OK. I've got those here. I'll make notes. So let's start with the clockwork radio and how it works. We'll obviously say how it's powered, i.e. that it's wound up.
A: Yeah and we also need to explain how the energy is stored.
J: OK … in a spring.
A: Fine. Keep it simple. But we also need to say that the thing which makes the mechanism so special is the inclusion of a gearbox, you know, which makes it possible to release energy extremely slowly. And that means that it can operate for a long time with minimal effort.
J: OK. Now the next section is, 'What are its benefits?' I suppose we just need to emphasise that it costs a lot less than radios which use batteries. And if we want to, we can explain that these can cost as much as a week's wages in some parts of the world.
A: Absolutely. And related to that of course, is the fact that people don't have to depend on buying anything in a store, which in remote rural areas is really important.
J: And then in the developments column, I think the most important thing we need to say is that the combination of the wind-up mechanism with a solar cell means that during the day it runs on the sun's energy and you only have to wind it up when it's dark, which makes it a much more attractive option.
A: And that's probably that for the radio.
J: Yep. So we'll then move on to the solar box cooker.
A: And again, let's keep the description of the mechanism very simple. We need to say that it uses sunlight rather than conventional fuels to cook food.
J: But we also need to explain two elements of why it's so efficient.
A: Yeah. The fact that sun's rays enter through a plastic cover.
J: Better call it a lid. I thought it was made of glass.
A: Not according to my research.
J: OK.

A: And then we just say that light is transformed into heat and …

J: because it has a longer wavelength, means that it gets trapped.

A: And so it cooks the food.

J: Good. Right. And then where do we begin on the advantages? There are so many.

A: I suppose we have to begin with the fact that you no longer need to cut down trees, which brings a whole raft of other benefits in its turn.

J: Sure … and related to that I think we need to say that because dung is no longer needed as a fuel for cooking, it can be used as a fertiliser.

A: Which leads to better harvests.

J: And then there's the fact that there is absolutely no smoke. I was reading somewhere that there is a huge incidence of lung complaints, especially among women and children who have to breath in smoke from conventional cookers.

A: So that's another plus point.

J: Yep. And then we need to say something about the way cook boxes have been improved. I think we can emphasise the fact that a reflector is often added at an angle to the lid to maximise the amount of light entering.

A: Yes. Good point. And also I read about the fact that the floor or base of the box is raised, which improves heat retention.

J: Oh and I think we should mention the fact that many of the new boxes have a sloping or inclined lid, which increases the surface area to capture the sun's rays.

A: Yes, that's a good point to finish on, I think.

J: So I'll write up that table on an OHT if you like and we're all set for our presentation.

A: Yes. Great. If there's any …

Unit 7, Focus on listening 2

EXERCISE 1

You will hear part of a presentation by a second-year Environmental Studies student on research into edible vaccines.

Student: I've chosen to give my seminar presentation on a very interesting piece of appropriate technology, designed to prevent sheep and goats from contracting a particularly virulent disease called goat's plague, which is a big problem across large parts of Africa, the Middle East and South Asia. The Indian Institute of Science in Bangalore has been working to produce genetically modified peanut plants to deliver an edible vaccine – in other words, vaccine which is given through the medium of food. In this case it is given through genetically modified peanut leaves, which are often used as animal fodder in India.

Why is edible vaccine considered much better suited to the local conditions and needs than ordinary vaccines injected by needles? Well, firstly, injected versions are very expensive to produce whereas edible ones are cheap, which must surely be one of the most important plus factors when choosing a mode of delivery. Secondly, a big drawback with injected vaccines is that they easily perish when they are not kept cool. By contrast, there are far fewer problems with storing edible vaccines – they can last a long time outside a fridge. You can imagine that in remote rural areas that is an enormous benefit. Another advantage is because this edible vaccine only contains one viral protein, it allows vets easily to pick out which animals are infected. It's apparently a common problem with injected vaccine that vets can't distinguish between sick and vaccinated animals.

However, edible vaccines do have their drawbacks. The major problem is ensuring that exactly the right dose is delivered. The amounts of vaccine which develop in a given genetically modified plant differ significantly depending on the growing conditions. Obviously too little of the protein might leave certain animals insufficiently protected. And there is also another shortcoming related to the issue of dosage of these vaccines – 99% of the protein actually perishes in the sheep or goat's stomach. We therefore cannot be sure just how much is getting through and working to protect the animal. These negative aspects really have to be addressed to ensure that animals receive maximum benefit. And finally, as with all GM crops – the transgenic peanut plants will have to be grown under strict supervision, if we are to ensure that it does not contaminate peanuts grown for human consumption. Now moving on to the next part of my …

Unit 8, Focus on speaking 1

EXERCISE 2

Do you prefer watching TV or listening to the radio?
Do you like sending letters or text messages to your friends?
Which do you prefer, talking to people on the phone, or talking face-to-face?
Do you like buying things in shops, or buying over the Internet?

Unit 8, Focus on speaking 2

EXERCISE 2

1 Erm, well, I suppose there are two basic kinds. Firstly, there are the more intellectual ones, the more serious ones. Then there's another kind which are not so serious, they are for – maybe less educated people. They have more articles about celebrities and crimes and things like that. And they have more pictures. Also, the language they use tends to be simpler. So, I suppose that's more or less what newspapers are like in my country.

2 Well, I used to be a teacher and one of the things we had to teach children was to make them wait their turn to speak, they were taught that it's rude to interrupt people, and that you should wait – you know, if you're a child in a classroom you should put your hand up if you want to speak, to ask a question or to say something. I think children are also taught to use a certain volume when they're speaking, that it's rude to speak too loudly, to shout out. And then I suppose there are things about politeness – you know, saying 'Please', 'Thank you', things like that ….

3 Well, I think it must affect their handwriting skills – I mean neatness and how easy it is for other people to read it. Because if children use the Internet a lot, they just don't get enough practice at holding a pen and forming letters. And then there's the effect that emails have on writing – I mean, people don't usually write full sentences in emails, or start and finish them like proper letters. So if children only send emails, their use of English might not be so good … They might not be very good at spelling, because if children use the computer's spell check, they don't have to memorise correct spelling in the way that people do who don't use computers.

Unit 8, Focus on speaking 2

EXERCISE 3a)

1 Are there any differences between the way news is presented on the radio and the way it's presented on the TV?
2 Do you think people are more interested in international news now than they were in the past?
3 What do you think are the advantages of talking face-to-face over talking on the phone?
4 Do you think there are differences in the way men and women communicate?

Unit 8, Focus on speaking 2

EXERCISE 3b)

1 Erm … I think the advantages of talking face-to-face over talking on the phone, are particularly that you can see the person's facial expressions. It's much easier to judge their mood, and their reactions to what you're saying, by looking at their eyes, the way they hold their head, and also if they're sitting comfortably, or if they suddenly tense up, or fold their arms. Whereas on the telephone it's very difficult to pick up on any of these things, because you can't see the person, and you have to go purely by the tone of voice. That can be quite useful for gauging a person's reaction, but on its own it's nowhere near as useful as being able to see their face.
2 I think news presented on the TV depends much more on the visual impact of the pieces that are presented. There tends to be less analysis, and less questioning of the interviewees. And er … they let the pictures speak for themselves, whereas on the radio, because there are no visual images available, there has to be much more questioning by the interviewers, by the presenters. Much more use of experts or commentators, they can't just rely on putting on a piece of film footage.
3 I think men generally tend to communicate either to exchange information, purely factual information, about their favourite make of car, a football game they watched on TV the previous night, or to use communication as some means of establishing dominance over each other. Who's sort of top dog. Whereas I think women tend to communicate much more as a means of bonding with each other, and to seek out things they have in common. And I think they generally tend to be better listeners, and are more comfortable talking about their emotions, and how they feel. Men don't really feel comfortable about admitting to fears or hopes or weaknesses, whereas women are much more comfortable talking about these things.
4 I think they probably are, yes. There's more coverage of it in the media – newspapers, TV – and so people will be able to know more about what's happening on the other side of the world, in other countries. And also, I think, very few countries now are self-sufficient in things like raw materials, food … and they depend on other countries much more so than they did in the past, for the things they need in their daily lives, like petrol, grain, meat. So what happens on the other side of the world can affect how much they have to pay for their daily needs and wants.

Unit 9, Focus on listening 1

EXERCISE 2

You will hear a local radio programme. A conference organiser is being interviewed about an exhibition on environmental issues.

Unit 9, Focus on listening 1

EXERCISE 3

(P = Radio presenter, J = Julia)

P: Good morning. On today's show, we're happy to welcome Julia Samson, who is organising the exhibition now on at Somerton Town Hall. Julia, what is the theme of the exhibition?
J: It's called the Earth Matters Exhibition and it's basically a showcase for businesses and organisations working to improve the environment. So we have organic farmers, you know, producing food without using harmful chemicals. We have shops which trade in ecologically friendly appliances, for example solar cells which heat your home with the power of the sun instead of using coal or oil. And so forth. Now, a lot of people ask me – what exactly is the purpose of the exhibition? Well, some of the stalls do allow the public and other businesses to buy their products. But the principal reason for running this fair is to raise awareness about what people can do to live a greener lifestyle. Now we can't run the exhibition as often as we'd like. We have plans to run it twice every year but at the moment we have it once a year, either in March or in September. We'd really like to encourage people to drop into the exhibition at any time. It's on from today, that's 23rd of course, till 28th March. And it's open from 10 a.m. to 8 p.m. Tickets cost just £4 for adults and £2.50 for the unwaged. You can buy them at the door of the Town Hall but you can also get them from Green Apple Health Foods – which is in the town centre opposite the library.

Unit 9, Focus on listening 1

EXERCISE 5

J: This time we have three new exhibits, which I think listeners will find particularly interesting. The first is the Cycle Safe stall and it's very easy to find. After you've walked through the entrance area turn immediately right and walk past Hydroponics. It's right next door to that. It's well worth a visit because it shows you how you can use a bicycle safely even on the busiest roads and they're organising lots of games and competitions so children will love it. The next new exhibit I want to tell you about is a wonderful new organic food outlet called Riverbank Farm Foods. It's right opposite the Education Centre, between the Book Stall and the exhibit for electric cars, so again you can't miss it. And Riverbank has lots of sample foods for you to try for free so do get along there. And finally, we'd strongly advise listeners to visit the Solar Homes exhibit, which is opposite Electric Cars and behind the gardening exhibit called Green Growth. There are lots of the latest devices on show and it's very educational. At this exhibit you can …

Unit 9, Focus on listening 2

EXERCISE 1

You will hear an Environmental Studies student talking to his tutor about an assignment he is working on.

Unit 9, Focus on listening 2

EXERCISE 2

T: Good morning, Wazim. Do come in.
W: Thanks very much.

T: Well, I've read through the work you've done so far and generally it's very good. Well done.

W: Thanks. I'm really interested in the topic and I've been working hard on it.

T: So starting with the work you've already done, I've just got a few suggestions for improving it. I particularly like your introductory section on why you've chosen to look at people's attitudes to the environment in our local area.

W: Thanks.

T: However, I would advise you to say quite a bit more on contamination of the river because it has been in the media so much.

W: Yes, I know what you mean. I think I glossed over that rather quickly.

T: Yes, so you need to develop that a bit more. And the second point I wanted to make is that, although your presentation is generally extremely good - particularly your diagrams and tables - there are quite a few mistakes in the part about toxic smoke. If I were you, I'd look carefully through that again.

W: I actually wrote that section at the last minute … you can always tell, can't you?

T: Well, that's soon fixed. And my final point is about reading. You've obviously done a lot on the causes and effects of acid rain but you only mentioned one book on the causes of floods. You ought to read a couple more.

W: I tried looking on the Internet but there was nothing relating to this local area. I think the library might be the best idea.

T: Yes, the Internet isn't the answer to everything.

W: Of course.

T: Now, that's everything I wanted to say about the work you've done so far. You now want to move onto the research stage, where you're finding out for yourself local people's attitudes and behaviour.

W: That's the main reason why I wanted to see you, to get ideas for how to approach that. I wanted to do something on people's attitudes to land-fill and the dumping of rubbish. What do you think?

T: That's a great idea. What research method do you think would be the most appropriate for that?

W: I wondered about setting up a small focus group with students discussing their opinions …

T: That's often quite hard to organise. Why not go for interviews instead – 10 to 20 people should be enough. And because you talk to them one-to-one I think it's easier to extract your data.

W: Yes, fine.

T: But I think you'll need to do that pretty soon. I suggest before the end of …

W: the week?

T: No, the month should be fine.

W: That's a relief! I can manage that.

T: Anything else?

W: Well, related to that I thought I'd try to find out how people felt about recycling … in particular I wanted to focus on paper.

T: Interesting … yeah.

W: But I'd like to do a wider spread, involving more people you know, in the wider community. So I thought I'd use questionnaires …

T: Sounds fine. But I think you should allow a much longer time for that – to prepare them and send them out, so I'd aim to get that done by the start of May.

W: I'll have to get moving on that!

T: Yes. Now, is there any other topic you'd like to investigate?

W: I wondered about looking at people's concerns about the ozone layer depletion.

T: That's obviously of great concern at the moment but can you think of something more localised … you know, practices in this particular community?

W: Well, I suppose I could look at using sprays … you know, whether people are following advice on this.

T: My advice is to focus on that.

W: So for the research method, I'd use questionnaires again.

T: Why not? But I also think it'd be a good idea to look at the statistics on this in the library. They cover the last decade so you could look at how they've changed over that period.

W: Yes. That'll give a bit of variety, won't it?

T: Absolutely.

W: I imagine I could do that pretty quickly. I'll aim to do that by 23rd June and I can follow up on it during the vacation if I need to get extra information.

T: And that should be plenty for the research stage.

W: Yes, I've got lots to be getting on with. Thank you very much.

Unit 9, Focus on vocabulary

EXERCISE 2

advise, advice, devise, device, describe, description, refer, reference, present, presentation, educate, education, complete, completion, exhibit, exhibition, discuss, discussion, produce, production, behave, behaviour

Unit 10, Focus on speaking 1

EXERCISE 1

Speaker A

Unfortunately I don't get very much. I have to leave my house at seven o'clock in the morning because the place where I work is a long way away. And I don't get home again till about seven in the evening. So by the time I've cooked the dinner and eaten it's more or less time to get ready for bed. Weekends are the only time I can unwind a bit.

Speaker B

To be honest, it's quite poor really. The thing is, I work in an office, so I'm sitting down most of the day, and I don't get much exercise or fresh air. Also, I eat in the office canteen, and the type of food they serve there isn't very nutritious. I keep meaning to enrol in a gym, and take my own food to work, but I'm lazy I suppose.

Speaker C

I'm afraid not. I've got a very demanding job, and I find it quite difficult to switch off. So I often lie awake thinking of the things I've got to do the next day. Sometimes I even get up and start writing things down!

Speaker D

I'm afraid I don't really. I don't get much time for reading anyway, and when I want to relax I prefer listening to music. That helps me unwind. If I started reading about health, I think it would make me stressed, so it wouldn't do me much good!

Speaker E

Unfortunately they don't, no. Most of them just sit at their computers playing games, or emailing each other. It's very unhealthy I know. I've only got a couple of friends who do anything active, they both do yoga. I know that's better than nothing, but even that's not very strenuous.

Unit 10, Focus on speaking 1

EXERCISE 2
1 Are there many sports clubs where you live?
2 Do you try to have regular exercise?
3 How careful are you about what you eat?
4 Where do people usually get information about health in your country?
5 Do you regularly take any tablets to improve your health?

Unit 10, Focus on speaking 1

EXERCISE 3
My favourite way of relaxing is to go down to a local beach near my house, called Horseshoe Beach. I just sit on the beach, you can get a chair there, and I usually take a book with me to read, one of my favourite books. Or sometimes I might just take some binoculars and look at the ships that go past. And sometimes I take my swimming things with me and have a swim. I usually do this in the summer time, I probably do it once or twice a week. Usually I try to get down there in the early morning, when I'm not working, to get a good position on the beach before everyone else arrives. And I enjoy doing this because I find it helps me to unwind, it helps me to get rid of any stress … And I also enjoy watching the people go by, the children and families who come down to swim … If I go for a swim, it's very refreshing and I enjoy being in warm water, and if there are any waves, I try body surfing … And that's my favourite way of relaxing.

Unit 10, Focus on speaking 2

EXERCISE 1c)
1 Some people think that modern lifestyles are less healthy than traditional lifestyles. Do you agree?
2 A lot of people say that schools should teach health education. Would you agree with that?
3 People often say that life is more stressful now than it used to be. Do you agree?
4 I think newspapers are responsible for worrying people too much about health matters. What do you think?
5 It's been suggested that having a good diet is very important for health. Do you agree with that?

Unit 10, Focus on speaking 2

EXERCISE 1d)
1 A: Some people think that modern lifestyles are less healthy than traditional lifestyles. Do you agree?
   B: Erm, I think so, because I know in my country people no longer just take the traditional diet of maize, rice and potatoes, with some vegetables and just a little meat. They tend to go now for fast foods, and there do seem to be a lot more fat people than I can remember when I was a boy. And I think probably we get less exercise, because everyone seems to drive around in cars now. There are still a few people who ride bicycles, or who take the tram, but most people don't really like to walk much now. So I think I would agree with that.
2 A: A lot of people say that schools should teach health education. Would you agree with that?
   B: Let me see … I think it probably is important. I think young people at school should be taught how to choose good, nutritious food, that's healthy for them and won't make them overweight, or spoil their teeth. And I think the other aspects of health such as disease – there are so many dangers for young people, and I do think they need education for it.
3 A: People often say that life is more stressful now than it used to be. Do you agree?
   B: Erm, I think I do … Because my parents and grandparents worked on the land, and their day was run really by the sun. When the sun rose, they got up to work and at midday when it got really hot they would stop and have a rest, and then go back to work till sunset … And then they'd come home from the fields and rest. But today we have to, you know, work to the clock, keep appointments and timetables. It doesn't matter how we feel, what the weather's like, we still have to do it. So I think there's a lot more pressure and stress on people because of the work they do.
4 A: I think newspapers are responsible for worrying people too much about health matters. What do you think?
   B: I think sometimes that's true, because newspapers have to sell. And so they often choose topics to write about that seem to be a bit scary, they make headlines out of things like new diseases, new health problems. But I think there's also a place for newspapers and magazines to tell us about new research, about health and food, and the kind of things to avoid … So I think you have to exercise your judgement about these things.
5 A: It's been suggested that having a good diet is very important for health. Do you agree with that?
   B: Well, I think to a certain extent it's true, yes. I think we have to be careful that we don't eat too much, particularly if we don't get much exercise, or else we can put weight on and become unhealthy. But I think some people take it to extremes and they go on silly diets that can make them too thin … And they don't seem to enjoy their food really. So I think you have to enjoy your food, and not worry too much about what you eat.

Unit 10, Focus on speaking 2

EXERCISE 2c)
1 Why do you think fitness clubs are becoming very popular in some countries?
2 People are generally living longer than they used to. What do you think are the main reasons for this?
3 In a lot of countries children are becoming overweight. Why do you think this might be?
4 Some big companies pay for their employees to join health clubs. What do you think are the reasons for this?
5 Why do you think a lot of people prefer traditional medicines to modern ones?

Unit 10, Focus on speaking 2

EXERCISE 2d)
1 A: Why do you think fitness clubs are becoming very popular in some countries?
   B: Fitness clubs? Erm … I think it's probably because … I think there are at least two reasons. One is because in many countries nowadays the majority of people don't do manual jobs … they work in offices and they're sitting all day, so

they don't get enough exercise in their job. So they have to go to a special place to do exercise. And I think another reason is probably because the magazines and newspapers and films and adverts we see all show people who are very slim and have good bodies, and I think a lot of people would like to look like them too.

2 A: People are generally living longer than they used to. What do you think are the main reasons for this?

B: I think people live in healthier conditions now. Erm … a lot of houses now have good sanitation, so they drink clean water, so there are no diseases or germs in the water they drink. So … houses are probably better ventilated and lighter, so we're healthier like that. And also I think medicine has improved a lot, the techniques, the drugs that are available, to cure people and to vaccinate them against diseases like smallpox and polio. And perhaps people know a bit more about diet and what the best things to eat to keep them healthy are.

3 A: In a lot of countries children are becoming overweight. Why do you think this might be?

B: Erm … I think children … this is perhaps the result of improvements in technology and … all children now have, all families seem to have a television, and a lot of children have some kind of computer games system that they can play. And I've noticed that a lot of children just spend all of their time, when they're not at school, just watching television and playing these computer games. So they don't run around, they don't have to do work to help their parents. And perhaps they eat too many burgers too!

4 A: Some big companies pay for their employees to join health clubs. What do you think are the reasons for this?

B: I think it's probably so that they get better productivity from their employees. People often have very stressful jobs, they work very long hours, often don't find time to take a lunch break, and complain about feeling very tense at the end of the day. And I think if you're healthy and take regular exercise, you're able to concentrate more, and to work harder. So I suspect it's because the companies think they'll get more work out of their employees if they keep them fit.

5 A: Why do you think a lot of people prefer traditional medicines to modern ones?

B: Well, it could be that … there've been a lot of scare stories recently about some modern medicines that have had very bad side effects, and have ended up making people more ill after they've taken them than before. And so people read these stories and they may think 'Oh well, all modern medicines must be dangerous.' Whereas people think their parents took traditional herbal remedies and it didn't do them any harm. And a lot of people think that if something's 'natural' it must be good. So I think that's probably the reason.

Unit 11, Focus on listening 1

EXERCISE 1
You will hear a woman giving a talk to people who would like to run their own businesses.

Unit 11, Focus on listening 1

EXERCISE 3
(M = Man, A = Amy)

M: Good morning and welcome to this month's Small Business Club meeting. I am very pleased to welcome Amy Lim, who owns and runs a catering business in the local area… She's going to talk to us today about the pleasures of running her own business. … Amy …

A: Thank you very much. Now, I started my business two years ago, selling very high quality ready-made meals, using all organic ingredients, sourced from the local area. And I have to say it has been the happiest time of my life, with sales doing extremely well. I've had to work very hard and this has meant a rather limited social life but I really value the fact that I'm my own boss and I can decide what I do, you know, when I think I'm ready to try something new and creative and when to continue with what I'm doing and so forth.

Now, I got the idea to produce these dishes when I was visiting a local supermarket and I looked at what was on offer in the ready-meals section – lots of low quality, unhealthy packs. And I thought, 'I could do so much better!' I discussed it with friends – some of them thought it was a great idea and others thought there wouldn't be a big enough market for such expensive products but I went ahead with my idea anyway! And, as I say, it's been very successful.

At the moment I employ two people: one to help me with the actual preparation and cooking and the other to work on the financial side, doing invoices and accounts and marketing. My business is expanding but I'm not ready to employ anybody new just yet. At the moment I'm negotiating with a local organic farmer who would like to sell my meals at his farm shop. We've already agreed that I will sell in his shop in the new year, but I just don't know how much. It probably won't be enormous – my sales in total at the moment are only about £7,000 a month and at least for the next few months I don't plan on increasing that. I think the thing which will make me take on new staff is if I just feel too exhausted and stop enjoying what I'm doing.

And plans for the long term future are a little vague at the moment. I've been thinking that in a couple of years' time, I'll start to sell on the Internet. My sales will increase quite a bit. I won't advertise because that might mean I would expand so fast that I couldn't continue to use all organic ingredients and I'm very anxious to go on doing that. But I think I'll need a bigger kitchen and packing area, otherwise we'll get very cramped.

Unit 11, Focus on listening 1

EXERCISE 5

A: Now, I've emphasised how much pleasure I get out of running my own business but, of course, one of the quickest ways to lose heart is to try operating without sufficient capital. So in the second part of my talk, I want to share with you how I got enough money to finance my business. The most significant part of my capital came from a grant from the Small Business Agency or SBA as everyone calls it. And this is how you go about getting it. The first thing you have to do is to draw up a business plan. Now don't make this too long and complicated. I would say it should just be up to two pages in length. I've seen some people's efforts go up to ten pages. Well, frankly I don't think anyone will read it if it's that long! The next thing is, it's worthwhile getting it checked. Now don't rely on an accountant for this. Your best bet is to go to your bank and get them to look through it. Only if they're happy should you go ahead with your application. If all is well, then you should finalise your submission. Then your next step is to send it to the SBA. Now they advise you not to do this by email but by post. However, they say this situation might change in the near future.

So when the SBA receive your grant application, they'll judge whether your business idea is interesting, that is, likely to benefit from their grant. If they think it's good, they'll invite you to interview. And then the successful candidates can get a maximum of £20,000. I got £18,000 which wasn't quite the top amount but still enormously useful, as you can imagine. Now if there are any questions, I'll be happy …

Unit 11, Focus on listening 2

EXERCISE 1
You will hear a psychology student giving a presentation about his project on 'the science of well-being'.

Unit 11, Focus on listening 2

EXERCISE 3

Student: For my project I chose to look at a subject which has interested me for a long time – why it is that some people are much happier than others – more upbeat and optimistic? I should say that I regard myself as a very happy person and so are most of my family, as far as I know. But that wasn't the reason why I chose this project. Some people think that nowadays we are becoming more depressed than we used to be but I'm not convinced by that and I came across some interesting research which tries to look at the subject from a positive point of view. It emerged from a movement called 'the science of well-being'. And I decided I wanted to investigate it for my project because it involves several different types of factors – it can be viewed not just from the mental or physical side but also from the social perspective.

Now, in a large-scale study of several thousand people of different ages, researchers found three main characteristics which appeared again and again in people who identified themselves as happy. The most significant factor was that you don't have to be someone who does something brilliant – discovers penicillin or composes a symphony, for example – but happy people do seem to know what their strengths are. This enables them to make the best of themselves and not to dwell on what they're doing badly. Another striking finding was that happy people tend to be very curious – not about family gossip or things like that, but about larger issues, like current events. I remember one person the researchers interviewed had never learned to read but he was happy because he kept up through TV news. And then, and this surprised me – people don't have to have lots of friends to be happy, but they do have to be able to appreciate what they do have – the good fortune they've had and how different their lives could have been if they hadn't been so fortunate.

Turning now to what the research says should be avoided if people are going to stay happy. The three things that stand out are as follows. First of all, reflection time on your own is good but not if people use that time regretting mistakes and blaming themselves for everything. Another point is that people shouldn't worry about getting angry sometimes – it's part of what makes us human and it can be healthy. But they shouldn't always try to find fault with others. This leads to a great deal of negativity. And the final thing which should be avoided if a person is going to be happy is always trying to compete. Of course it can be fun to try to beat another person in a game but not if this becomes your only aim. It's much better to enjoy taking part in the game rather than being obsessive about winning it.

Now I've tried to do a lot of reading on the subject of well-being research and I have to say it does have its critics. It is widely accepted that this 'positive' approach does help us understand what happiness is and why some people are very unhappy. However, this has been dealt with many times before. The critics basically say that it is the old science under a new name with only very small changes in approach.

Well, that might be the case. It may bring us very little closer to finding out exactly how our brains work but I think that sometimes even a very small change in perspective can bring real and long-lasting benefits. Above all, I feel that well-being research might help us to move away from simply prescribing drugs for depression. It helps us to explore alternative ways of dealing with unhappiness.

I'd like to finish my short presentation by mentioning one of the people who was interviewed by the research team. Ada Clarke is exactly 100 years old and still going strong, still giving piano recitals in her local town. She regards herself as a very happy person and that this positive spirit has kept her healthy over her long life. But the reason I'm mentioning her now is because not one of the factors she says make her happy is on the list I mentioned before. Every human life is unique and we cannot guarantee what will make each one of us happy.

Unit 12, Focus on speaking 1

EXERCISE 1
1 Do you live in a town or a village?
2 What kind of building do you live in?
3 Have you always lived in this building?
4 What do you like most about the building where you live?
5 What do you like least about the building where you live?
6 Is there a garden outside your home?

Unit 12, Focus on speaking 1

EXERCISE 2
A public building I really like is the old railway station in Kuala Lumpur. It's right in the centre of the city. It's a very striking building – it stands out from the others around it because of its architecture – it looks sort of middle-eastern. It has a lot of pillars

and arches. But it's not a modern building – I think it's about a hundred years old. And of course, it's used for trains. It used to be the main station for the whole of Malaysia, and there were trains passing through it to all parts of the country, and to Singapore and Thailand as well. But now there's a new station, so the older station building is just used for local, commuter trains. But it's still a big tourist attraction too, so we get lots of visitors just coming to have a look at it. And … the reason why I like the building so much is … well I just like its appearance, it's a beautiful building I think. And it's also nice to have some historic buildings in a modern city – it gives variety.

Unit 12, Focus on speaking 2

EXERCISE 1c)

1 How important is it for people to have a permanent home?
2 How necessary is it for building designers to consider energy use?
3 How important is it for public buildings to look good?
4 How necessary is it for governments to regulate building work in towns and cities?

Unit 12, Focus on speaking 2

EXERCISE 1d)

1 A: How important is it for people to have a permanent home?
   B: It's very important to have a permanent home because home is the place where you feel safe and secure. You can relax there and do whatever you like. And you can decorate it or change it in whatever way you like … And you need to know that it's permanent for you, and that you haven't got to move off and away in a few days or weeks.
2 A: How necessary is it for building designers to consider energy use?
   B: Well, it didn't use to be in the past, but now I think it's very important because we know now how unpredictable energy sources are … oil is becoming more and more expensive, and now we have this problem with the climate and climate change, global warming … And I think it's very important to have buildings that are energy-efficient, to minimise the amount of energy they use, because of the amount of damage that we can do to our climate and our planet.
3 A: How important is it for public buildings to look good?
   B: I think it is very important. People who live in the cities, that's all they see, when they go to work, when they come home. So it's important that the public buildings look nice because it makes them feel proud of their city or their town, they'll feel that it's a good place to live. And people like to look at beautiful buildings, well-designed buildings.
4 A: How necessary is it for governments to regulate building work in towns and cities?
   B: Oh, I think it's essential, because there've been lots of cases where buildings have been poorly designed, there've been some terrible accidents where buildings have collapsed. Or they've been built too close together, and the environment is spoiled because they're too high and the streets are too dark. And so it can be very dangerous. So the government has to make regulations, I think.

Unit 12, Focus on speaking 2

EXERCISE 2a)

Well I think one of the main things architects will have to take into account in future is energy use. It's going to be more and more important to use renewable energy where possible, so I think we'll see buildings with more natural ventilation than we have now. And more natural light as well – so more windows or just larger ones I think. And as well as solar panels I expect we'll see wind turbines attached to individual buildings to generate heating and light. So I think that'll be the most significant development. Secondly, I think that as land becomes more and more scarce, architects will have to design a greater number of high-rise buildings, instead of individual houses on single plots of land. But as we're more aware now than we used to be of people's need to identify with a community, architects will have to provide more communal facilities like play areas for children in their designs. And finally, I think architects will be experimenting with new building materials that we haven't seen before, especially synthetic ones with special properties.

Unit 12, Focus on speaking 2

EXERCISE 2b)

1 What do you think houses of the future might look like?
2 What are the most likely trends in city planning in the next 50 years?
3 What effect might new technology have on house design in the future?

Unit 12, Focus on speaking 2

EXERCISE 2c)

1 A: What do you think houses of the future might look like?
   B: I think they'll have to be quite a bit smaller, with the population growing as it is. To get more houses. They maybe won't be able to have such big gardens, or any garden at all. And I think they'll have to be much more energy-efficient, so smaller windows, double glazing. Erm … they might have to try and recycle the heat that's produced in the houses to make the most of the energy that's used. I think that's it, really.
2 A: What are the most likely trends in city planning in the next 50 years?
   B: I think something that all cities will have to think very carefully about is public transport, because it's highly likely that oil will either run out, or become so expensive that petrol engines will either become really expensive or even disappear altogether. And most people will have to use public transport. So I think cities will have to be designed to make better use of public transport, and also to be more pedestrian-friendly, bicycle-friendly. I think they'll also have more green spaces, more parks, to try and absorb some of the carbon dioxide and other greenhouse gases that are being produced.
3 A: What effect might new technology have on house design in the future?
   B: I think a lot more things will be automatic in houses. There'll be locks like the ones in some hotels – you just swipe them with a card which is programmed for an individual. Heating and lights will probably come on

automatically when someone enters the house, and go off again as they leave. Fridges will have electronic displays showing what food is inside, or what new things need to be bought. So houses will look more streamlined, because there won't be as many switches and wires and handles.

Assess your speaking, Part 1

(*E = Examiner, C = Candidate*)

E: Do you enjoy reading?

C: Yes I ... I do

E: What kind of things do you usually read?

C: Oh I read ... er ... the history books, about ... And some novels

E: Is reading a popular hobby in your country?

C: Oh, I don't know ... Er ... reading is ... er ... maybe I think reading is popular in my country. Yes.

E: OK. And how often do you read English books?

C: Er ... Oh no ... Recently I don't er ... read English books. But now I read ... er ... read Daphne du Maurier's novel ... er ... borrowed ... borrowed from my host family. It's very difficult for me!

E: Did your parents read to you when you were young?

C: Er ... no ... they didn't.

E: Why not?

C: Er ... when I was a young child ... sorry ... when I am a child, I was a child, my mother is ... was very busy. So my parents didn't ... er ... didn't ...

E: OK. Thank you.

Assess your speaking, Part 2

C: I go swimming in the hall, once a week ... Er ... This is because ... er ... it is nice to keep fit, and yes, so I like swimming very much. It is very relaxing ...

E: OK. Do any of your friends go swimming as well?

C: Yes, I go with my friends.

E: And where do you go swimming?

C: Where? The swimming pool.

E: Why do you go there?

C: Er ... because I like swimming. It's a very nice place.

E: Good. OK.

Assess your speaking, Part 3

E: What kinds of leisure activity are most popular in your country?

C: There are, I think, lots of leisure activities. A traditional activity in my country ... it's riding horses ... and camel racing is very popular. ... And the other thing is er falcon hunting and especially in the winter season ... However ... there are lots of other hobbies and activities which are popular... like quad bikes, fishing ... Fishing is popular because we have a lot of coasts ... my country is like an island so you can fish anywhere ... so I think everybody does lots of activities ...

E: People often say that life is more stressful than it used to be. Do you agree?

C: Would you mind repeating that?

E: People often say that life now is ... er ... more difficult, more stressful, lots more stress in life than there used to be. What do you think? Do you agree?

C: I think no, because ... fifty to a hundred years ago ... people used to work all day ... Planting and working on the farm, and some people were fishing the whole day ... to just bring the food to his family to eat ... and there were no ... facilities to move ... I mean ... to transport ... just maybe horses ... now they have cars and they have chairs to sit in, and I think it's more ... more comfortable now ... especially if a person works in a big company. You can have your food there or you can bring it in the cafeteria and can sit and talk with a friend ... I think before it was difficult more than now.